BOREHAM

a history of the racing c

Bryan Jones
and
John Frankland

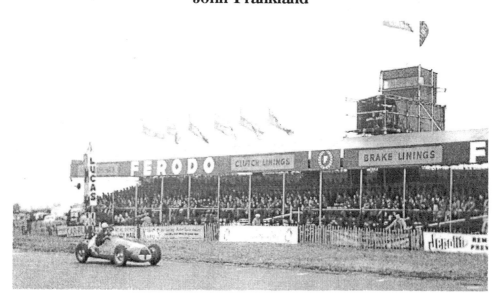

Ian Henry Publications

ISBN 0 86025 493 3

The photograph by Les Downes on the title page is of
Harry Schell (Maserati Platé) passing the Grand Stand at Boreham

Published by
Ian Henry Publications, Ltd.
20 Park Drive, Romford, Essex RM1 4LH
and printed by
WBC Book Manufacturers, Ltd.
Waterton Industrial Estate, Bridgend, Glamorgan CF31 3XP

FOREWORD

I was more than a little surprised to receive a request to write a Foreword for this book, after all it has been nearly fifty years since racing ceased at the circuit, and did I even remember anything of the races which I took part in? How good to learn that the history, of which I played a very small part in helping to create in much younger days, is not just committed to the memory of only those who are old enough to have seen some of the racing at Boreham. But now two authors have got down to researching and writing for posterity, those exciting races which took place there.

Although many old wartime airfields came into use for only short periods of time as racing circuits, and then ceased to operate as such for various reasons, they all played a very big part in the resurgence of interest in many parts of the country in post war motor racing, and that is an important factor to remember. There were many, and varied reasons, for the demise of these old airfield circuits, not least of all for the fact that many were in the wrong geographical position to make them pay. Motor racing is a very costly sport to run, and to meet the costs involved the circuits have to be in a location where they can easily be travelled to, and will therefore attract huge crowds of spectators from any part of the country without too much difficulty. This theory I think has been proved with the 50th anniversary of motor racing at Silverstone, a circuit located more or less in the centre of England.

A day of some success for me at Boreham took place at the *Daily Mail* International Festival of Motor Sport on 2nd August, 1952. I was 'on the podium' on three occasions, once for winning the 100 miles Sports Car Race in a Jaguar, for taking third place in the Formula 2 race in an ERA G Type, and third place in the Formula 3 race in a Cooper Norton. My sporting adversaries on that occasion were the likes of Ken Wharton, Roy Salvadori, Mike Hawthorn, Reg Parnell, Alan Brown, Luigi Villoresi, Froilan Gonzalez, Peter Collins, and others.

I returned to Boreham in January, 1964, not this time to race, but to appraise, or should I say indulge, in a 'burn up' with two particular cars that I was interested for various reasons to drive, and which belonged to friends of mine. The weather I remember was "foul', in fact it snowed a little, and with an east wind blowing, not the best of days for such an event. So much for nostalgia.

I recommend this book to all who have interests in motor sport and motor cycle racing, not least to those who heard the stories from their fathers and others, of those good old days at Boreham in the 1950s.

Here, to read at your leisure, are the old racing stories created by those racing legends of yesteryear.

Stirling Moss, O.B.E.

Stirling Moss (Jaguar) is presented with the Cup for winning the 100 Mile Sports Car Race, Class C by the Hon. Mrs Gerald Lascelles, on 2 August, 1952. (*photo: Autosport*)

INTRODUCTION

In July each year, motor sport enthusiasts from all over the British Isles and abroad converge on a former Second World War airfield on the border between Northamptonshire and Buckinghamshire. It is time for the British Grand Prix and all roads lead to Silverstone.

It could so easily be another Second World War airfield - Boreham - to which those enthusiasts head on their annual pilgrimage for, early in the 1950s, there seemed to be the very real possibility that it would be Boreham rather than Silverstone which would become the country's premier motor racing circuit. In the post-war years very many redundant airfields were pressed into service for motor sport activities. Some flourished briefly for national events but were never intended to be more than temporary expedients and fell into disuse. Boreham, four miles from Chelmsford in the centre of Essex, seemed to be in a different league.

Under the auspices of the progressive West Essex Car Club who organised motor racing there and the Chelmsford & District Auto Club who were responsible for the motor cycle meetings, the sport's big names - and those making their names - Hawthorn, Moss, Villoresi, Gonzalez, Collins, Wharton, Salvadori, Parnell, Kavanagh and Surtees, were all drawn to the venue. Within just three short years the circuit had progressed from minor speed trials to full international events. But then activities unexpectedly ceased.

The Ford Motor Company took over the circuit after racing ended and in due course it became the centre of the company's motor sport operation, especially rallying. Under Ford's enlightened ownership the old circuit has seen occasional use for nostalgic motor sporting events and even for the testing of Formula One cars. The sound of F1 engines wailing over the flat Essex countryside has been a poignant reminder of what might have been. The extraction of gravel at the site is now creating what has been described as the largest man-made hole in Europe and even these evocative sounds will soon die away.

This then is the story of Boreham Circuit. It is hoped that what is recorded here does justice to all who took part in those now increasingly distant events and, indeed, to the hundreds of American servicemen who built the airfield in the first place.

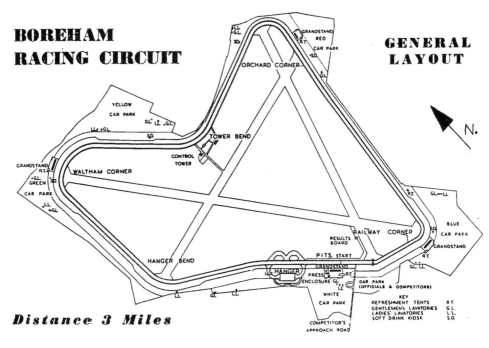

BOREHAM RACING CIRCUIT

GENERAL LAYOUT

GRANDSTAND
RED
CAR PARK

ORCHARD CORNER

N.

YELLOW
CAR PARK

TOWER BEND

CONTROL
TOWER

GRANDSTAND
R.T.
+GL
GREEN
CAR PARK

WALTHAM CORNER

BLUE
CAR PARK

GRANDSTAND

RAILWAY CORNER

RESULTS
BOARD

HANGER BEND

PITS START

HANGER

GRANDSTAND
PRESS
ENCLOSURE GL

WHITE
CAR PARK

CAR PARK
(OFFICIALS & COMPETITORS)

KEY
REFRESHMENT TENTS   R.T.
GENTLEMEN'S LAVATORIES   G.L.
LADIES' LAVATORIES   L.L.
SOFT DRINK KIOSK   S.D.

COMPETITOR'S
APPROACH ROAD

Distance 3 Miles

WALTHAM CORNER

TOWER BEND

ORCHARD CORNER

HANGAR BEND

RAILWAY CORNER

Boreham Airfield, looking north-west, c.1970 (*photo: Eric D Probert*)

AIRFIELD CONSTRUCTION

In the months preceding the Allied armed forces landings on the beaches of Normandy on D-Day, 6 June, 1944, a major bombing offensive was to be carried out by planes of the Allied air forces, and in particular the United States Army Air Forces.

This offensive was to be against specific targets in northern France and the Low Countries, which were thought to be of major use and importance to the German forces in defending against the Allied forces once they had landed in France.

Before this operation could be carried out, it was necessary to build sufficient airfields to accommodate the countless number of planes which were to take part.

The generally flat countryside of Essex, together with its geographical position in relation to the targets to be attacked, was most probably the main reason why one of the eight airfields built for these bomber groups was built at Boreham.

The work of constructing the airfield, together with all its associated buildings including the bomb dump, was carried out by the Americans. The 861st Engineer Aviation Battalion of the United States Army, arrived at the green field site on 13 May, 1943, they were under the command of Lt.Col. Stanley H Lomax. A total of 560 men arrived from America by boat train and truck, and were obliged to erect a sufficient number of tents (which they called the Tented City) in which to live, until they had erected brick built accommodation.

In order to meet the timing requirements for the D-Day landings (the precise date not being known at this time), following the bombing offensive, Lomax and his men were given 12 months in which to complete the work and be ready for the arrival of the bomber aircraft from America.

The gigantic operation was to be carried out in shifts of 12 hours day and night 7 days a week. Work at night, air raids permitting, was with the aid of flood lights.

The airfield was to Class A specification, it had a three runway layout, the lengths being 6,000 feet of main runway and two others each at 4,200 ft. The perimeter track (in post war years to be used for motor cycle and motor car racing) was just over three miles in length. The total area of the site was 620 acres which before commencement of building had been covered by orchards, fields and Duke's Wood covering 86 acres. This wood ran partly over the north-east corner of what was to be one of the 4,200 ft long runways, and over nearly half of the other 4,200 ft runway on the eastern side of the airfield. The wood was totally removed from the site.

Approximately 130,000 tons of concrete were used in building the airfield, with 50 miles of electrical conduit and cable. Two huge aviation fuel tanks, with a total capacity of 150,000 gallons were buried beneath the surface of the site, and

Building the airfield
The 'tented city' accommodation for the airfield builders (*photos: Bruce Preble*)

two large T2 type aircraft hangers also built. 212 Nissen huts were built on seven sites on the north and north-east sides of the airfield, for just over 2,600 men.

All the civil engineering equipment used in the building programme, was brought in from the U.S.A. - bulldozers, earthmovers, scrapers, cranes, dumper trucks etc..

Every conceivable type of tradesman was amongst the workforce - bricklayers, electricians, carpenters, surveyors, draughtsmen, steel construction workers, soil chemists, and blacksmiths etc. The Americans said of the work involved in the project "... tell the world that it was the hardest job they ever undertook to do. The weather itself was also a big enemy, for during the winter, it was raining continuously and wind and damp cold would go right through your clothes. But the work went on regardless of rain, cold or Jerries. It was hell to us, but at the end of nine months, three months ahead of schedule, another base was ready for operation against the enemy."

On completion of the airfield building programme in Essex during early 1944, the total number of operational airfields was 23, fourteen used by the United States Army Air Force (8 by Marauder Bomber Groups of the 9th USAAF, including the one at Boreham) and nine by the R.A.F.

The pressure of work may have been the cause of a breakdown in Stanley Lomax's health, for during the last week of May, 1944, he was taken seriously ill and was hospitalised at the 121st Station Hospital at Braintree, where he died on 5 June, 1944. He was therefore never to witness D-Day, one of the greatest days in the war, which he and his men through their hard work, had helped to achieve. Lt. Col. Lomax is buried amongst 3,811 fellow Americans at the American Military Cemetery, near Cambridge.

AVIATION HISTORY

During 1943, when the Americans were building the airfield at Boreham, the 394th Bombardment Group (M) - 9th United States Army Air Force, who were to be the airfield's first occupants, were still involved in flight training in America. The Official Activation Orders for the Group were issued on 5 March, 1943, by Headquarters Army Base Command at MacDill field, Tampa, Florida.

So began the three year life span of a Martin B26 Marauder twin engined medium bomber group, later to set new bombing records and fame across the flak filled skies of Europe, as the famous Bridge Busters. They were to be the last but one B26 Bomb Group to come off the famous MacDill field production line. On 5th April, 1943, a West Point Military Academy graduate, Lt.Col. Thomas B Hall, was appointed Group Commander, a post he was to hold during the Group's stay at Boreham. After training at MacDill, further training followed in Oklahoma, Michigan and Indiana.

It was, however, from Kellog field in Battle Creek, Michigan, that the first of the four squadrons of this Group departed for England on the south Atlantic ferry route during 29th January, 1944. The journey included overnight stops at all places where they landed to re-fuel, these were Savanna (Georgia), West Palm Beach (Florida), Boriquen (Puerto Rico), Georgetown (British Guiana), Belem (Brazil), Ascension Island, Roberts Field (Liberia), Dakar, Marrakech (French Morroco), St Mawgan (Cornwall), before finally landing at Boreham on 24 February, 1944. The flight had taken 26 days, and the distance covered was 11,000 miles.

All four squadrons of aircraft arrived safely. The bombardiers and gunners of the Marauder aircrews did not take part in the trans-Atlantic flight, in order to reduce the all up weight of the aircraft, and they were transported to England by ship. The available number of aircraft for bombing missions, including spares was between 48 and 60.

The Marauder Bomber Groups based in Essex were to provide a tactical support function for the Allied ground forces. The Normandy landings had not yet taken place in early 1944 when the Bomber Group arrived at Boreham. During the months leading up to D-Day, this Group was to take part in the bombing offensive by attacking targets in France, which were thought to be of vital importance towards the defence of enemy held territory after the Allied troops had landed. Targets most frequently attacked were, road, rail and river bridges, airfield gun positions, railway marshalling yards and construction sites. The latter sites were established to be V1 Flying Bomb launching sites, intended to come into operation after D-Day.

A number of training flights were carried out over England before the crews of the Marauders were ready for their first bombing mission which took place on 23 March, 1944, just 13 days after their arrival.

The target was an airfield at Beaumont-le-Roger in France. Lt.Col. Thomas B Hall, the Group's Commanding Officer, led the 36 aircraft mission. It was described as 'good'; 50.5 tons of bombs were dropped and all aircraft returned safely. During the period up to D-Day, the Group carried out 57 missions, dropping 2,366 tons of bombs. This cost the Group eight aircraft and the lives of eighteen aircrew.

On D-Day, the Group flew two missions, the first of 34 aircraft, was carrying 61 tons of bombs, the target being coastal gun positions at Varreville. Due to bad weather and low cloud, four of the Marauder bombers collided and crashed in two separate accidents over southern England on the outward flight, twenty-three crewmen were killed, and three civilians on the ground. The second mission later in the day was carried out without loss.

Following the successful troop landings on the beaches of Normandy and the progress of the advance, the time had arrived to progressively move the eight

Essex-based Marauder bomber Groups to bases nearer the advancing Allied armies, thus reducing the distance for the bombers to fly in their quest to support the land battle.

As a result of this plan, the 394th Bomb Group left Boreham on 24 July, 1944, for the air base at Holmsley South, near Christchurch in Hampshire. The cost of carrying out 96 bombing missions from Boreham, during which they had dropped 4,547 tons of bombs, had been 61 aircrew killed and 16 aircraft destroyed.

Following the departure of the Americans, no significant aviation events took place, until an advance party of the 315th Troop Carrier Group arrived on 22th March, 1945, in more than eighty C47 Dakota aircraft. Two days later these aircraft carried men of British 6th Airborne Division to take part in operation 'VARSITY', the crossing of the river Rhine from the west bank, by Allied troops near Hamminkeln.

At the end of the war in May, 1945, the airfield remained disused, but parts of the Nissen hut accommodation under the control of the Essex County Council, was rented out to local families to overcome the post-war shortage of houses in the Chelmsford area.

The airfield was finally closed in April, 1946, and the land between the runways was used by Co-Partnership Farms for the growing of crops. It was not until late in the 1940's that local people finally left their Nissen hut accommodation and the huts were demolished.

Martin B26 medium bomber taking off from Boreham (*photo: 394 B.G. Collection*)

MOTOR SPORT IN BRITAIN - THE POST-WAR YEARS

The World War represented a watershed for many facets of life in Britain. In culture and the arts, economic life and in politics, upheavals were the order of the day. A landslide election victory, without precedent since 1906, brought the Labour Party to power in 1945, heralding a remarkable programme of sustained economic activity and the bringing into public ownership of some 20% of the nation's industry including coal, railways, civil aviation, gas, electricity and road transport.

Wartime blueprints for a new Britain had a profound effect on the country in post-war years; the Beveridge Report (1942) laid the basis of a comprehensive social security, the Uthwatt Report (1942) outlined a new approach to town planning, and the Butler Education Act (1944) laid a framework of a new comprehensive secondary education system for all. It was a remarkable period of change and new beginnings.

In the overall scheme of things, with the havoc wrought by six years of war on such obvious things as road, rail and sea transport and the supply of raw materials, motor sport occupied a fairly low level of priority in the national consciousness. When car owners opened their garage doors to wheel out their racing machines they soon began to realise that, for them too, the war years represented the end of an era; a watershed in their beloved sport no less than in matters of far more importance.

Since 1907, the Brooklands Motor Course at Weybridge in Surrey had provided Britain with a permanent circuit of some importance used not only for circuit racing but also for numerous record attempts. During the war, as Bill Boddy describes in his history of Brooklands, the circuit had been adapted for military purposes and had been damaged by air raids. A workshop had been set into the Members' Banking, a large hangar had been built on the Railway Straight and a new vehicular access had been cut through the southern banking.

Despite these rather drastic alterations there was a general assumption that the government would eventually restore Brooklands as a motor course. This was not to be and it soon became apparent that the Air Ministry felt that it would be cheaper to buy the Brooklands site for industrial development rather than to reinstate the track. Early in 1946 a meeting of shareholders of Brooklands (Weybridge) Ltd voted in favour of selling the site to Vickers Ltd when it was realised that the earliest practical date by which racing could resume was 1950. Racing at Brooklands was over.

The other prominent, and very different, circuit in the pre-war years was Donington, near Derby, where Auto Union and Mercedes-Benz cars had spectacularly demonstrated their dominance in the 1937 and 1938 Donington Grands Prix. Racing originally came to Donington Park in 1931 when a short course for motor cycle racing was laid out on the gentle slopes of the park. This was the English mainland's first enclosed road racing circuit. The popularity of meetings held there was such that an extended circuit 2.19 miles long was laid out in time for the 1933 season and by 1937 the lap length had been increased to 3.125 miles.

Donington Park was requisitioned by the War Office and became Vehicle Reserve Depôt (Breedon), the largest military transport base in the country. As so often happened at such requisitioned properties, the speed with which the site had been possessed and put into alternative use was not matched by the speed of its subsequent clearance and reinstatement and it was to be more than ten years after the end of hostilities before some attempt was made to clear away the debris of war from the site: this despite a noisy campaign mounted by enthusiasts to restore it as a venue for racing. The clearance was by no means complete and the pre-war track was never reinstated. The Park had been built on, trees had been felled and the whole area was left in a terrible state. The ready-made hard surface of the track surface had attracted a motley collection of Nissen huts, vehicle parts, air raid shelters and service buildings.

It would be unfair to hold the War Office solely responsible for the loss. It had apparently agreed to quit Donington Park if the Society of Motor Manufacturers and Traders could show cause why the circuit was essential to the industry as a testing ground. The SMMT had failed to provide such justification.

Remarkably, Britain's third purpose-built major motor sporting venue at Crystal Palace in South London had also fallen victim to the requirements of the war effort. Although its loss was not the body-blow to motor sport suffered by the loss of Brooklands and Donington it was nonetheless sorely missed by enthusiasts. The circuit's pre-war life had been relatively short. It had been laid out in the grounds of Crystal Palace Park and was opened in 1937.

It has often been compared with the continental road circuits of the era and, before the war brought matters to a halt, witnessed some superb racing especially amongst the ERA fraternity. At the end of the war the circuit was not in a state to allow an early resumption of racing. The Ministry of Defence gradually removed the debris of war - including some unexploded bombs - from the site but it was to be eight years before renovation work under the direction of the London County Council once more made motor sport at the venue a reality. The post-war circuit was a shortened version of the original course.

The war had indeed dealt a series of serious blows to the infrastructure of motor racing in this country. As the sport struggled to re-establish itself in the immediate post-war years it could not call upon any of the permanent venues which had been in use in 1939.

Paradoxically, however, the tragic conflict, in its wake, provided the means whereby the sport was able to revive and rebuild itself, albeit in a very different form from that which existed in the pre-war years. All over the country, many of the military airfields - both RAF and USAAF - had served their purposes and now lay silent. Their runways and perimeter roads had been constructed very rapidly but, for the most part, provided good quality tarmac surfaces which, it was realised, were ideally suited to the needs of motor sport enthusiasts. There was a general desire to restart motor sport as soon as possible and, with permanent circuits lost, these airfield venues seemed to provide an answer.

Even in 1945, at a Council meeting of the Junior Car Club (the forerunner of the British Automobile Racing Club), Gordon England had suggested that a disused airfield might be a possible venue for a race meeting and Kidlington in Oxfordshire was mentioned as a possibility. It was, however, a group of enthusiasts in the Eastern Counties who were first off the mark when, in June, 1946, the first post-war race meeting in the country took place at Gransden Lodge airfield in Suffolk. This was Britain's first airfield circuit and it used a combination of runways and perimeter roads to produce a circuit of 2.13 miles. The pioneering organisers were not from any of the major, well-established clubs but were members of the Cambridge University Automobile Club.

The example set by the University clearly inspired the Junior Car Club to renew their efforts to find a similar venue for themselves and, in due course, the disused Westhampnett airfield, on the Goodwood estate of their president, the Duke of Richmond and Gordon, was pressed into service. The first meeting on the 2.6 mile perimeter road of the airfield was held in September, 1948.

In the meantime, the RAC Competitions Committee had set its sights higher and had plans for Britain's first post-war Grand Prix in hand. Building a circuit from scratch was out of the question but a search of redundant airfields had been narrowed down to a choice between two centrally placed establishments. Snitterfield, near Stratford-upon-Avon, and the former Wellington bomber base at Silverstone straddling the Northamptonshire/Buckinghamshire border. A lease was arranged for the short-term use of the latter venue and the new circuit's first meeting, the RAC Grand Prix - the British Grand Prix in all but name - took place on 2nd October, 1948.

DIVINE AROMA

So Castrol R is back in pungent glory,
Nostalgic, oleaginous and sweet,
And half an hour at Boreham or at Goodwood
Shall set your jaded nose upon its feet.

Its twin-cylinder G.N's and belt-drive Nortons,
It's Brooklands on Bank Holiday as well,
And mucking up a perfectly good engine
Just to get the golden glory of the smell.

The savour of burnt almonds is perfection
Now wedded to a castor base at last,
The thin blue haze makes mirage in the sunshine
To conjure up the paddocks of the past.

And when you point your bonnet to Valhalla
To learn anew the old enthralling game,
As you change up just beyond the spiral Nebulae,
What else is strange, the smell will be the same.

Attributed to W R Charnock
via Patrick Murrell

No.85 Whitehouse (998 cc Cooper-H.R.D.) and No.80 G E Matthews (Jaguar) in a speed trial on 26th March, 1950. Matthews was later to put up the fastest time of the day (*photo: Autocar*)

THE ORIGINS OF BOREHAM CIRCUIT

One might imagine that the revival of circuit racing in any form would have been welcomed unreservedly by motor sport enthusiasts who had been deprived of their sport during the long war years. Rather surprisingly this was not the case and there was a degree of opposition from some quarters where it was felt that airfields were quite unsuitable for circuit racing. The use of such flat and featureless venues was derided by those accustomed to seeing racing on the tree-lined straights and village streets of continental circuits. The new airfield circuits, it was felt, would be too easy and too forgiving; there simply were not enough hazards and the circuits would provide an entirely inadequate training ground for drivers who would face such hazards on circuits elsewhere in Europe.

There can be no denying that the new venues, for obvious reasons, lacked the gradients and man-made hazards found on many true circuits and that a combination of their necessarily rather exposed positions and featureless outlooks was not a promising basis on which to attempt to reproduce the kind of atmosphere to be found at continental events of the day. It was, however, very much a case of using what was available; a temporary expedient to meet a particular need.

A requirement in early post-war years was that airfields had to retain a capability of being returned to operational use within 48 hours. In such circum-stances, spectator protection amounted to straw bales and a rope barrier and, perhaps more importantly, a respectful distance between track and spectating public. The immediacy of public road circuits could not be replicated.

Whatever misgivings there may have been it became increasingly clear that airfields were to play a major part in the future of motor racing in this country and by the mid 1950s, following the example set by the pioneering Gransden, the runways and perimeter roads at Charterhall, Ibsley, Castle Combe, Full Sutton, Davidstow, Snetterton, Winfield, Crimond, Camston, Thruxton, Turnberry, Brough, Fersfield - and Boreham had echoed to the sounds of racing exhausts and squealing of tortured tyres. The few undulating 'road circuits' introduced during this period, notably Brands Hatch, Oulton Park and a re-established, and shortened version of, Crystal Palace brought some welcome relief in more than one sense of the word but, for the most part, enthusiasts enjoyed their sport in the spacious surroundings afforded by redundant airfields. After the first tentative steps into airfield racing, the concept had seemed to gather pace quite quickly. Almost in the same way the severe pruning of a plant brings forth vibrant new growth, the drastic loss of Britain's pre-war circuits seemed to result in a blossoming of new venues.

The first new 'shoots' at Boreham can be detected as early as 1948, when Alan Rippon, a racing driver living in nearby Chelmsford, investigated the airfield

Alan Rippon, a staunch advocate for the use of Boreham Airfield as a motor racing circuit (*photo: via Anthony Skingley*)

as a possible place at which to carry out trials of an experimental car which he and C J M Abbot were contemplating constructing. Permission was obtained from the site owners, Co-Partnership Farms Ltd and the car was ready early in 1949. The roads and runways, however, were in no fit state for motor vehicles and Mr Rippon and a group of friends who, in later years, he was to describe as "the early settlers" of Boreham set to and cleared large pieces of concrete from the track in preparation for its new use. With the example of Silverstone fresh in people's minds this small group of enthusiasts may have seen the potential of the site for circuit racing but no record can be found that indicates that they contemplated using the venue for anything other than for testing purposes.

The availability of non-public roads and wide open spaces at Boreham had attracted the attention of a second group of motorists by the end of the 1940s. Their interests similarly lay in high speed motoring but for primarily non-sporting reasons. They were members of the Essex Police Wing Advanced Driving School, Chelmsford, under the guidance of chief instructor Inspector R Priestley. This school, described by the perhaps biased correspondent of the *Essex Weekly News* as "one of the best of its kind in the world" was not averse to its students mixing work and pleasure and its students undertook competition work around the country, gaining numerous awards in rallies and driving tests. It was this school's participation in local driving tests that brought it into contact with the West Essex Car Club and which, in turn, alerted this club to the wider possibilities which existed at the old USAAF Boreham airfield on its doorstep.

The West Essex Car Club was to play a vital rôle in the events which were to unfold at the venue in subsequent years. The club's origins lay in an informal gathering of enthusiasts who, through travelling to motoring events throughout the country, became acquainted. In 1947 they proposed a club to bring together others in the locality who shared their interests. 1948 saw the club officially constituted - there were farmers and farm workers, young businessmen and shop workers among the early members. Initial activity was confined to dances, film shows, minor rallies and driving tests but members were keen to expand into more serious mainline motor sporting activities. The track at Silverstone seemed to offer the best opportunity for the organisation of a speed event and the club investigated the possibility of organising a race meeting in conjunction with seven other like-minded clubs.

What the club described as their "sincere enthusiasm for a return of motor sport after the war" was coupled with a desire to see a fair share of this type of sport in the county of Essex. With this in mind, the club's energetic Competition Secretary, George Matthews, was pursuing another possible venue. In November, 1949, he reported to a WECC Committee meeting that he "had hopes of obtaining permission for the use of an airfield which, if Silverstone were to be unobtainable, might be suitable for a race meeting." The committee decided that whatever the outcome of the Silverstone negotiations might be "the Competitions Secretary should continue his endeavours to secure the use of the airfield" and he was authorised to make whatever financial arrangements he considered reasonable in order to secure the use of the airfield. At this delicate stage of negotiations the venue remained unnamed in reports of committee meetings. Even at this early stage in the club's short history, the membership's hopes of finding a venue for speed events had already been raised and dashed several times. Valentines Park in Ilford, Matching Green, Stapleford, North Weald and even Canvey Island had each been the subject of negotiations that had not borne fruit. It had to be admitted, however, that the site at Boreham Airfield began to look promising.

In December, 1949, George Matthews met the principals of Co-Partnership Farms Ltd, the owners of Boreham airfield. In this company the club found an organisation receptive to their ideas. The Co-Partnership concern benefitted from having within its ranks farmers of some vision including a number who were motorists themselves which in itself was no foregone conclusion at a time when horsepower, in a literal sense, had not yet been totally supplanted by tractor power on Britain's farms. The helpful attitude that Alan Rippon and the Police Driving School had met in preceding years was extended to the West Essex Car Club and negotiations reached a successful conclusion. The use of the venue for a speed trial - a straight line acceleration test - on the main runway was agreed.

Wheelspin, the bulletin of the West Essex Car Club, proudly announced in its Editorial of its first issue of 1950, "The privilege of publishing a grand piece of news falls to *Wheelspin* in announcing that the Club has secured permission from the owners and the R.A.C. to run a Closed Speed Trial at an airfield in Essex. This is, we hope, the first event of many to follow, as apart from speed trials, the venue is quite suitable for putting on club races, etc., including circuit racing".

At this stage, permission from Co-Partnership Farms Ltd was solely for speed trials for which the club had agreed to pay five guineas in the case of 'Closed' events and ten guineas in the case of 'Invitation' events. The 'Closed' classification of this first event meant that it would be open to West Essex Car Club members only and led to a spate of applications for membership. An emergency meeting held just eight days before the event duly accepted the applications of 21 new members. The first speed trial in the history of the club was about to become a reality.

SPEED TRIALS MEETING - 26th MARCH, 1950

In the autumn of 1949, the West Essex Car Club, (formed only one year earlier) saw the use to which Boreham airfield could be put, and following negotiations with Co-Partnership Farms, who were the owners of the site, held their first ever event there. It was termed a 'Driving Test', and occurred at the end of the Chelmsford Car Rally.

It was a rather bare looking airfield at which competitors gathered on an early Spring day in 1950 for the event. The meeting was a closed club event run mainly for the enjoyment of the club's members. For an event of this nature, the entry of almost 100 cars was impressive - even allowing for the participation of members of the local Chelmsford Police Drivers' School - and perhaps indicated the extent of untapped enthusiasm for speed events in this part of the country.

By using the main 6,000 feet airfield runway, rather than the perimeter track later used for circuit racing, it was possible to set out a one kilometre standing-start course. The generous 150-feet width of this runway meant that cars could be despatched in pairs in what *Autocar* described as a 'miniature Brighton speed trial' event. Classes ranged from standard saloon cars to racing cars and the entry displayed that pleasing mixture of ex-Brooklands cars and post-war vehicles so typical of meetings of this period. Amongst the categories of sports and racing cars were a J2 Allard, two Silverstone Healeys, an O.B.M. in sports car trim belonging to Oscar Moore, Tony Crook's 2 litre blown Alta, D Parker's 500 cc Parker Special and a sprint Jaguar belonging to George Matthews. This latter car was a SS Jaguar 100-based special (chassis 18008) which had been developed by the works in the late 1930s and had been bought by Matthews in 1948.

Mechanical misfortunes befell Symonds' Austin which had a cylinder suddenly fill with water and Whitehouse's Cooper-H.R.D., which holed a piston. More significantly however the Tony Crook Alta lost a timing chain tensioner after two very fast runs; this misfortune leaving the way clear for the sprint Jaguar to take fastest time of the day albeit by only 0.26 seconds from the crippled Alta which before its troubles, had done sufficient to win the racing car class.

This was the first ever speed event organised by the young Essex Car Club and, after just a few delays, the meeting ran smoothly throughout what was almost a full day of competition. It must have been doubly satisfying to the organising club that one of their most stalwart members George Matthews had taken FTD (fastest time of the day). He had been a Brooklands competitor and in post-war years a keen hill climb and sprint exponent. At all subsequent circuit racing meetings held at Boreham, he assumed the responsibilities of Clerk of the Course and Secretary of the Meeting.

Even at this early stage it was hoped that circuit racing might come to Boreham but as competitors headed homeward on that March Sunday evening few could have imagined that they had been pioneers at a venue which, during an all too brief two-and-a-half years, would witness some of the sports' top stars competing in international events.

1 KILOMETRE STANDING START

T A D Crook

FASTEST TIME OF THE DAY
| G E Matthews | Jaguar | 76.74 mph |

FASTEST RACING CAR
| T A D Crook | Alta | 76.06 mph |

FASTEST UNSUPERCHARGED CAR
| R Way | Frazer-Nash-BMW | 31.23 seconds |

FASTEST SPORTS CAR IN ANY TRIM:
| R Ayrson | Bugatti | 32.32 seconds |

FASTEST STANDARD OPEN CAR
| G E Matthews | Jaguar | 34.16 seconds |

FASTEST STANDARD SALOON CAR
| A K Watson Police Driver | Jaguar | 38.64 seconds |

FASTEST CAR DRIVEN BY WOMAN DRIVER
| Mrs J Mortimer | Healey | 34.16 seconds |

MILL TROPHY (Fastest MG Midget with standard body)
| R W Jacobs | MG T.C. | 41.50 seconds |

RACING CARS
| G H Symonds | Austin | 31.45 seconds |

SPORTS CAR IN ANY TRIM up to 1000 cc
| R W Jacobs | MG | 33.11 seconds |

1100 to 1500 cc
| G E Phillips | MG | 34.18 seconds |

STANDARD OPEN CARS up to 1100 cc
| R A May | MG | 43.24 seconds |

1100 cc to 1500 cc
| R W Jacobs | MG T.C. | 41.5 seconds |

1501 cc to 3000 cc
| F A Spiller | MG | 38.8 seconds |

UNLIMITED
| R K Clarkson | Allard J-Type | 36.6 seconds |

STANDARD SALOON CARS up to 1100 cc
| J V Lewis | Riley | 50.75 seconds |

1100 to 1500 cc
| H W Dalling, Police Driver | MG | 46.0 seconds |

1501 to 3000 cc
| M H Buckler | Healey | 39.06 seconds |

UNLIMITED:
| A H J Whitehead, Police Driver | Jaguar | 39.13 seconds |

SPEED TRIALS MEETING - 1st APRIL, 1951

Sunday, 1st April, saw the first of the WECC's 1951 meetings. The event was for members only, but still well attended with over a hundred cars competing, in seventeen classes of speed trials over a distance of one kilometre from a standing start, over what was described as "the broad runways of the airfield".

It was said that the variety of entry ensured that there was much to see and hear, and took one back to the pre-war days at Brooklands. The day was very cold and started by being very wet, although it cleared towards lunchtime, some rather flooded patches were left on the course.

Racing began at 10 a.m. and the last race was completed by 5 p.m. It was a credit to the WECC that the event was very efficiently run without delays or incidents, with many spectators watching the racing with enthusiasm. Again it was said that it made a good curtain raiser to circuit racing which was to be held at Boreham later in the season.

Top honours for the day's events with the best time went to the bearded A J (Archie) Butterworth. He was driving his 'unpretentious' 4.5 litre Steyr-engined four wheel drive A J B. The car was described as 'most astonishing'. It had no secrets or mystery devices to assist in its performance. An unblown engine, cart springs front and rear, modified Jeep axles and transmission, a very substantial chassis, and plain disc pattern wheels.

The V8 Steyr engine with a compression ratio of 14-1, giving about 180 plus b.h.p. was the secret to success. The getaway for this incredible vehicle it was said, had to be seen to be believed. Butterworth's time over the kilometre was just 25.12 seconds, a new record.

John Appleton was driving his specially developed Riley Maserati on which he had spent a considerable amount of money since the mid-1930's. The basis of the vehicle had been an 1100 cc Maserati with a four cylinder engine. This had been changed for a four cylinder blown 1100 cc Riley engine with better results. A big blower was fitted, a new chassis and single seater body, new brakes and eventually a three bearing crankshaft replaced the old two bearing.

The car entered by Tony Crook, spun its wheels at the start of the race, and the enormous engine roar was similar to that remembered from more than twelve years previously. It clocked 31 seconds.

A good dozen or more XK120 Jaguars were there, but perhaps because they were becoming a common sight at the time, were not warranting any more than a glance, although still good competitive cars.

Don Parker was present with his new JBS 500, fitted with a speedway J.A.P. engine. The rear wheels of the car had to be jacked up and a wheel spin given before it would start, but the staccato sound of its engine was no longer there, replaced now by a pleasant efficient sounding burble.

The well known sprint special Jaguette of Gordon Parker was also competing. Six short exhaust pipe stubs accounted for the excessive noise which caused a few ladies to retreat. It was fitted with a six cylinder 2.66 litre pre-war S.S. Jaguar engine, mounted in a Magnette chassis, this engine had replaced a 1.25 litre M.G. engine and improved the power to weight ratio. The results for Parker being 28.69 seconds over the one kilometre.

In the sports car classes, MGs of all kinds were competing. George Phillips and Dick Jacobs were running neck and neck in MG T.D.s which weighed 18 cwt each, until the former's gearbox failed.

Amongst the many midgets was an historic K3 Magnette, one of the original MILLE MIGLIA cars of 1933. It had a Powerplus blower and single S.U. carburettor. It was owned by M Potter-More who was making his first sprint with the car. He was no match, however, for the PB Midget of E J Hasendonck which shot away into the distance.

Another classic vehicle in black cellulose taking part was the actual ex-Fontes-Hindmarch 4.5 litre Lagonda which had won the Le Mans 24 hour race in 1935.

The bracing of the rear brake backplate had to be seen to be believed. It was described as 'certainly a noble vehicle', even though the same type of Meadows engine, minus furbishings, was fitted to many a pre-war Albion lorry.

True to form, the Bugattis were there and the glorious 'Bug' sound rang across the airfield, as M Hukins in his 2.3 litre with wire wheels and semi-elliptic rear springs, shot away with A S Raven in his most un-Molsheim single seater with type 44, 3 litre engine.

The car constructed by Jack Andrews created considerable interest. A Ford V8 powered rear engined sports car, with a beautifully made and finished bodywork, mounted on a large diameter steel tubed chassis. All wheels had independent suspension, and the rear wheel drive was through an ordinary Ford 3 speed gear box.

Another competitor's vehicle, the Buick Special belonging to W C Turner, was also of some interest. Built by the owner, who had no professional experience or special equipment, in "his own back yard". It had an excellent body form, radiator and wing treatment, and lines which could match many sports cars at that time. The 3400 cc Buick engine, fitted into a chassis of circa 1932 vintage, propelled the vehicle smartly off the starting line with a curious high pitched note.

There were many other intriguing looking cars taking part including David Brake's immaculate Cooper, several Frazer-Nashes, a fine looking Mille-Miglia model, an MG engined sports Cooper, a Norris Special, a 1100 cc Alta, and a Hudson, a prominent pre-war sprint car, the 328 based O.B.M. driven by Terry More, one or two Silverstone Healeys and an impeccable Le Mans Aston-Martin and a new A40 Sports Austin first introduced at the Earls Court Motor Show in 1950.

1 Kilometre standing start

BEST TIME OF DAY
A J Butterworth   A.J.B.   25.12 seconds (new record)
AWARD FOR FASTEST RACING CAR
J B Norris   Alta   27.5 seconds
FASTEST SPORTS CAR (any trim)
Gordon Parker   Jaguette   28.69 seconds
AWARD FOR FASTEST UNSUPERCHARGED CAR (up to 1500 cc)
C A Booker   Cooper   28.47 seconds
FASTEST OPEN STANDARD CAR
W B Black   Allard   33.82 seconds
FASTEST STANDARD SALOON
T A D Crook   Bristol   37.6 seconds
SALOON CARS UP TO 1100 cc
J V Lewis   Riley   48.48 seconds
SALOON CARS 1100 to 1500 cc
A   G Baker   MG   46.75 seconds
SALOON CARS 1501 to 3000 cc
G H Grace   Riley   39.58 seconds
SALOON CARS over 3000 cc
F J Covington   Jaguar   39.62 seconds

Don Parker

OPEN CARS UP TO 1100 cc
A C Westwood   Fiat   44.2 seconds
OPEN CARS 1100 to 1500 cc
J T K Line   MG   40.0 seconds (fastest standard MG Midget)
OPEN CARS 1501 to 3000 cc
F Spiller   Healey   36.45 seconds
OPEN CARS over 3000 cc
J Craig   Jaguar   34.0 seconds
SPORTS CARS up to 1100 cc
S G Greene   MG   41.0 seconds
SPORTS CARS up to 1500 cc
A G Baker   MG   30.64 seconds
SPORTS CARS 1501 to 3000 cc
S G Greene   Frazer-Nash   32.9 seconds
SPORTS CARS over 3000 cc
P Larrinaga   Allard   34.06 seconds
500 cc RACING CARS
D Parker   J.B.S.   32.8 seconds
501 to 1100 cc RACING CARS.
D N Brake   Cooper   28.6 seconds
1100 to 1500 cc RACING CARS
R J W Appleton   Appleton Special   31.0 seconds

WEST ESSEX CAR CLUB

OFFICIAL   PROGRAMME

CHELMSFORD SPEED TRIAL

1/-

BOREHAM AIRFIELD,
on Sunday, 1st. April 1951, at 10 a.m.

18

1501 to 3000 cc RACING CARS
M Hukins   Bugatti   39.72 seconds
Over 3000 cc RACING CARS
A S Raven   Bugatti   29.8 seconds
(only one award could be taken by one entrant)

No.78 J V Lewis (1087 cc Riley) - Winner, Saloon cars up to 1100 cc, 48.48 seconds (*photo: Essex Chronicle Series, Ltd.*)

Main runway (6,000 feet long) looking north-west. All speed trials were carried out here, over a distance of 1 kilometre (3,281 feet)

CAR RACE MEETING - SATURDAY, 26th MAY, 1951

After a certain amount of prevarication during 1950, Co-Partnership Farms, Ltd., encouraged by the success of the first motor cycle race meeting in September, gave consent for circuit racing on the perimeter roads of the airfield. The company indicated that, rather than hand matters over to the WECC on a temporary lease arrangement, it wished to be more deeply involved and to be responsible for the overall management of events. There would be no direct financial input from the organising club and indeed it would receive remuneration for running the events; a sum of 50 guineas per meeting was mentioned. Some necessary repairs to the track were carried out and, for the benefit of spectators, the entire outside of the circuit was encircled by what the club described in its bulletin as "a flourishing green belt of freshly sown grass" which was provided to enable spectators to circulate unhampered from one vantage point to another.

The air of keen anticipation surrounding the new venture was heightened when the RAC announced that it was not going to renew its lease of Silverstone after the end of 1951. Was it possible that Boreham, the layout of which had many similarities with Silverstone, could take over as the country's premier motor sport venue? Even before a wheel had turned in anger on the new circuit, pundits were speculating on this possibility. Writing in the *Essex Weekly News* under the heading 'Motor Mecca for Essex' on the eve of the first meeting, 'Sentinel' wrote, "It is no exaggeration to say that all over Britain tomorrow the interest of car racing enthusiasts will be centred on Boreham, Essex. For there, at the first open car race meeting to be held on the airfield track, the future of our car racing in this Country will, to a large extent, be decided". With the predicted end of Silverstone, it was felt that Boreham may well have been on the verge of becoming "the new home of British car racing".

"Only Boreham, it seems can provide equal or better facilities. Goodwood has always been a strong favourite, but there the course is smaller, and further from London, Brands Hatch, in Kent, has only a three-quarter mile lap, Donington, a pre-war circuit, offers many difficulties; and other tracks are too far in the North. Boreham presents an ideal centre, close to London, served by main roads and railway lines. It will certainly be more convenient than any other for the thousands of followers of a sport that grows ever more popular."

It was considered as probably a good sign for the track's future that a senior official from the Italian Embassy in London would be present at the meeting: the Italian teams having complained about the running of the Silverstone meetings.

Clearly the West Essex Car Club was keen to make a good impression and the club, which in due course became known for the generous starting money which it offered, had assembled a fine entry for this first race meeting. The Formula Libre race for the Boreham Challenge Trophy was oversubscribed and the club

The start of the first-ever circuit race at Boreham (1500 cc sports cars - 5 laps). Leading is No.78 W Croysdill (Lester MG), second from left W Archie Scott Brown (MG) (*photo: Don Moore*)

Alan Rippon and support team. L to R: Tony Skingley, ?, 'Ginger' Hamilton, John Broad, Alan Rippon (*photo: via Anthony Skingley*)

had attracted the largest ever number of Formula 3 (500 cc) cars to a circuit event. It was probably a combination of the good entry and the novelty of motor racing in this corner of Essex that brought a large crowd to the circuit. Estimates of the attendance varied, somewhat wildly, between nearly 20,000 and 35,000. Pedestrians were charged 3/6 (17½p), cyclists 4/6 (22½p), motorcyclists 6/- (30p) and cars including occupants £1.

In the morning practice session, Reg Parnell in his 1.5 litre Maserati 4CLT demonstrated the potential of the course when, after just four practice laps, he lapped at an average speed of 91.25 mph. The course was marked by white-painted oil drums; spectator protection was one or two rows of well-spaced straw bales and a post and rope fence. The start and finish straight was marked by a banner hung across the track from striped poles, and the ubiquitous time-keepers' double-deck bus.

The circuit itself was a generous 50 feet wide track, 3 miles long, each corner adopting the name of a local feature. After a slight left-hand kink soon after the start the track swept through a slightly off-camber right hander Hangar Bend. A wide open 150 degree turn at Waltham Corner led to Tower Bend, near the old airfield control tower, which despite a surface change was a nearly flat-out left-hander. The following right-hander at Orchard Corner was a critical part of the circuit as it led into the fastest part of the course - Dukes Straight - named after the wood which covered much of the area before the airfield was built. Railway Corner, at the end of this straight, was the nearest point to the London to Norwich railway line. It was the slowest corner of the track and brought cars back to the start-finish straight.

After morning practice, racing got under way slightly later than the advertised 1 p.m. start in overcast but dry conditions. When the meeting's official starter, Charles Fothergill, brought down the union flag a new era in the life of Boreham was heralded in and a field of 14 cars comprising mostly MGs set off on a 5-lap, 15-mile scratch race for sports cars up to 1500 cc. Although the grid had been lined up on the basis of a driver ballot, this haphazard system did not prevent the eventual winner W Croysdill in his Lester MG from taking a two to three length lead over the rest of the field by the time they turned into Hangar Bend on that first lap. He was unchallenged throughout and averaged 73.83 mph to lead home George Phillips' MG, R Thurgood's HRG, G Samson's MG and R Richards' RBW. Railway Corner, which by the end of the meeting had unofficially been re-christened 'Gilhooley Corner' had claimed its first victim when J Stocks spun his MG wildly but harmlessly.

The two 5-lap qualifying heats for 500 cc Formula 3 cars which followed were needed to reduce the 49-strong entry to a more manageable 30 cars for the final later in the afternoon. In reality, non-starters, which disappointingly included the works Coopers, had already reduced the number. Heat One was an Eric Brandon benefit, the Ecurie Richmond driver taking his Cooper Norton to a clear win ahead of a race-long duel between Les Leston (JBS-JAP) and George Wicken (Cooper JAP), the latter leading across the line on every lap apart from the most important one.

Ecurie Richmond's other driver, Alan Brown, appeared to be following in his team-mate's wheeltracks in Heat Two but retired with a seized engine at the halfway stage whilst leading. The 20-year-old Peter Collins, driving a JBS for the first time, inherited the lead and took the victor's laurels. The young Kidderminster driver was already demonstrating the quality that would take him to Formula 1. In fact, Collins led home a 1-2-3 finish for the numerically less favoured JBS cars ahead of hordes of Coopers. For the young JBS outfit, mounting a serious challenge to Coopers' supremacy in the formula, this was a most encouraging result at a time when spirits were low. Its gifted co-founder, designer and works driver, Alf Bottoms, had tragically lost his life in the Luxembourg Grand Prix just three weeks earlier.

As the Formula 3 cars returned to the paddock to be prepared for their final, two more 5-lap scratch races for sports cars kept the large crowd entertained. These races, like the opening event were qualifying races for the main sports car race, scheduled for the last event of the day, when all the capacity classes would be brought together; the first seven finishers from each qualifying race went through to the final. In the 1501-2500 cc race Tony Crook (Frazer-Nash) ran out an easy winner after an initial challenge by Dick Jacobs' MG. The latter fell victim to the slippery 'Gilhooley' corner allowing the closely following Ken McAlpine (Connaught), after expertly avoiding the errant MG, to take second place. Jacobs fought his way back to third ahead of Tom Meyer (HWM) and H Kemp-Place (Healey) at the finish. With Frazer-Nash, Connaught, MG, HWM and Healey occupying the first five positions, Britain's specialist sports car companies were well represented.

The rain that had threatened for much of the day was now making the track greasy and in the over 2500 cc sports car race that followed several drivers were caught out by the worsening conditions, amongst them Wicken, Binns and Jelley, all in Jaguar XK120s. It was another Jaguar XK120 driven by Hugh Howorth which took the chequered flag. Guy Gale's old but well-driven 4-litre Darracq finished in second place, the only non-Jaguar in the top five. Behind him in third place was D Pierpoint.

Heavy rain had set in for the 15 lap Formula 3 final but pole position man Eric Brandon showed himself to be master of the conditions as he gradually pulled clear of Wicken. When the latter's Cooper-Jap broke its driving chain and Gray (Cooper), Parker (JBS) and Moore (JBS) had spun out of contention, the chasing group comprised Peter Collins (JBS), Paul Emery, in the distinctive front-engined, front wheel drive Emeryson, Ken McAlpine (JBS) and the Cooper-JAPs of Donald

Beauman and Norman Pugh. It developed into a most confusing race for spectators: those who managed to maintain sodden lap charts in the downpour were faced with keeping track of spinning cars on every lap. Railway Corner (Gilhooley) alone claimed at least ten victims - one third of the entire field! Whilst most managed to resume racing, Major Peter Braid (Cooper) ended his race ignominiously perched on top of a straw bale, although this was relatively tame by his own high standards: in 1949 in a Formula 3 race at the Blandford Army Camp circuit he had somehow contrived to park his car on the roof of the camp's guardroom. It was clearly a struggle to stay on the track but Brandon duly completed the task without mishap to claim the first prize of £100 at an average speed of 71.22 mph and was followed home by Collins in a safe second place. Ken McAlpine in third made it two JBS cars in the top three.

The meeting's only handicap event - a 5-lap race for MG cars brought yet more drama at Railway Corner when A Lusty's red TD spun on the second lap making W Scott Brown (TD) and J Burgess (TC) take avoiding action; all three, according to one report "waltzed around like curling stones gone mad". One of the drivers on scratch, F Davis in his Leonard modified Magnette, drove a finely judged race to make up the 100 second deficit on the limit men to take first place. D Moore, one of these limit men, finished second in his 847 cc PA model with W Knight (Special) third.

The 'First Race in Great Britain exclusively for the famous Jaguar XK120 cars' which followed was billed as one of the meeting's special attractions in advertisements for the meeting. Unlike today, when one-make races and championships proliferate, it was relatively rare to find such a race in the early 1950s. Sadly it proved to be dull with Howorth taking an early lead with the rest of the field strung out behind him. He took his second win of the meeting in his XK120 at the somewhat reduced speed, reflecting the conditions, of 70.95 mph. The 'disappointment of the day' was how a local newspaper described the race, musing that perhaps 'no one wanted to crash four figures worth of car'. While Howorth took the Jaguar Challenge Trophy, cups for second and third went to George Wicken and D Pierpoint.

Although, rather strangely, the 15-lap Formula Libre race for the Boreham Challenge Trophy did not feature in local advertising for the meeting (unlike the Formula 3 and XK120 races) it would have been keenly anticipated by knowledgeable enthusiasts in the crowd. The race meeting was a closed club event, that is, open only to members of the organising club and invited clubs, but the quality and number of entries was surprisingly high in this race and gave spectators the chance to see Britain's most experienced Grand Prix driver, Reg Parnell, in his Maserati 4CLT. Parnell had driven for the all-conquering Alfa Romeo team at the previous year's British Grand Prix - thus becoming the first British driver to drive for a foreign team since Dick Seaman drove for Mercedes-

Stewards await action as Reg Parnell (Maserati- 4 CLT. 1.5 s/c) approaches from the right in poor conditions (*photo: T C W Wigg*)

No.114 H Howorth (XK120 Jaguar) - Winner, 'Jaguar Challenge Trophy'

Benz before the war. Just three weeks before his Boreham appearance he had famously taken the top prize money against the cream of Formula 1 at Silverstone's rain-shortened International Trophy driving, on that occasion, Tony Vandervell's 4.5 litre Ferrari 375 'Thinwall Special'. He was to become a keen advocate of Boreham during the circuit's short life. Other notable entries were the 1950 British hill climb champion Dennis Poore in his ex-Hans Ruesch 3.8 litre Alfa Romeo 8C-35 and Tony Rolt in the Rob Walker 1.5 litre Delage-ERA.

At the start, on a streaming wet track, Parnell leapt into a clear lead. The other occupants of the front row, Rolt, Poore and Booker (Cooper-JAP), seemed to be left standing and Sydney Allard swept past them into second place in his Allard sports car. The 5.4 litre Cadillac-engined car amazingly hung on to this position for two laps.

Poore then began motoring to great effect in his big green Alfa Romeo and not only passed Rolt's Delage and the Allard but also began closing the gap to Parnell. On the eighth lap - half distance - he had caught the leader and successfully made his challenge on Dukes Straight. Parnell tried to respond at the next corner but he chose his spot badly; the next corner was the treacherous 'Gilhooley' which duly embraced its most significant victim of the afternoon. Parnell blamed himself for the misjudgment which nearly carried him into the crowd, narrowly missing a loudspeaker pole, but clearly the Maserati was suffering from a locking nearside front brake.

With Poore now well ahead, Allard and Rolt took advantage of Parnell's indiscretion and motored by, with Rolt eventually passing the rapidly driven sports car into second place. Parnell treated the crowd to crowd to a comeback drive after losing at least one-and-a-half minutes and brought his battered Maserati back up to third place. Insufficient laps remained for him to progress any further although he did make one determined attempt to get past the second-placed Delage at the end. Poore, meanwhile, was unchallenged in the lead and completed the race at an average of 80.36 mph, well below the morning's practice speeds but commendable in the prevailing conditions. His reward was the Boreham Challenge Trophy, £100 and circuit's outright lap record of 2 minutes 10 seconds (83 mph). Behind Allard a dice for fifth place was resolved when Eric Thompson driving R Ayrson's Bugatti managed to pass and stay ahead of Miles Martin's ERA R2A. Despite the large number of non-starters - only 13 cars started out of an entry of 30 and 6 reserves - it had been an absorbing and entertaining race.

The final, and wettest, race in a perhaps over-ambitious 10-race programme was the Sports Car Race Final of 10 laps. It was, by this time, about 7 p.m. As a result of poor weather, numerous incidents and perhaps reflecting the club's inexperience, the meeting was now running about one-and-a-half hours late.

During this race it seemed that almost everyone spun, some managing two or three spins. Through the chaos and murk, the well-driven, venerable 4-litre

Darracq of Guy Gale emerged to take the final chequered flag of the day. A fist-shaking duel behind Gale saw Tony Crook (Frazer-Nash) displace the race's initial leader Howorth (Jaguar XK120) for second place. The track surface had seemed to offer minimal grip in the rain and in the latter stages of the meeting the crowd, in *Autosport*'s words, "saw some of the most astonishing incidents ever to be witnessed in motor racing". Boreham had made its mark but perhaps not in the way that its instigators had hoped...

SPORTS CARS UP TO 1500 cc		5 laps
W Croysdill	Lester MG	73.85 mph
G E Phillips	MG	
R Thurgood	MG	

500 cc Formula 3 HEAT 1		5 laps
E Brandon	Cooper-Norton	79.76 mph
L Leston	JBS-JAP	
G Wicken	Cooper-JAP	

500 cc FORMULA 3 HEAT 2		5 laps
P Collins	JBS-Norton	79.06 mph
J Westcott	JBS-Norton	
D Parker	JBS-JAP	

Peter Collins (J.B.S.)

SPORTS CARS 1501 to 2500 cc		5 laps
T A D Crook	Frazer-Nash	77.36 mph
K McAlpine	Connaught	
R W Jacobs	MG	

SPORTS CARS 2501 cc upwards		5 laps
H Howorth	Jaguar	78.40 mph
G Gale	Darracq	
D Pierpoint	Jaguar	

Eric Brandon

500 cc FORMULA 3 FINAL		15 laps
E Brandon	Cooper-Norton	71.22 mph
P Collins	JBS-Norton	
K McAlpine	JBS-Norton	

MG HANDICAP		5 laps
F Davis	MG Special	68.47 mph
D Moore	MG PA	
W Knight	MG Special	

Dennis Poore

'JAGUAR CHALLENGE TROPHY' for JAGUAR XK 120s   5 laps
H Howorth   Jaguar XK120   70.95 mph
G Wicken   Jaguar XK120
D Pierpoint   Jaguar XK120

'BOREHAM CHALLENGE TROPHY' for FORMULA LIBRE   15 laps
D Poore   Alfa Romeo   80.36 mph
A Rolt   Delage ERA
R Parnell   Maserati

SPORTS CARS - FINAL   10 laps
G Gale   Darracq   75.50 mph
T A D Crook   Frazer-Nash
H Howorth   Jaguar

(photos: J B Palmer)

No.48 Dennis Poore (Alfa-Romeo) Formula Libre race winner

No.78 W Croysdill (Lester MG) Winner, Sports car race, up to 1500 cc

No.1 Les Leston (J.B.S.) leads No.41 George Wicken (Cooper) in Formula 3 500 cc race

CAR RACE MEETING - 30 JUNE, 1951

Despite the difficulties created by the adverse weather, reactions to the West Essex Car Club's first race meeting were generally favourable. *Autosport* thought that "undoubtedly the three mile circuit has tremendous possibilities for Grand Prix racing" but, perhaps mindful of the inordinately high number of spins during the day, added "re-surfacing is essential". *Autocar* was similarly positive and said that "situated on good roads near London, this venue should prove extremely popular; the circuit in plan is much akin to Silverstone, and the lap speeds are in the same region". It noted, what many drivers had found out to their cost at Railway Corner, that "the circuit is in parts uneven and one corner in particular is very slippery in the wet". There was some suggestion that the tricky Railway Corner should not only be re-surfaced but should be banked for safety but Reg Parnell expressed himself very pleased with the track and did not consider this necessary: "whichever way the corner goes it is the same for everyone and that's where driving counts more than anything" was his commonsense response. In fact, Parnell considered the track to be much superior to Silverstone and in support of his view that Boreham could outstrip Silverstone "in every phase of the game" he pointed out that the track was interesting to drive on - more so than Silverstone, it gave spectators a much better view, it was more accessible for the public and was closer to London.

Reg Parnell's conclusion, expressed in an exclusive interview published in the *Essex Chronicle* was that Boreham would become Britain's top track and also one of the best Grand Prix circuits in Europe. In a glowing report to readers Reg Parnell's interviewer, John Parker, wrote that "every racing correspondent has been praising the track and its potential" and that the drivers themselves, despite the slippery surface, were practically lyrical". The general public, he reported, had gone home quite happy "and reports have in nearly every case been outspokenly favourable". One should perhaps make allowances for local bias, but clearly the track had created a reasonably good impression.

The suitability of the track for future international events was uppermost in people's minds even at this early stage and, in the respect, the views of the visiting Vice-Consul of the Italian Embassy were solicited. It was thought that "his assessment of the possibilities may well bring the crack Italian team to Boreham next year". Reportedly he had nothing but praise for the new track, which augured well for the future. The Italian Government, after all, effectively owned Alfa Romeo through its Instituto Riconstruzione Industriale, so perhaps the idea of a Vice-Consul in London having any influence on the Italian team's affairs may not be so far-fetched as it first seems.

For the time being, though, such thoughts lay in the future. Attention soon became focused on the WECC's next race meeting on 30th June. In the light of experience at the previous meeting some improvements were already in hand at the circuit. More public address loudspeakers were installed and communications between the paddock area, the starting grid and various positions around the course were the subject of improvements which, according to committee minutes, included 'a proper mobile loudspeaker'. The club's pre-race publicity for the event developed the theme of the emerging rivalry between Boreham and Silverstone and quoted national newspapers which had apparently proclaimed Boreham to be "an excellent successor to Silverstone" (*Daily Telegraph*) and 10 mph faster than Silverstone (*Daily Mail*).

WECC obliquely took up this faster-than-Silverstone theme when it described Boreham as Britain's fastest and longest circuit. It may indeed have been fractionally longer than Silverstone (by a couple of hundred yards) but the somewhat extravagant claim to have been faster does not stand close examination.

In May, Silverstone had been lapped at 97.19 mph, almost 6 mph faster than the best practice lap (Parnell's) at Boreham later in the same month. Silverstone also had the distinction of recording the first official 100 mph lap in 1951: a feat not achieved at Boreham (in practice) until the following year. Whilst the claim may have made for good publicity, the figures reveal that in 1951 the Essex venue never did edge ahead of its Midlands rival in the speed stakes. The best that could be said was that the two circuits were quite evenly matched.

Held on the same day as the nearby Chelmsford Carnival, the second car meeting nevertheless attracted a reasonably sized crowd to the circuit. Reports initially suggested that there may have been as many as 50,000 there but, again, one account considered that about half that number may have been present. In fact, a large discrepancy in reported attendance figures seems to have been a particular characteristic of Boreham's meetings, so much so that it led to speculation in the local press that people were actually finding ways into the circuit without paying and that the different figures represented 'official' and 'actual' numbers of people attending. There would, of course, have been some unofficial entrances into a site of this size but it seems hardly plausible that literally thousands of people could have poured through such entrances on a regular basis ... or could they? There was one unconfirmed report in the following year that a farmer near Waltham Corner was running a car park and letting people into the circuit across his land!

Whatever uncertainties there were about the attendance figures, there was one certainty about that second motor race meeting: an indeterminate number of people enjoyed much better weather than at the previous meeting. It was a gloriously warm and sunny day.

The young WECC was still finding its feet in the finer points of organising race meetings and event one, the first of two Formula 3 heats, started some 40 minutes behind schedule. A clashing event at Silverstone meant that the Formula

3 entry was smaller than the record-breaking entry at the first meeting. Twenty cars were to be admitted to the final on this occasion: ten from each heat. Though lower in numbers, the entry was certainly not lower in quality.

The first heat saw the Cooper versus JBS battle rejoined with Bob Gerard, in his first Formula 3 season, Eric Brandon and a 20-year-old Bernie Ecclestone representing the Surbiton marque and Peter Collins, the practically bald Ron 'Curly' Dryden and Les Leston with the JBS cars. Four drivers, initially in the order Dryden, Ecclestone, Collins and Brandon pulled clear of the field as the race got under way but, despite being a qualifying heat, there was no question of these drivers taking it easy in the knowledge that they would comfortably qualify for the final. A thrilling scrap ensued. Dryden dropped back and Collins relieved Ecclestone of the lead on lap 2. Ecclestone stuck with Collins and on the last of the 5 laps re-took the lead only to be outdragged by Collins between the final bend and the finish line. The comfortable winner of the previous month's Formula 3 race at the circuit, Eric Brandon, could only manage fourth on this occasion behind 'Curly' Dryden, but with only a second between first and fourth places there was everything to play for in the final.

The slightly slower second heat was a complete contrast and provided an easy win for Brandon's Ecurie Richmond team mate Alan Brown. Brown drove his Cooper to finish half a lap ahead of K Watkins (Emeryson). Coopers filled the next three places with R W Brise, M Barclay and J Brise comfortably heading for the final.

The winner of Boreham's first ever car race, W Croysdill, probably wished he had the Lester MG he had used on that occasion when the third race of the afternoon got under way. Instead, his entrant Acland and Tabor Ltd had provided him with a Lancia for the 850 cc supercharged, 1500 cc unsupercharged, sports car race. Although this had the speed to figure well - it initially ran third - it fell back and had to be nursed home. Instead it was another Lester MG, a new car entered by the works and driven by Jim Mayers, which mounted an early, but unsuccessful challenge on the race winner's 16-year-old Riley Sprite. The driver of this winning Riley was listed in the programme and race results as 'J Hawthorn' and was none other that John Michael Hawthorn in his first year of circuit racing and already showing glimpses of the potential that would take him to the World Drivers' Championship in 1958. The win was amongst many in a year which culminated in his winning *Motor Sport*'s Brooklands Memorial Trophy at the end of the season. Gerry Ruddock (HRG) took third while, behind, an exciting scrap between R Thurgood (HRG) and T Line (MG) was resolved when Railway Corner claimed Line as another victim.

A small, nine-car field competed in race 4, a 10-lap scratch race for sports cars 851-1500 cc supercharged, 1501-2500 cc unsupercharged. After his fist-shaking dice during the previous month's meeting, Tony Crook (Frazer-Nash) had further occasion to sign language his displeasure during this race. The object of his displeasure was not one of his fellow competitors, for none of them got close enough to challenge him for the lead, but rather it was a visiting light aircraft! This aircraft, which had arrived earlier in the meeting, took off to fly above the leaders. Despite the obvious dangers created by this aerial distraction there was, as *Autosport* reported, "little the flag marshals - lacking Very pistols - could do about it". Behind the fist-shaking Crook, a group of Healeys initially led by F Spiller, occupied the next three places. By the chequered flag this group had been reshuffled to finish in the order A Stokes, H Kemp-Place and Spiller. The WECC bulletin subsequently revealed that the aircraft was a Miles Magister carrying a cine photographer who was taking colour films of the racing for inclusion in the club's film of the 1951 season at Boreham.

It seemed to be more a case of the survivors, rather than the qualifiers, who lined up for the next race, the 15-lap Formula 3 final, with just 18 cars filling the 20 available grid places. It was heat-winner and fastest man in practice, Alan Brown, who was quickest away closely pursued by team mate Eric Brandon, Ecclestone (Cooper), the JBSs of Curly Dryden and Peter Collins, D Gray (Cooper) and Les Leston in another JBS. After initial baulking by Ecclestone, Dryden took third place on lap 3 and was second by lap 6. It was on this lap that the leader, Brown, presented the crowd at the now notorious Railway Corner with a new variation on the spins, marker-tin-flattening and straw-bale-bashing they had already witnessed by "actually motoring for some distance with two wheels on the straw bales". Naturally this was not the quickest way round the corner and Dryden and Brandon were gratefully through into first and second positions before Brown amazingly regained the track ahead of Ecclestone.

Unfortunately, Dryden's excellent climb from fourth to first was in vain. Alerted to a tyre problem on his JBS by the wildly-gesticulating second-placed Brandon, poor 'Curly' retired at Tower Bend with a flat tyre. Ecurie Richmond's two drivers thus inherited first and second positions which they maintained to the chequered flag; Brandon taking the win after a strong last lap challenge by the recovering Brown. The team thus continued its remarkably successful Formula 3 season in what was so often a very closely fought formula. After finishing fourth in his heat, it must have been a particularly satisfying result for Eric Brandon who, nevertheless, regretted the departure of Dryden: "I would have enjoyed it a lot more if Curly's tyre hadn't burst. It would have been a very close race between us". In what was adjudged to be one of the best races of the day, Bernie Ecclestone completed a Cooper 1-2-3 by finishing about 0.2 seconds behind the Ecurie Richmond duo.

Race 6 was a 10-lapper for sports cars over 1501 cc supercharged or over 2500 cc unsupercharged and saw a resumption of the May meeting's fierce and entertaining duel between Tony Crook (Frazer-Nash) and Hugh Howorth (Jaguar

XK120) only this time their battle was for the lead rather than for second place - and what a battle it turned out to be. Crook's Frazer-Nash, a 2 litre car - had already won Event 4 for smaller capacity sports cars and was actually too small to comply with the 2500 cc lower limit for this race. Such niceties did not seem to concern the WECC nor indeed Mr Crook who headed the field for the first three laps at which point Howorth slipped by and led for the next three laps, despite taking a swipe at the long-suffering markers and bales at Railway Corner on lap 5. Perhaps exercising greater caution, Howorth allowed the Frazer-Nash back into the lead as they entered this corner on the following lap. Crook's regained lead lasted but one lap of this enthralling race as laps 7 and 8 belonged to the XK120. However, ending the penultimate lap Howorth surprisingly repeated his earlier error at Railway Corner sending oil drums and straw bales flying once more. The Jaguar driver regained control but Crook, his Frazer-Nash in avoidance also taking to the grass, was through back into the lead. Despite a final moment of over-exuberance resulting in a dramatic slide at the very fast Tower Bend, Crook held on to the end to complete a satisfying double. Obviously the exhilarating duel with Howorth had spurred him on to greater effort and his second win of the day, at 82.99 mph, was a remarkable 6 mph faster than his win in the same car earlier in the day. Behind these two, the Jaguar of D Pierpont initially held off the Allards of Leslie Allard and K Watkins, but Allard eventually took a deserved third place. A McGregor's 4 litre Alvis and S Boshier's Jaguar XK120 added to the mayhem at Railway Corner where, according to *Autosport*'s meticulous reporter, this particular race "left the track patterned with parabolas and 22 marker tins flattened or bent".

Tony Crook, not content with entering two different capacity sports car races, also filed his Frazer-Nash as an entry in the following event, a 15-lap race for racing cars up to 2000 cc unsupercharged, 1100 supercharged but on this occasion he did not feature at the head of the field. Before the starting flag came down, Ron Willis in his Frazer-Nash had left the line - for which he received a one-minute penalty - and led the race for two laps, eventually falling victim to Railway Corner. Ray Merrick in his unconventional 1132 cc Norton-JAP engined Cooper took the lead from the penalised Willis on the second lap with Oscar Moore's Formula 2 HWM in close attendance. Drive of the race came from Connaught backer Kenneth McAlpine who powered his A-type Connaught up from 8th at the start to relieve Moore of second place on lap 12. Merrick and McAlpine were then head to head for the rest of the race; the larger engined Connaught holding a slight straight line advantage, the nimble Cooper faster through the corners. Into the last corner of the last lap, McAlpine was leading and it looked as though he had only to use the superior power of his Lea Francis engine to keep him ahead to the line. Alas, in the excitement, McAlpine momentarily selected neutral and Merrick nipped by to regain the lead and to win at 85.03 mph: a great win for the little Cooper. Two 2 litre cars, an HWM (D Moore) and a Frazer-Nash (Bob Gerard) completed the top four.

This meeting generally had smaller grids than the first meeting and the final event for racing cars over 1100 cc supercharged or 2 litre unsupercharged really hit rock bottom with just four cars coming to the line from an original entry list of more than 15. The quality of the racing, however, could not really be faulted. Archie Butterworth in his own creation, a fearsome looking V8 4.5 litre, 4-wheel-drive, ex-army Jeep chassised device called simply 'AJB', led for two laps until overtaken by the Rob Walker Delage-ERA driven by Tony Rolt. Butterworth hung on grimly but had to concede defeat by some 10 seconds. The other two runners, Howorth in his hard-working Jaguar XK120 and Dunham in his Alvis, had a race-long duel for third spot, the Jaguar's superior straight line speed eventually proving sufficient to bring Howorth home third albeit about a minute and a quarter behind the winner. It was the day's fastest race: Rolt's average being 87.34 mph.

An advertisement in the race programme invited spectators, after the races, to spend an evening at the Chelmsford Carnival celebration in the King's Head Meadow, Chelmsford, where they could enjoy further excitement in the form of motor cycle thrills, a 'Great Firework Display', massed bands and a modern funfair. The final chequered flag of the day had fallen at about 6.45 p.m., more than one-and-a-half hours behind schedule but, nevertheless, some racegoers no doubt would have made the short journey into town to join the evening's festivities at the end of an excellent day's racing.

In due course the WECC was informed that attendance at the event, far from the reported 25-50,000, had only been in the region of 15,000 and that as a result Co-Partnership Farms had incurred a loss. The Club discussed ways of improving crowd figures. A reduction in admission prices was suggested as £1 for a car was thought to be a lot of money if it contained only one or two occupants. The general feeling however was that prices were in line with similar meetings at Goodwood and Silverstone. A further, more esoteric, explanation put forward by one member was that the word 'track' in advertisements gave the wrong impression. "Track," he suggested, was "psychologically unsound as it suggested speedway."

500 cc FORMULA 3 HEAT 1		5 laps
P J Collins	JBS	79.97 mph
B Ecclestone	Cooper	
R M Dryden	JBS	

Tony Rolt (Delage), the eventual winner of Racing cars scratch race, leads Archie Butterworth (A.J.B.)

500 cc FORMULA 3 HEAT 2   5 laps
A Brown   Cooper   79.16 mph
K Watkins   Emeryson
R W Brise   Cooper

SPORTS CARS up to 850 cc S and 1500 cc U/S   10 laps
J Hawthorn   Riley   78.26 mph
J C C Mayers   Lester MG
G A Ruddock   HRG

SPORTS CARS 851 to 1500 cc S and 1501 to 2500 cc U/S   10 laps
T Crook   Frazer-Nash   77.66 mph
A Stokes   Healey
H Kemp-Place   Healey

500 cc FORMULA 3 FINAL   15 laps
E Brandon   Cooper   80.76 mph
A Brown   Cooper
B Ecclestone   Cooper

SPORTS CARS 1501 cc S and 2501 cc U/S upward   10 laps
T Crook   Frazer-Nash   82.99 mph
H Howorth   Jaguar
T L Allard   Allard

RACING CARS up to 1100 cc S and 2000 cc U/S   15 laps
R Merrick   Cooper   85.03 mph
K McAlpine   Connaught
D Moore   HWM

RACING CARS over 1101 cc S and 2001 cc U/S   15 laps
A P R Rolt   Delage Era   87.34 mph
A J Butterworth   AJB
H Howorth   Jaguar

Paul Emeryson in his Emeryson, 26 May, 1951

CAR RACE MEETING - 11th AUGUST, 1951

A crowd numbering between 13,000 and 20,000 gathered for the West Essex Car Club's third and biggest race meeting of the year. Club members had been able to put in additional practice for the event when, about a fortnight earlier, a mid-week evening practice session had been arranged at the circuit. A significant addition to the programme was the name of the *Daily Mail* as sponsor of the Formula 3 and Formula Libre races in the 10-race meeting. The newspaper was to play a key role in events at the circuit in the following season.

Two 5-lap heats for the popular 500 cc Formula 3 cars started proceedings. The first race was won comfortably from pole position by Peter Collins in his JBS-Norton. Jack Leary (Cooper) gave chase, but was never really in a challenging position. By mid race these two had opened up a big gap over the rest of the field which was led by the works Cooper driven on this occasion by team-backer Bill Whitehouse but John Green in Reg Parnell's JP-Norton inherited the chasing position on lap 4 when Whitehouse retired and this was how they finished. The fast-cornering front-engined Emeryson of H Williams in fourth place led home a closely packed group of cars with Gill, Gray, Fraser and Chelmsford's own Alan Rippon, all in Coopers, occupying fifth to eighth positions just ahead of Pelling in the second Emeryson. Collins winning speed was 80.18 mph and this turned out to be the fastest race speed of the day because this was the only race run on a dry track. The rest of the programme was run in ever-worsening conditions as the rain, initially a thin penetrating shower, had turned to a relentless downpour by the end of the day.

The second heat was run in treacherous conditions and brought tragedy to Boreham. The field was headed on the first lap by the familiar Ecurie Richmond Cooper of Alan Brown followed by Bernie Ecclestone's Cooper and Arengo's Arengo, with the JBSs of Don Parker, J Habin and Curly Dryden in hot pursuit. Halfway round that first lap, as the mass of cars swept through Orchard Corner, two cars touched. Whether this was a direct result of the slippery conditions or a racing accident is not recorded in the motoring journals covering the event, although the local newspaper reported that David Brake lost control of his Cooper entering the bend and struck J Brown's similar car. Brown's car slid off the track and came to rest on a straw bale but poor Brake's car turned over three times as it left the course into the oil drums and straw bales. St John Ambulance men were with the grievously injured driver within seconds and he was rushed to hospital but died from serious head injuries within a few minutes of being admitted. It was Formula 3's first fatal accident in Britain.

The race went on, with drivers vainly struggling for grip on a surface "with seemingly nil adhesion," as *Autosport* described it, with many cars spinning wildly and pointing in every direction. On lap 3, the leader came unstuck at

Railway Corner which had already claimed Arengo. Curly Dryden benefitted from these indiscretions to inherit a lead that he retained to the end. Don Parker moved through to second but spun, giving the place to Ecclestone who promptly spun himself, thus handing second place back to a recovering, and probably rather surprised, Parker thus completing a JBS 1-2. Behind Parker, Jack Moor in his Wasp, who had started well down the grid but simply kept his car heading in roughly the right direction amidst all the spinning cars, gained a creditable third place. It had been a tense race bringing little enjoyment to participants or to the bedraggled spectators.

Three 7-lap sports car races were next on the programme. In the first, for cars up to 750 cc supercharged or 1100 cc unsupercharged, spectators witnessed 23-year-old Colin Chapman in "Lotus, that ultra rapid 750 cc Austin derivative," as one report described it, in a good scrap with Harewood's PB type MG Midget, Sparrowe's Morgan and C Le S Metcale's Balilla Fiat. The final order was MG, Fiat and Morgan. Colin Chapman's mount was the Lotus MkIII; the first Lotus designed specifically for circuit racing but there is no record of it in the final results; perhaps Chapman simply had to give best to the larger-engined cars on this occasion. The race provided a welcome contrast to the hectic Formula 3 encounters. Drivers adapted to the tricky conditions with caution and the winner's average speed was a modest 64.1 mph. By this time the spectators were resigned to a thoroughly wet afternoon but, as *Autosport*'s reporter put it, they "clung on tenaciously to their vantage points, donning strange mantles of infinite variety - yellow oilskins, fishermen's hats and waterproofs of every colour, the familiar ex-W.D. gas cape much in evidence."

Cars in the next event, a 7-lap race for 1100 cc supercharged and 1500 cc unsupercharged sports cars splashed round the course only marginally faster than the smaller cars in the preceding race. The race produced the first ever win for the Cooper MG of Lionel Leonard. This car, registered JOY 500, sported attractive polished aluminium bodywork, produced by Leonard himself, based on the contemporary Ferrari 166 Barchetta. This eye-catching car was pursued home by S B Wells in a 1.5 litre Riley, Dick Jacobs in an MG TD and W Knight in another MG.

The next 7-lap race featured larger capacity sports cars (up to 1500 cc super-charged and 2000 cc unsupercharged) and produced a Frazer-Nash 1-2. Boreham regular Tony Crook took an initial lead in his red version but was passed on lap 2 by a similar car driven by Eric Winterbottom. Peacock provided Frazer-Nash back-up in third position having managed to get ahead of R Willis's modified BMW. But this Frazer-Nash domination did not last. Willis took his BMW ahead of Peacock and with Crook dropping back with engine trouble the BMW was soon in second place. The determined Peacock hung on and after a stirring battle regained the advantage on the last lap. Peacock thus finished second although he was some way behind the green Frazer-Nash driven by Winterbottom which completed the race at 71.56 mph.

A relatively small field of just 10 cars assembled for the 10-lap William Lyons Trophy Race for Jaguar XK120s. The race got under way in clouds of spray, the early leader being Hugh Howorth. His car, which he prepared himself to very high standards was adjudged by Jaguar works team manager 'Lofty' England as "undoubtedly being the best XK120 in this country". His lead over Duncan Hamilton at the end of the first lap was a couple of lengths. T Wood, J Craig, Roy Salvadori and J Swift were next up. The scrap between Wood and Craig for third place became rather too close and at about half distance they entered Orchard Corner together and did not emerge until some time later, both with tell-tale damaged bodywork. At least the combatants had delayed long enough at Orchard to be identified; one car spun at the same place but, the observer reported, "was too darned quick to see who it was, but he was driving an XK120 Jaguar!" Swift gratefully accepted third place, having already passed Salvadori.

The end of lap 7 saw the elimination of the leader Howorth when the notorious 'Gilhooley' (Railway Corner) claimed him as a victim. Unfortunately a marker drum got wedged underneath against a rear wheel and this took some time to extract. Hamilton and Swift in their modified cars and Salvadori in his standard production car had all passed before he regained the circuit and they finished in that order. For Salvadori it was a particularly satisfying result. Three months earlier, at Silverstone's International Trophy meeting, he had suffered serious head injuries when he rolled his Le Mans Frazer-Nash at Stowe Corner. Given the Last Rites, he was not expected to survive longer than an hour after arrival at hospital. In fact, he remained unconscious for several days but then began to make a gradual and miraculous recovery. In this, his first race since that accident, he was pleased and relieved to discover that he was still competitive and able to race seriously again.

It did not seem possible, but weather conditions deteriorated further as event 7 - the keenly anticipated Formula 3 final - got under way. The 30 competitors were enveloped by spray, smoke and driving rain as they splashed round on their first nerve-wracking lap. Perhaps the poor visibility affected reporters: *Autocar* would have us believe that poleman Peter Collins "duly streaked off in the lead", whilst *Autosport* contended that "Curly Dryden's JBS and Williams's Emeryson were fastest away."

Soon cars were spinning and being delayed at almost every corner and the mutually agreed order at the end of the first lap bore little relationship to the order in which they had left the grid. Fast starters Collins, Leston and Ecclestone had all slipped down the order and a decidedly reshuffled field went by in the order Dryden, Williams, Moor (Wasp) and Brown (Cooper) - four different makes in the first four positions. Collins (JBS) in fifth place was recovering after a rapid spin at Railway Corner. The same corner claimed the leader, Dryden, on the second lap, letting Alan Brown into the lead. Brown, in later years, remembered Boreham as the venue for some of the wettest racing in his long career but clearly the conditions suited him on this occasion. His progress, from a lowly grid position, in the terrible conditions had been remarkable.

Collins, too, was showing his true class and the recovery from his first lap trouble was completed as he took the lead on lap 3. Alas Collins' lead was short-lived; a detached plug lead sent him into retirement. Moor in the Wasp was the interloper in what was otherwise becoming a Cooper benefit. The Coopers of Brise and Gill occupied third and fourth positions but, in a race of total unpredictability, they had soon fallen off the circuit. Early leader, and heat winner, Dryden then moved back on to the leader-board and at two-thirds distance displaced the Wasp for third. Alan Brown was never challenged after Collins' demise and when the chequered flag signalled the end of the 15 laps the order was Brown (Cooper), Dryden (JBS), Moor (Wasp) and Parker (JBS) although, in all honesty, in this hectic, incident-filled race, almost any order might have been possible behind the steady winner!

Event 8 was Boreham's first ever Formula 2 race. It was won with some ease by Ray Merrick in a car giving away more than 800 cc to the true 2 litre Formula 2 cars in the race - the Cooper Formula 3 car into which had been fitted a special 1132 Norton-JAP twin cylinder engine and which had featured strongly at the circuit's previous meeting. George Abecassis in a single seater HWM challenged momentarily but fell back. Another HWM, driven by Oscar Moore, took up the vacated second spot and third and fourth positions were occupied by two Cooper-JAPs of C Booker and J Barber but at Orchard Corner, which had so tragically claimed David Brake's Cooper, first Booker overturned his car and, astonishingly, a lap later Barber did the same thing at the same spot; in the process almost running into those attending to the earlier accident. Fortunately only minor injuries were sustained by the drivers.

Clearly, conditions were treacherous in the extreme. In fact, *Autosport*'s reporter felt moved to resort to nautical terms to describe the scene: the leader Merrick 'navigated' his corners with caution, Ken McAlpine now in an inherited third spot was "working hard at the tiller" of his Connaught and Peacock was 'next astern' in his Frazer-Nash. On laps 10, 12 and 13 of the 15-lap race, McAlpine, Peacock and Abecassis - the latter's HWM back on song again - moved ahead of Moore's fading HWM into second, third and fourth positions respectively and this was the order in which they finished behind the untroubled Merrick in his amazing little Cooper.

The day's penultimate event, a 7-lap race for unlimited sports cars, brought out some of the protagonists from the earlier XK120 race. The open-topped XKl20s, Allards, Connaught and Frazer-Nashes provided scant protection in the continuous rain but Tony Rolt was at least dry, if not as fast, in the Aston Martin DB2. Rolt's slower pace was, no doubt, partly explained by the fact that he was enjoying a cigarette in the cosy confines of the Rob Walker entered car!

The race provided Duncan Hamilton with his second win of the day. He led from start to finish although Leslie Allard in his Cadillac-engined Allard clung on well to take second. Third spot went to Salvadori after a fine drive through the field and despite a dramatic high-speed spin on the very last bend. A second Allard, driven by K Watkins, finished fourth.

Finally, at about 7.30 p.m., the ambitious programme reached its climax: the *Daily Mail* 50 Guineas Championship Trophy for Formula Libre Racing Cars. It seemed rather late for the big race of the meeting. Unfortunately the promising line-up was depleted by a number of non-starters including Dennis Poore (Alfa Romeo), Pat Garland (Talbot), Goodhew (P3 Alfa Romeo) and the three ERAs of Reg Parnell, Ashmore and Bond. Another potential non-starter was Tony Rolt in Rob Walker's ERA-engined Delage but Parnell's misfortune did at least allow his ERA engine to be cannibalised to get a grateful Rolt into the race.

Gloucester garage proprietor, Brian Shawe-Taylor, was in excellent form in his ERA 8C. His driving, as he slid his car in four-wheel drifts at each corner in clouds of spray was the highlight of an otherwise rather dull race. Rolt in second place could not match Shawe-Taylor's pace but at least the effort to get him in the race seemed as though it would be rewarded with the runner-up spot: his progress on the streaming wet track being likened to an extremely fast launch. Alas those efforts came to nought: his engine failed on the 15th and last lap allowing Graham Whitehead in ERA R10B into second to complete an ERA 1-2. Initially James in a Maserati 4CLT had held a strong third place but a lengthy pit stop dropped him down the order. Duncan Hamilton, competing in his third race of the day had little chance to complete a hat-trick of wins and finished third followed by the two HWMs of Abecassis and Moore - all rather spaced out. Shawe-Taylor had driven brilliantly; his average speed over the 45 miles in atrocious conditions being a remarkable 78.8 mph.

Less than an hour of daylight - such as it was - remained when proceedings came to an end at about 8 p.m. Many of the large crowd had persevered to see the final race and they now began to make their way home to dry out. It was to be almost midnight before all vehicles had left the circuit; some club members toiled into the night to attend to sundry cars and motorcycles whose ignition systems had been drowned by the deluge. "Unquestionably," *Autocar* remarked, "this meeting would have scored an outstanding success given better weather"!

It was the WECC's final race meeting of the year. Although a date in September had been allocated to Boreham for a meeting tentatively proposed as the 'Tim Birkin Trophy Meeting' this clashed with other events in the country and as a result the number of entrants was too small to make the meeting viable.

500 cc FORMULA 3 HEAT 1   5 laps
P J Collins   JBS   81.50 mph
J Leary   Cooper
J Green   JP

500 cc FORMULA 3 HEAT 2   5 laps
R M Dryden   JBS   76.53 mph
D Parker   JBS
E J Moor   Wasp

SPORTS CARS up to 1100 cc S and 1500 cc U/S   7 laps
E Harewood   MG   64.10 mph
C le S Metcalfe   Fiat
J Sparrowe   Morgan

SPORTS CARS up to 1100 cc S and 1500 cc U/S   7 laps
L Leonard   Cooper MG   63.30 mph
S B Wells   Riley
R W Jacobs   MG

SPORTS CARS up to 1500 cc S and 2500 cc U/S   7 laps
E Winterbottom   Frazer-Nash   71.56 mph
R Peacock   Frazer-Nash
R Willis   BMW

'W LYONS TROPHY' for JAGUAR XK120s   10 laps
D Hamilton   Jaguar XK120   73.57 mph
J Swift   Jaguar XK120
R Salvadori   Jaguar XK120

500 cc FORMULA 3 FINAL   15 laps
A Brown   Cooper   70.70 mph
R M Dryden   JBS
E J Moor   Wasp

FORMULA 2   15 laps
R W Merrick   Cooper-Nor-JAP   73.97 mph
K McAlpine   Connaught
R Peacock   Frazer-Nash

SPORTS CARS unlimited   7 laps
D Hamilton   Jaguar   71.34 mph
T L Allard   Allard
R Salvadori   Jaguar

"DAILY MAIL CHAMPIONSHIP TROPHY" FORMULA LIBRE   15 laps

B Shawe-Taylor	ERA	78.80 mph
A G Whitehead	ERA	
T L Allard	Allard	

Special Trophy Meeting

NATIONAL CAR RACING BOREHAM

RACE TRACK . CHELMSFORD . ESSEX

Special Attractions
★
500cc Formula III
Daily Mail Trophy Race
★
Formula Libre
Daily Mail Trophy Race

Jaguar XK 120 Race
for the W. Lyons Annual Trophy

Saturday
AUGUST 11th

First Race 1.30 p.m.

ADMISSION including tax
CARS   £1
MOTOR CYCLES   6/-
CYCLES   4/6
PEDESTRIANS   3/6
CHILDREN   2/-
COACHES with occupants   £6

Organised by the WEST ESSEX CAR CLUB. (RECOGNISED BY THE R.A.C.)

Duncan Hamilton
(Jaguar)

R M 'Curly' Dryden

43

PREPARING FOR 1952

At the end of 1951, members of the West Essex Car Club and their colleagues in the Chelmsford and District Auto Club could look back with reasonable satisfaction on their first season of circuit racing at Boreham. They had been successful in gaining good-sized entries for most of the races and, perhaps more importantly, had attracted some of Britain's top drivers. Reg Parnell, the only Briton to score World Championship points during the year was already a firm favourite at Boreham and other top British drivers Brian Shawe-Taylor, Duncan Hamilton, Tony Rolt, George Abecassis and reigning British Hill Climb Champion Dennis Poore had all put in at least one appearance. Added to these were the flowering talents of Mike Hawthorn, Peter Collins and Alan Brown; each of whom was heading toward his Grand Prix debut in the following season.

Considering the purely domestic nature of racing in that first year, crowd figures must have been reasonably encouraging to the organising clubs if not totally satisfying to the circuit owners themselves. Unfortunately, two of the three motor race meetings had been badly affected by the weather but the perseverance of the crowd at August's damp meeting was in itself a source of encouragement. A local newspaper reported, "As Saturday's great crowd at Boreham Airfield huddled together five deep to gain protection from the driving rain, one of the organisers of the meeting turned and said 'If they stick this they'll stick anything.'"

Those spectators had enjoyed good viewing insofar as airfield circuits allowed them. One could walk right round the circuit and find viewing points anywhere, few places being outside the range of the circuit's public address system supplied by MIMCO, the special products division of the Marconi International Marine Communication Company Limited.

There was a feeling that, far from being a temporary expedient to meet a particular post-war shortfall in motor racing venues, Boreham had 'arrived' and that this first season really was the start of something significant in the motor racing world. "Boreham will win through as premier race track" were the confident tones found in the *Essex Chronicle* and echoed elsewhere.

Naturally there were criticisms. For a newly formed club operating at a new venue this was, perhaps, inevitable. The inordinately late finishes to the day's events - on one occasion 8 p.m. - was a reflection of the club's inexperience and over-ambitious programmes. For spectators or competitors coming from a distance such late finishes were a trifle inconvenient.

The RAC itself was apparently a little unhappy about some aspects of the first season's meetings and summoned representatives of the West Essex Car Club to London to "discuss certain alleged shortcomings in the organisation of the Boreham race meeting" but whatever it was that had ruffled RAC feathers seemed to have been dealt with successfully by the hard-working Competitions Secretary,

George Matthews, and his colleagues. The public commentary was the subject of some criticism. John Eason-Gibson was accused of weak wisecracking and aroused envy and despair by using the public address system for relaying personal requests for liquid refreshment to the caterers' tent. "He was completely dry and warm in a bus! We needed it much more!" wrote one local reporter. Ironically the same commentator was singled out for praise by the motoring correspondent of the *Braintree & Witham Times,* who thought that the spectators' interest was maintained by the informed and often humorous observations of the commentator but the writer recalled "intense personal irritation at one speakers forced attempts to whip up excitement with superlatives clearly unjustified by events."

On a very much more serious note the circuit had witnessed a fatality during the year. David Brake had been fatally injured in a Formula 3 race. It has to be said, however, that this sad event was treated less sensationally in the motoring press than might be the case today and did not reflect on the safety or otherwise of the circuit. It was adjudged that the use of straw bales to mark the courses on airfield circuits were dangerous when hit at speed and should more properly be used as a second line of defence to protect spectators. Through the use of oil drum markers, Boreham had tried to do this and despite some claims to the contrary it seems unlikely that the safety features at the circuit could be faulted on this particular occasion.

A matter requiring remedy which became obvious from the very first meeting was the track surface itself. For some reason this was particularly slippery and the addition of rain seemed to affect it more adversely than drivers might reasonably expect. Railway Corner or 'Gilhooley' was particularly affected in this respect. Pundits considered that a new track surface should be laid as a first priority.

More seriously, as far as the future of the venue was concerned, was that the owners, Co-Partnership Farms Limited, lost money in that first year and considering the high level of spectator interest this must have sounded alarm bells. The crippling Entertainments Tax, which took nearly 50% of the circuit's gross takings, offered no encouragement to organisers in the early 1950s and swallowed up funds that were needed for investment. However, rather than be beaten by the financial situation, the circuit's backers felt that the season had shown what Boreham could achieve and that to realise its full potential the project had to be put on a better financial footing. Investment and improvements were needed to bring the circuit into direct competition with Silverstone and to enable it to hold international events. In fact, there still remained a serious doubt over Silverstone's future and Boreham seemed poised to take a significant step forward as a frontline circuit and a possible Silverstone replacement.

There were notable developments taking place at this time which seemed destined to provide the foundations for this step forward. Firstly, it appeared that the *Daily Mail* newspaper had decided to back racing at Boreham for 1952 at least. The circuit's organising clubs were not in a position to provide the large funds that would be needed to develop Boreham and an outside backer was absolutely vital to the future of the circuit. Negotiations had taken place on and off during the course of the 1951 season and the *Essex Chronicle*, on the eve of the season's final meeting, said that it understood that the national daily had "finally decided after several months of negotiations to back fully car and motor cycle racing at Boreham". It was rather less than an official announcement and in the following week's edition the paper somewhat more moderately reported that Co-Partnership Farms were "engaged on delicate negotiations with the *Daily Mail* who wanted to back the track". Both sides, the local paper suggested, "know that Boreham is a winner with International meetings and 100,000 crowds practically certain next year". By December, 1951, the West Essex Car Club was told that the newspaper's backing had been confirmed

In 1952 a member of the Chelmsford and District Auto Club, the organisers of the motor cycle meetings at the circuit, was reported as saying that the *Daily Mail* "have got the track on lease" but at this distance in time it has not been possible to determine, either from the *Daily Mail* or elsewhere, whether matters ever really progressed as far as that. What does seem likely however is that the *Daily Mail* had one eye fixed on the successful involvement of its rival, the *Daily Express*, at Silverstone. The *Express*'s support of the British Racing Drivers' Club at Silverstone dated from 1949 and, in fact, was to last for ten unbroken years. The general manager of the *Daily Express* was Tom Blackburn who saw the publicity value of a link with events at Silverstone. It was a publicity stunt that grew into a true partnership as Blackburn's interest in the sport blossomed. In due course the newspaper took on an organisational role which involved event promotion, overall cash control, programme selling and other operational tasks. It has been generally recognised that the *Daily Express*'s support was crucial in Silverstone's early years. A similar link with a rival national daily newspaper would obviously have been of immense value to the young West Essex Car Club, as well as the Chelmsford and District Auto Club and in 1951 the *Daily Mail*'s expression of interest seemed to show that such a liaison was a distinct possibility.

The second notable development, linked with the *Daily Mail*'s involvement as sponsor and which augured well for the circuit's future, was the founding of a separate company specifically to maintain and develop the circuit. The Motor Racing Company Limited, whose registered office was 60a Piccadilly London W1, was incorporated on 22 March 1952 with issued capital of £10,000. The coming season was to see some of the results of this company's determination to bring the circuit into what they saw as the new era" when Boreham would emerge "as a grown arena fitted for high speed duels and great audiences." The company described its early achievements in the programme of the June 1952 meeting:

"New surfacing makes the track speedier and more exciting. Mike Hawthorn, newest star of this sport, has already broken its lap record of 91.3 mph and proclaimed it enthusiastically "a really outstanding track.

"Only a month ago came a new bridge over it. Primarily, that benefits officials, drivers and mechanics on their way to the control centre, pits and paddock, but it serves the spectator too. It means smoother and slicker racing.

"Now, for the first time, Boreham opens to you covered grandstands at the most exciting points with seats for 3,500 people - one opposite the pits, others at Waltham Corner, Orchard Corner and Railway Corner.

"New pits, staggered for swift recognition and easy entry by racers in difficulty, will bring faster returns to the struggle of contestants with mechanical trouble. Every grandstand now has its own catering, with separate service for spectators outside the enclosure. Kiosks all round the course provide soft drinks.

"Minute by minute news of all that happens will reach you through the loudspeakers around the track, and over the pit stands the new score board, biggest and most informative of its kind, showing lap by lap the position, speed and time of the six leaders.

"You will have noted already the meticulous care spent on making your approach smooth and expeditious - the result of exacting conferences of authorities and planners.

"Boreham has arrived! The Motor Racing Company wishes you all 'Good watching and a pleasant day'. It promises further improvements for the future and expects to offer comfortable watching soon to more than 100,000 of you."

Jaguar Cars had financed the bridge over the track and Shell were responsible for the provision of the impressive scoreboard. It was planned that a tunnel would be constructed later on under the track to give access to the paddock. Investment and optimism were running high as Boreham's second full season got under way.

At a more mundane level, new regulations brought in by the sport's governing body, the RAC, required competitors to wear crash helmets. To help competitors to meet this requirement the West Essex Car Club decided to purchase six crash helmets, in popular sizes, and to hire them to competing members for a small charge. These were available at the first event of 1952 - the club's annual sprint meeting.

SPEED TRIALS MEETING - CARS - 6th APRIL, 1952

Blizzard conditions prevented this sprint meeting organised by WECC from taking place the week earlier. The weather was only slightly better for Sunday, 6 April, when a steady drizzle fell all day, and high winds were blowing. Clubs whose members were invited to take part in the events were Half Litre Club, East Anglian M.C., Herts County A.&A.C., Thames Estuary A.C., Eastern Counties M.C., London Enthusiasts' C.C., M.G.C.C., and club members of WECC. Nearly all 163 entries who had agreed to take part in the previous week's event which was cancelled turned up.

The poor weather conditions did not prevent the lowering of nearly every record in the saloon and open class events. The weather appeared to affect only the racing cars, as the organisers and competitors were in their usual high spirits, and a good number of spectators arrived for the afternoon.

This sprint meeting was the third at Boreham, and was run along the main runway, starting at Railway Corner. The saloon car class races were run in the morning, starting with low capacity engined cars, progressing to the highest.

Despite a good run by A G Baker in his 1.25 litre MG, with a 2 seconds reduction in the previous record, had a time of 44.2 seconds, but J V Lewis (43.6 seconds) and S L Ince (44.0 seconds) bettered the record driving 1.25 litre Rileys.

Tony Crook in a 2 litre Bristol with a time of 36.4 seconds, lowered his own record by 1.2 seconds, beating G Dunham in a 3 litre Alvis with a time of 37.5 seconds, and G H Grace, 38.2 seconds, who beat a number of Healeys and a 2.5 litre Riley.

Tony Crook broke a second class record with a time of 31.8 seconds, driving his Frazer-Nash when beating S G Greene with an excellent time of 32.1 seconds.

W B Black, driving a 3.4 litre Jaguar in the largest of the Open Class cars, beat his own record with 31.4 seconds. In the over 3 litre racing class he also won with two runs of 31.6 seconds, and was placed third with 31.8 seconds in the 'any trim' Sports Class. The winner of the 'Any trim' class, driving an 8 litre Bentley was Forrest Lycett, with a time of 29.7 seconds, beating by only 0.5 seconds the supercharged Jaguette of W Coleman. A W Richards in a J.B.S., won the Racing Class for up to 500 cc cars in a time of 33.6 seconds.

The record of Don Parker in this class with 31.84 seconds was not approached. Parker's own efforts were limited to his first run time of 34.4 seconds, due to the breakdown of his car on the second run.

The fastest times of the day were established in the 1500 to 3000 cc racing class. J B Norris in a 1970 cc Alta held the record in this class with 27.5 seconds, but could only manage 28.2 seconds. L W Boyce, driving a 2986 cc Maserati, won with a time of 28.1 seconds and third in a 3000 cc Alfa Romeo was J Goodhew in 28.4 seconds.

SALOON CARS up to 1100 cc

| J M Edmondson | Fiat | 50.2 seconds |
| F T Holloway | Ford | 50.83 seconds* |

1101-1501 cc

| J V Lewis | Riley | 43.6 seconds* |
| S L Ince | Riley | 44.0 seconds |

1501-3000 cc

| T Crook | Bristol | 36.4 seconds* |
| G Dunham | Alvis | 37.5 seconds |

Over 3001 cc

| C R Leonard | Jaguar | 38.8 seconds |
| S A Mitchell | Jaguar | 40.0 seconds |

OPEN CARS up to 1100 cc

| W A Bristow | MG | 42.0 seconds* |
| P H Wren | MG | 44.6 seconds |

1101-1500 cc

| T Line | MG | 39.2 seconds* |
| W F Ashdown | MG | 41.5 seconds. |

1501-3000 cc

| T Crook | Frazer-Nash 31.8 seconds* |
| S G Greene | Frazer-Nash 32.1 seconds |

Over 3001 cc

| W B Black | Jaguar | 31.4 seconds* |
| Mrs J Sarginson | Jaguar | 32.1 seconds |

SPORTS CAR IN ANY TRIM Up to 1000 cc.

| D Moore | MG | 37.2 seconds* |
| K Rolfe | Fiat | 39.0 seconds |

1001-1500 cc

| A G Baker | MG | 31.6 seconds |
| L J Coe | Riley | 32.0 seconds |

1501-3000 cc

| R C Willis | B.M.W-Bristol 30.8 secs* |
| T Crook | Frazer-Nash 31.6 seconds |

over 3001 cc

| F Lycett | Bentley 29.7 seconds |
| W Coleman | Jaguette 30.2 seconds |

RACING CARS up to 500 cc

| A W Richards | JBS | 33.6 seconds |
| D Gray | Cooper 33.8 seconds |

501-1100 cc

| F B Stowrey | Cooper 29.9 seconds |
| A G Baker | MG | 31.4 seconds |

No.29 K Watkins (Allard J2X-Cadillac 5.4 litre)

1501-3000 cc

L W Boyce   Maserati 28.1 seconds
J B Norris   Alta   28.2 seconds

Over 3001 cc

W B Black   Jaguar 31.6 seconds
J H Sarginson   Jaguar 32.4 seconds

*   NEW RECORD

B Mason (2.5 litre Jaguar) leads I C Lucas (1.7 litre Connaught)

(photos: Motorsport)

Frazer-Nash cars (2 litre)
Roy Salvadori leads D A Hely

Don Gray's Cooper-J.A.P., showing a crash bar fitted rear of the driver's seat, rare in the 1950s (*photo: Autosport*)

CAR RACE MEETING (including 'Tim' Birkin Memorial Trophy race) - 17th MAY, 1952

The opening motor race meeting of the 1952 season, again organised by the West Essex Car Club, was run in bright sunshine under blue skies. A crowd, estimated at 22,000, saw an admirable day's racing, run with precision and with every race starting on time over a greatly improved circuit.

Practice day on the Friday indicated that the course was now giving faster racing times. Dennis Poore (3.8 Alfa Romeo S.) lapped in 1 min. 55.8 secs., at 93.4 mph, Mike Hawthorn in an unblown 2 litre Cooper Bristol, recorded 1 min. 56.6 secs - almost 93 mph. Fastest of the very large 500 cc entry was Don Parker (Kieft-Norton) in 2 mins. 9.4 secs., 83.5 mph.

In the opening event, a five lap race for 1100 cc. S., and 1500 cc. U/s cars, Pat Griffith (Lester MG) and Ken Downing (Connaught) made the running. Chris Sears (Frazer-Nash) spun round, and spent the remainder of the race trying to catch up. It was easy for Downing after Griffith spun spectacularly at Orchard Corner on the second lap. Archie Scott-Brown (TD. M.G.), and Tom Dargue (MG) scrapped for most of the race, but Dargue, producing extra acceleration with the lighter car up the hill after 'Gilhooley' corner.

Ken Watkins (Cadillac-Allard) in the larger sports-car five lap race, won easily. Guy Gale in his blue Mille Miglia Frazer-Nash outpaced a number of XK 120's, with S J Boshier being the fastest. Bill Black spun at 'Gilhooley'. Then his engine went off song and he had to retire. Watkins the race winner, was outstandingly good, and appeared to be in top gear throughout the race from just after the start to finish.

The remarkable number of 44 cars entered the 10 lap Formula 3 event, with only two non-starters. Motor racing at its best was the scene at the start of the race, with row upon row of brightly painted cars and with every driver showing a look of grim determination on his face. George Wicken (Cooper Norton) quickly went into the lead, with Les Leston (Cooper Norton) and Don Parker in pursuit.

The event was turning into what appeared to be a three man race, with Wicken and Leston interchanging positions with the wily Parker playing his usual waiting game, lapping at 83 mph. Behind these three were Charlie Headland (Kieft Norton) followed by John Habin (Erskine-Staride-Norton), Ken Smith (Smith Norton), and Paul Emery (Emeryson Norton). Of the slower starters A J Nurse (Cooper-Norton), R Bicknell (Revis Norton), and Don Truman (Cooper Norton) began to tear through the field. Leston passed Wicken, but Wicken re-took the lead on lap three. The unlucky Headland did battle with the straw bales at 'Gilhooley' and left the race, letting Ken Smith into fourth place. On lap four Leston came round followed by Parker but there was no sign of Wicken. His

Pits and race results board (near Railway Corner at lower end of main runway) [No.33 S Lawrence (Bentley), No.19 T W Dargue (MG), No.14 S Wells (Riley)]

The start of Event 2 - Sports cars scratch race, 5 laps. No.24 E Murkett (Jaguar), No.23 S Boshier (Jaguar [3rd]) No.22 W Black (Jaguar), No.29 K Watkins (Allard) [winner], No.26 G Gale (Fraser-Nash [2nd]) (*photos: Les Downes*)

gearbox had split and although he kept going for two more laps, he eventually retired. Lap six saw Parker take the lead with Leston very close behind and Ken Smith moved up to a deserved third place with Habin and Nurse determined to take it from him. Nurse had made a fine recovery and was now driving his Cooper with great skill. The crowd applauded the Parker-Leston duel and the Smith-Habin-Nurse battle. Lap seven saw Nurse streak past Habin and Smith to go third, Smith now being one gear short. Truman had made a fine recovery from being in last place on lap one and was now in sixth place. With two laps to go Parker was still in the lead, and with one lap left Leston dropped a valve and was out of the race. Don Parker won the race to set new 500 cc lap figures with 2mins. 8.3secs. (84.25 mph) averaging 82.59 mph for the 30 miles covered. Nurse finished second 37.2 seconds behind; Habin third and Smith fourth.

The 'Tim' Birkin Memorial Trophy Race, organised by the Bentley Drivers Club, was over five laps, with each driver receiving a time handicap. It was described as a grand sight. H J Wilmhurst (4.5 litre) put up one of the best performances and easily averaged the highest speed of the race, drove the fastest lap and came home in third place from a 38 seconds handicap.

Gerry Crozier (8 litre), driving from scratch, never looked like challenging the leaders. A Hollington (4.5 litre) took the lead after two laps and kept it to the end. His main challenge came from Allen (4.5 litre) who, when overtaking the eventual winner, had the misfortune to lose an accelerator connection. Peter Woozeley (4.4 litre) entertained in a different way, colliding with numerous straw bales during the race and scattering clouds of dust and wisps of straw over the spectators. It had been a fine race. Second man D McClure, off the same handicap of 1 min. 53 seconds as the winner, only made second place by 0.8 of a second.

Ken Watkins (Allard), with a handicap of 18 seconds, scored his second win of the day in the 5-Lap Any Capacity Race, with Ken Downing (Connaught), handicap 30 secs., runner up, and Guy Gale (Frazer-Nash) in third place with a handicap of 3 seconds. Eric Thompson (ERA-Delage) off scratch, and thought to be in with a chance of winning, departed from the race in lap three, but on the form shown by Watkins, it was doubtful if anyone could have beaten him, on one lap he went round at nearly 85 mph.

The Formula Libre, over a distance of 10 laps, was the final event of the day. It was described as 'a highly diverting race'. Dennis Poore on the first lap, driving his big Alfa Romeo, took the lead from both Mike Hawthorn in his Cooper Bristol, and Graham Whitehead in an E.R.A.. On the second lap Poore was 2.6 seconds ahead of Whitehead who also passed Hawthorn. Behind this trio were Ken McAlpine (Connaught), Joe Kelly (Alta), J Barber (Cooper J.A.P.), Eric Thompson (ERA-Delage) and Ken Watkins (Allard). Poore then suffered a faulty scavenge pump causing surplus oil to be sprayed on his Alta tyres, this

Mike Hawthorn (Cooper-Bristol) Formula Libre race winner on the starting line; background No.6 J Barber (Cooper)

A scene in the pits. Competitors in the Formula 3 500 cc 10 lap race. No.37 C Hale (Emeryson), No. 11 E Mitchell (Cooper), No.9 N Pugh (Cooper) (*photos: Les Downes*)

giving him wheel spin and steering problems. The oil thrown up from the tyres of Poore's Alfa caused Hawthorn to reduce speed and fall back from the Alfa. Hawthorn then removed his oil covered visor and by the end of lap four had not only regained lost ground but had taken the lead. Whitehead also came in for the oil treatment, and he too was forced to remove his goggles before passing Poore whose Alfa appeared to be slowing down. Thompson who was now in fourth place, and McAlpine for some reason had retired. A smoke screen was coming from Barber's Cooper, and he was overtaken by Watkins, who was trying hard to keep up with the single seaters - Poore was still going in his big Alfa which was becoming uncontrollable, and by this time Hawthorn had a 13 second lead over Whitehead on lap six, and was content to keep his rival safely in sight, although the E.R.A driver never gave up trying. The race ended with Hawthorn the winner, Whitehead second 8.8 seconds behind, Eric Thompson third and the unlucky Poore fourth. During the race, Hawthorn broke the outright lap record at Boreham, with a speed of 92.02 mph, which was a fantastic achievement in a 2 litre un-supercharged car.

SPORTS CARS 1100 cc S. & 1500 cc U/S   5 laps
Ken Downing   Connaught   75.77 mph
S Wells   Riley
T W Dargue   MG
Fastest lap: Downing, 78.14 mph

     Over 1100 cc S. and 1500 cc U/s.   5 laps
Ken Watkins   Allard   79.91 mph
Guy Gale   Frazer-Nash)
S J Boshier   Jaguar
Fastest lap: Watkins 83.2 mph

RACING CARS - FORMULA 3   10 laps
Don Parker   Kieft Norton   82.59 mph
A J Nurse   Cooper Norton   80.30 mph
J Habin   Erskine-Staride-Norton   79.91 mph
Ken Smith   Smith Norton   79.75 mph
Don Truman   Cooper Norton
Fastest lap: Parker 84.25 mph (New 500 cc record)

'TIM' BIRKIN MEMORIAL TROPHY - (Handicap race for Bentleys) 5 laps
A Hollington   70.7 mph
D McClure   69.32 mph
H Wilmhurst   76.61 mph
Fastest lap: Wilmhurst 78.95 mph

SPOTS CARS - ANY CAPACITY (HANDICAP)   5 laps
Ken Watkins   Allard   82.0 mph
Ken Downing   Connaught   77.57 mph
Guy Gale   Frazer-Nash   79.02 mph
Fastest Lap: Downing 84.91 mph

FORMULA LIBRE   10 laps
Mike Hawthorn Cooper Bristol   88.82 mph
Graham Whitehead   E.R.A. S   88.17 mph
Eric Thompson ERA-Delage   85.86 mph
Dennis Poore   Alfa Romeo S   85.40 mph
Fastest lap: Hawthorn 92.02 mph

Preparing for the start of 500 cc Formula 3 10 laps race. No.18 D Parker (Kieft) [winner], No.39 G Wicken (Cooper) (*photo: Les Downes*)

CAR RACE MEETING - 21st JUNE, 1952

The second car race meeting in 1952 attracted a fair gathering of spectators, and was run in cool and dry conditions. With the big International Meeting in August a few weeks away, only six events took place.

The first event, a handicap race for sports cars up to 1500 cc was over five laps. The start between Scratch and Handicap competitors was described as taking a veritable age, one competitor, Jim Mayers, in a Lester MG giving away two whole minutes. E W Heath and J C Stokes, in 1087 cc MGs were first lap leaders, with Mitchell in a 847 cc MG in third place. Mayers was chasing Cliff Davis in a Cooper MG, which had a five second start on him. He caught it on the second lap only to spin on lap three at Waltham Corner, allowing Davis to overtake him again. The undaunted Mayers put his foot down, but the Irishman, Joe Kelly, had now thrust his Jupiter into third place, but Mitchell, in his MG Midget, lost time hitting bales of straw at Orchard Corner. On the final lap, Cliff Davis caught the leader Heath, and C le S Metcalfe (Fiat) passed Kelly, then strayed amongst the straw bales. Next it was Davis's turn, and the leader harried by Mayers in the Lester MG, lost time in a spin at Railway Corner, letting Mayers go ahead to win by seven seconds.

The unlimited capacity sports cars race was also over five laps. A D Stevens (Lea Francis) fought off a number of bigger cars for four laps before being overtaken first by F K Morley in an Allard at Orchard Corner and then by J Goodhew in a 4.5 litre Lagonda, and J B Swift and Roy Salvadori, both in XK120 Jaguars. The last lap was a fierce race for the line between Swift and Salvadori both of whom had caught the Lagonda driven by Goodhew. Swift was the winner by a margin of one second.

Oscar Moore, off scratch in his H.W.M.Jaguar, failed to finish in the first three, but took the honour with the fastest lap at 85.98 mph.. Ken Watkins crashed badly at Orchard Corner in his J2 Cadillac Allard, turning over twice. The car was badly damaged at the front, but he escaped with only minor injuries.

Event three on the programme was the keenly anticipated Formula 2 race over 10 laps. Competing here was Reg Parnell in a Cooper-Bristol owned by A M H Bryde, J Baker in a Rebrab, Dick Jacobs driving S G Greene's 'Replica' Frazer-Nash, Gerry Dunham in a single seater Rover-Marauder, Bill Dobson in a 2 litre Ferrari, and amongst others, three single seater Connaughts.

Parnell took the lead followed by the Rebrab which was emitting smoke, Dobson and Downing (Connaught); W B Black (Connaught) stalled at the start and lost almost a lap. By the second lap the Cooper-Bristol driven by Parnell had a 12 second lead from Ken McAlpine in a Connaught, Dobson, Baker and Downing. In lap three Downing was fourth and then Baker in the Rebrab dropped out, as did Air Vice Marshall Donald 'Pathfinder' Bennett in his Cooper-Vincent.

John Cooper greets his winning driver, Reg Parnell (1971 cc Cooper-Bristol) Formula 2 scratch race
The Cooper-Bristol driven to victory by Reg Parnell (*photos: Don Osborn*)

There was no stopping Reg Parnell in the green Cooper-Bristol, but the Connaughts were running well and sounding very healthy. Behind, a fierce duel was developing between Dick Jacobs in the Frazer-Nash and Gerry Dunham in the Rover-Marauder, who was cornering at the limit and drawing closer and closer, then on the last lap he overtook Jacobs at Orchard Corner, but his speed was too great, the Marauder spun completely round, the engine stalled and he was out of the race. Parnell won easily with 19 seconds to spare over McAlpine in the Connaught, with Dobson in the 1949 Ferrari third and Downing fourth.

A race between identical cars appeals to many race fans as a means of proving the various abilities of the drivers taking part. The 'W Lyons Jaguar XK120 Trophy' over 10 laps was just such a race.

Hugh Howorth in a red and blue car met a very strong competitor in Roy Salvadori driving a buff coloured machine. Howorth took the lead at the start, but on the approach to Waltham Corner, Salvadori overtook him with Ian Stewart (Ecurie Ecosse) third and J H Hemsworth fourth. Around Orchard Corner and on to Railway Corner they sped, fourteen various coloured Jaguars. Only the screeching of tyres on the surface of the track could be heard above the sound of Jaguar engines. Salvadori was still in the lead after lap one, but at Hangar Bend Howorth overtook him and J K Hemsworth in his white car overtook Stewart in the Ecosse car, which was not running too well. On the run down to Railway Corner and, holding braking to the very last, Salvadori overtook Howorth again.

On the next lap J B Swift overtook Stewart to go into fourth place, and on lap six the Ecosse lost two further places to E W Holt and Michael Head. Whilst all this was going on, Howorth, with superb driving, again took the lead from Salvadori at Hangar Bend, only to lose it again to him on lap seven, when due to excessive speed at Orchard Corner, he was forced to momentarily go off course, allowing Salvadori to go through. J B Swift then spun completely at Orchard Corner and Michael Head was now hot on the trail of Hemsworth and with Ian Stewart and Graham Whitehead retired with engine problems attention was on the battle between Salvadori and Howorth, the latter slightly behind.

At Orchard Corner they were level, then Howorth eased ahead, as it slid outwards, Salvadori drew up with both running neck and neck until the superior acceleration of Howorth's car told, taking him into a lead of a car length. Behind all this excitement, Michael Head overtook Hemsworth to go into third place, the two cars approaching Railway Corner close together; Hemsworth's car slid outwards and collided with numerous oil drums sending them flying. With his car somewhat battered, he took it straight into the paddock, which let E W Holt into fourth position. Howorth ran out as winner by 2 seconds, with Salvadori, after a great exhibition by the two drivers, in second place. Head was third. The remaining cars passed the finishing line in the order, Holt, Air Vice-Marshall Donald Bennett, D T Russell, Sir James Scott-Douglas, and E A Murkett.

The fifth event was for sports cars of any capacity, a five lap scratch race. Ron Willis in a B.M.W.Bristol shot away from the start to take the lead. Salvadori and Hemsworth, both in Jaguars, and Oscar Moore in an H.W.M. Jaguar pursuing the leader. Moore, with foot down, caught up with Hemsworth, who spun round at Railway Corner, and then came level with the duelling pair of Willis and Salvadori. On lap four Moore shot into the lead under Jaguar Bridge. Then Howorth, with possibly another trophy in his sights, put on more power and passed Willis to finish third, just one second behind Salvadori, with Moore winning by 2.6 seconds ahead of the two Jaguars.

The sixth and final event of the day was a Formula Libre 10 lap scratch race. Amongst the runners was Reg Parnell in a 4 CLT Maserati; Dennis Poore in a 3.8 litre Alfa Romeo; Archie Bryde in a modern Cooper-Bristol: Graham Whitehead in a 'C' Type E.R.A.; Downing, McAlpine and Black, all in Connaughts; Guy Hale (3 litre Maserati); Oscar Moore (H.W.M.Jaguar); Joe Kelly (E.R.A.); Dobson (Ferrari); Richards (H.A.R.); Sir James Scott-Douglas (Ecurie Ecosse Jaguar); and Fay Taylour, the prominent lady driver, in a 1.2 litre Alfa.

The really big Alfa of Dennis Poore was given its head from the start of Boreham's long straights and fast bends and quickly ran away with things at a tremendous speed. Apart from an attempt at Orchard Corner to allay the plans of Dennis Poore by Reg Parnell on lap one, Poore led from the start to finish and created a new lap record of 94.41 mph, beating Mike Hawthorn's 92.02 mph.

With Poore running away with things, it was a competition amongst the remaining competitors as to who was to take the next three places. Parnell lay second for six laps in the Maserati amongst the Parnell-Downing-Whitehead group, but it was thought that Downing was a likely challenger in his unblown Connaught Formula 2 car. It was not to be, however, and the real threat came from the E.R.A. driven in magnificent style by Graham Whitehead, who was in fourth position for four laps. Through Railway Corner and past the starting area he hung on and then at Waltham Corner the E.R.A. overtook Parnell to go into second place. Amongst the other competitors, Fay Taylour returned to the paddock after a slow two laps, but re-appeared later in the race. Sir James Scott-Douglas was busily reducing the distance between his Jaguar and the 1100 cc Kieft of Clive Lones, but the Jaguars were having a bad day and the Kieft was still ahead by the time Dennis Poore in his Alfa had received the winner's flag. Whitehead was second after a brilliant drive 4.2 seconds ahead of Reg Parnell who took third place, and Downing fourth in his Connaught.

No.81 Fay Taylour (1.5 litre Alfa supercharged) Formula Libre race
Part of paddock area (*photos: Don Osborn*)

SPORTS CAR (Handicap) up to 1500 cc   5 laps
J C C Mayers   Lester MG   79.49 mph
F C Davis   Cooper-MG
J Kelly   Jowett-Jupiter
Fastest Lap: Mayers 83.44 mph

SPORTS CAR (Handicap) over 1500 cc   5 laps
J B Swift   Jaguar   80.48 mph
R F Salvadori   Jaguar
J Goodhew   Lagonda
Fastest Lap: Moore 85.98 mph

Reg Parnell

FORMULA 2 (Scratch race)   10 laps
R Parnell   Cooper-Bristol   89.62 mph
K McAlpine   Connaught
W A Dobson   Ferrari
K H Downing   Connaught
Fastest Lap: R Parnell 91.53 mph

'W Lyons Jaguar XK120 Trophy'   10 laps
H Howorth   84.29 mph
R F Salvadori
M W Head
Fastest Lap: H Howorth 85.86 mph

SPORTS CAR SCRATCH RACE (Any capacity)   5 laps
O Moore   H.W.M.-Jaguar   83.88 mph
R F Salvadori   Jaguar
H Howorth   Jaguar
R Willis   BMW-Bristol
Fastest Lap: O Moore 86.96 mph

FORMULA LIBRE SCRATCH RACE   10 laps
R D Poore   Alfa Romeo   92.59 mph
A G Whitehead   E.R.A
R Parnell   Maserati S
K H Downing   Connaught
Fastest Lap: R D Poore 94.41 mph

John Cooper

DAILY MAIL INTERNATIONAL FESTIVAL OF MOTOR SPORT - 2nd August, 1952

"On this, the peak day of a young circuit's new story, 130 drivers including first-class racers from six foreign lands and many of the most famous British aces, are to compete in Boreham's first International meeting" is how the programme notes heralded Boreham's big day on 2nd August, 1952. The efforts of the circuit's owners and race organisers were coming to fruition. With generous *Daily Mail* sponsorship, the West Essex Car Club and the Motor Racing Company were poised to present a day of top-class racing which would put Boreham firmly on the international motor racing map.

The overall quality of entries at the meeting was so high that *Autocar* was moved to remark that "such a day's motor sport is very rare in Britain." The four-race programme included two 100-mile races for Le Mans type sports cars: one for under 2 litre cars and one for over 2 litre cars - and an oversubscribed International Formula 3 race. The highlight of the meeting, and the race which naturally attracted the greatest pre-race publicity was a 200-mile race for Formula 1 and Formula 2 cars.

Early in the 1952 season, after a single race for the current 4.5 litre unsupercharged or 1.5 litre supercharged Formula 1 cars at Turin, organisers realised that, following the withdrawal of Alfa Romeo, Ferrari would face little opposition and that entries would be rather poor. BRM appeared to offer rather uncertain opposition. Race organisers turned to Formula 2 (which was then for 2 litre cars) for their premier single seater races and consequently for two years the Drivers' World Championship was based on races for the smaller Formula 2 machines. Britain followed suit and a Formula 2 World Championship event was planned for Silverstone but race organisers in this country were reluctant to forsake Formula 1 completely particularly as the country's ambitious Fl BRM project, after six years, was still struggling to make a significant impact. There were, in consequence, a number of races organised for Formula 1 cars in Britain.

The organisers' attitude was summed up in the Boreham race day programme: "Motor racing, after all, is a speed game. You paid your money today to see cars go fast; to see the pick of Europe's finest drivers pitting their skill one against the other in coaxing every possible ounce of power out of their snarling engines and getting round the three-miles track in the shortest possible time."

All good stuff! It went on...

"If they can lap at 100 miles an hour - and everyone expects the BRM at least to set a new lap record in excess of that speed today - you will get more excited than if they go round at 90. Realising this the organisers of today's meeting said "Let's give them, at this first big International meeting on our new Boreham circuit, the fastest cars available and the most exciting possible race."

100 mile sports car race. No.99 C le S Metcalfe (Fiat), winner Class G; No.24 Mike Hawthorn (Frazer-Nash Mille Miglia); No.22 Ken Wharton (Frazer-Nash), winner Class E (*photo: Ford Motor Co., Ltd.*)

No.15 F C Davis (Cooper-MG), 100 mile sports car race, 34 laps. Second place, Class F (*photo: Les Downes*)

No.40
Stirling Moss
(3442 cc
Jaguar),
winner Class C
(*photo:
Les Downes*)

They also had in mind that the BRM organisation, in spite of its faults and defects, and despite the frequent disappointments which the car itself has inflicted on the British public, deserved an opportunity to prove itself in a major race on Britain's fastest circuit."

Reviewing the meeting in the *Essex Chronicle* newspaper R A F Handley wrote colourfully of what he thought may well be the BRM's final chance: "I hope they prove themselves. I hope they beat the guts out of all the foreign competitors with a snarl of 'I told you so'".

Such talk undoubtedly drew the crowds although, once again, the actual numbers seem in dispute: 40-50,000 (*Autocar*) or 75,000 (*Motor Sport*) - both significantly below the anticipated 100,000.

Unusually, when viewed from the perspective of later years, those spectators were expected to pay a mere 6/- (30p) admission compared with the 5/- (25p) charged at June's club meeting. Today's massive price differentials were still a long way off.

Practice had been held on the previous day, leaving Saturday free for racing. The crowds were still pouring into the circuit when the cars in event 1, a 34-lap, 100-mile race for under-2000 cc sports cars lined up in front of the pits for the 10.30 a.m. start of their race.

As the flag fell for the Le Mans type start, 28 drivers sprinted to their cars and, in an impressive display of Frazer-Nash unity, the similar Le Mans Replica cars of Ken Wharton, Roy Salvadori and Tony Crook gained an immediate advantage. One car, the Frazer-Nash Mille Miglia, driven by Mike Hawthorn was momentarily left behind when its engine refused to fire. This was to produce the drive of the race from the young Hawthorn and, as *Motor Sport* described, "doing prodigies with the wheel" he moved through the field, gaining 17 places on the first lap alone. His reputedly slower Mille Miglia model was not expected to offer serious opposition to the Le Mans Replicas of the leading trio, but he climbed to fourth position by lap 4. From the start of the race there had been threatening clouds and rain now began to fall. Lap speeds fell as cars skated with wheelspin on the increasingly slippery track but this did not slow Hawthorn's progress up the leader board. On successive laps, at about one-quarter distance, he amazingly relieved Crook and Salvadori of third and second positions respectively.

By lap 10 the deficit between Hawthorn and Wharton was seven seconds and decreasing. Three laps later they were together and, as they entered Railway Corner for the 12th time, Hawthorn slipped through into the lead. Wharton was not giving up however and, as the rain stopped, a great duel ensued. Wharton, who set the fastest lap of the race at 87.95 mph, had retaken the lead by the end of the 20th lap only to be slightly baulked by Metcalfe's class-leading Fiat at Waltham Corner on the next lap, allowing Hawthorn to audaciously slip between

No.43 W Black (Jaguar) in 100 mile sports car race   No.50 K Watkins (Allard)

No.31 Reg Parnell (Aston Martin) leads No.53 M W Head (Jaguar) at Railway Corner. Parnell won Class D (*photos: Les Downes*)

the two to lead the race once more. Within another lap however Wharton had tigered back to the front and just as the crowd were anticipating a thrilling finish from the two closely matched combatants, Hawthorn's mount faltered with clutch trouble and failed to complete the 26th lap. Wharton's pit crew signalled to confirm to their driver, what he must have already seen for himself at Orchard Corner: "Haw Out."

In the end it was a comfortable win for the pre-race favourite. For Hawthorn, it would have been a particular disappointment as he was striving to maintain his 56 to 43 points advantage over Stirling Moss in the season's B.R.D.C. Gold Star table. The winner of this prestigious award was determined by positions gained in international races and was, in all but name, the year's 'British Champion'. Taking over Beckwith-Smith's Frazer-Nash entry for the occasion had seemed to offer Hawthorn the possibility of not allowing the gap to close too much at a meeting where each race was classified as an 'international' and where Moss was entered in three races to Hawthorn's two.

The absorbing duel for the lead had rather overshadowed events in the rest of the field. Wharton led a Frazer-Nash benefit in the large class: the Le Mans Replicas of Salvadori, Crook and Peacock took second, third and fifth places with fourth place occupied by the Mille Miglia variant of J 'Dickie' Stoop. In the 1100-1500 cc class Jim Mayers was unassailable in his Lester-MG and led home his Monkey Stable teammates Griffith and Ruddock in a 1, 3, 4 finish; the interloper who spoiled their party in second place was Cliff Davis in his Cooper MG. C Le S Metcalfe's black Fiat won the under-1100 cc class. Second in class fell to A Baker (MG PB) after relieving the similar car of E Heath of the position on the penultimate lap of the race.

Despite the efforts of the organisers to improve access, the crowds were still coming into the circuit at midday having experienced queues which were described as "reminiscent of those vast queues at early big Silverstone meetings". Those who had made it to the trackside for the 12.10 pm start of event 2 were to witness the shortest race of the day: a 10-lap event for international Formula 3. This had attracted a large entry although the only representation from abroad was the Beels Racing Team from Holland with its two Beels Specials.

The top-class entry included all the 1952 Formula 3 regulars, including Stirling Moss who, although entered in his usual Kieft, had arranged to borrow a works Cooper for the event; the Kieft, in his words, "finally having run out of steam." As The *Motor* wryly observed "a director of Kieft Cars was thus competing against Kieft in his rival's product!"

The 33-car 5-4-5 grid made an impressive sight as it surged towards Hangar Bend led initially by pole position man George Wicken (Cooper). By the end of that first exciting lap Wicken had fallen to third with Alan Brown (Cooper) and Stirling Moss occupying the first two positions. Within a couple of laps the order

No.42 Sir John Scott Douglas (Jaguar) spins off the track in a cloud of dust in 100 miles sports car race (Event 3) (*photo: Les Downes*)
No.4 Mike Hawthorn (Cooper-Bristol 1971 cc) winner of the Formula 2 race; 3rd overall position

had reshuffled to Brown-Parker(Kieft)-Moss-Brandon(Cooper) and Wicken, these five running in a constantly changing nose-to-tail group. A second group comprising Webb (Kieft), Loens (Tiger Kitten), Truman and Leston (Coopers) was chasing hard. By half distance, as once more it began to rain, Wicken had retired with carburettor problems but Webb had pulled clear of the chasing group to challenge Brandon in the leading group.

With two laps to go, Parker who had started from 8th position on the grid passed Brown at Railway Corner to take his Kieft into the lead but at the same corner on the last lap Brown re-passed and, with both hands thrown up in elation, took his Ecurie Richmond Cooper over the finish line to win by a matter of yards. Moss would have had mixed emotions being beaten by a Kieft, but was happy to salvage third place as he struggled with a pair of broken goggles.

Brown's teammate Brandon lost and then regained fourth place as he battled with the surprisingly fast Webb all the way to the line. Les Leston completed the top six. First of a number of non series-built machines in the race was Ken Smith in his Smith-Norton in 10th place. Fellow front row starter Paul Emery (Emeryson) joined Wicken in retirement along with nine others who suffered mechanical problems including, sadly, the two Dutch visitors.

Fastest lap of the race was credited to Alan Brown who was timed at 1 minute 59.6 seconds. This represented what *Autosport* described as "the almost unbelievable speed by a 500 cc car of 90.3 mph... the fastest lap ever recorded by a 500 cc car in the British Isles". If correct, this lap time was indeed remarkable, being an astonishing 6.2 seconds improvement over Wicken's pole position time. In later years, Alan Brown recalled being credited with a fastest lap of over 90 mph in the Cooper - a feat he simply did not believe!

The rain had stopped and the track was drying as an impressive line-up of large capacity sports cars assembled Le Mans-style in front of the pits. The (non-works) Jaguar C-types looked set to dominate the 3000 cc class and, in the under 3000 cc group, a pair of 2.7 litre Ferraris faced two works 2.6 litre Aston Martin DB3s. The latter cars were entered on the basis of an extended test session. The prestigious Goodwood Nine Hours in mid-August was the Aston Martin team's main objective and they needed to gain experience with the cars' hypoid gears which had caused the retirement of all three factory cars at Le Mans a few weeks earlier.

Even at this early stage in his career, Stirling Moss was renowned for his rapid Le Mans getaways and he did not disappoint on this occasion. A lightning sprint to his C-type Jaguar standing at the head of the line of cars saw him emerge as a clear leader at the end of the first of the 34 laps. Moss's experience was in stark contrast to the fortunes of the two other C-type drivers: Duncan Hamilton made a terrible start and was engulfed by much of the field whilst worse befell Ian Stewart. A combination of unscrubbed race tyres on Stewart's Ecurie Ecosse C-type and an excess of enthusiasm sent him sliding helplessly across the grass at the first right-hander, Hangar Bend, through the inadequate straw bales and into the crowded ranks of spectators. Injuries were sustained by seven spectators, four of whom were immediately removed to hospital suffering from broken legs and other injuries. It could have been so much worse. In the spirit of the age, which seemed to have a more cavalier attitude to such accidents, the race continued at unabated speed as the injured spectators were tended to.

Two of the smaller capacity cars followed Moss on the first lap; Parnell (Aston Martin) and Tom Cole from America in the fast Ferrari very close behind. Duncan Hamilton had soon made up for his slow start and had moved up to fourth place on lap 2. Abecassis in the second DB3 had even more time to make up; his engine had refused to fire for many agonizing seconds and he had been last away.

Up at the front, Cole had snatched second place but could not shake off the inspired Parnell, the two taking corners side by side on several occasions. Neither could resist the rapidly recovering Hamilton whose C-type gained its rightful place - second behind Moss - and ahead of the battling smaller capacity cars. Cole had mercilessly punished his Ferrari's brakes in his early efforts and began to fall back, yielding his second in class at one third distance to the hard-charging Abecassis who thus consolidated Aston Martin's supremacy in the 3-litre class.

In a race considerably enlivened by the rapid progress of slow starters, Salvadori in the second Ferrari moved up from third last position on the first lap to displace Cole's failing sister Ferrari with 6 laps of the 34-lap race remaining. In doing so he moved to fifth overall and third in class. Alas, Abecassis's similar dramatic climb through the field came to nought; his Aston Martin began to falter. On lap 29 the driver slowed as he passed his pit, shouting and gesticulating wildly. Whether or not his pit crew understood the meaning of these actions is not recorded but on the following lap, with just four remaining, the DB3 stopped at the pits where frantic work by the pit crew enabled their driver to complete just one more lap. It was not enough and second place was lost; a blocked fuel filter being the reported cause of the car's retirement. This late development moved the Ferraris of Salvadori and Cole into second and third in class behind the surviving DB3 of Parnell.

At the front, Hamilton in the drum-braked C-type was never in a position to seriously challenge Moss in the disc-braked version despite highly entertaining cornering techniques. Moss ran out a convincing winner at 88.09 mph.

Behind the leading protagonists, Ecurie Ecosse founder member Bill Dobson brought the team's XK120 into sixth overall and third in the unlimited class which provided some comfort for the Scottish team which, after Stewart's accident, had also seen their other XK120 blow up approaching Railway Corner and spin two-and-a-half times before coming to an otherwise harmless rest much to the relief of its distinguished occupant Sir John Scott-Douglas, Bt.

No.25 Froilan Gonzalez BRM having final preparations carried out for the big race
No.17 Luigi Villoresi (Ferrari) Winner Formula 1 race (*photos: Les Downes*)

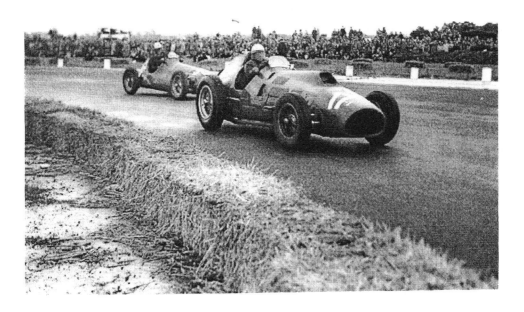

Further back an entertaining skirmish between D Russell's XK120 and Peter Clark's Aston Martin DB2 went the Aston Martin's way after half distance although, strangely, Clark was reported as competing without a crash helmet!

Within a quarter-of-an-hour of the sports cars returning to the paddock, the rain which had been threatening again after the earlier showers came down in earnest. The cars for the main race, the *Daily Mail* International Trophy Race, were lined up on the grid during this downpour. Despite the rain, the 31 Formula 1 and Formula 2 cars made an impressive sight.

Scuderia Ferrari had entered one car, a 4.5 litre type 375 for Luigi Villoresi and there were two more of these impressive cars privately entered for Francisco Landi and Louis Rosier. It was hoped, rather than expected, that the V16 1.5 litre supercharged BRMs in the hands of Ken Wharton and Froilan Gonzalez would provide the main opposition. When Gonzalez joined Villoresi in lapping the circuit at an average speed in excess of the magic 100 mph in practice these hopes seem to have been given some foundation.

Best represented Formula 1 marque was Talbot Lago; two-car teams from Ecurie Rosier and Tony Lago were joined by Philippe Etancelin in his own car. The Ecurie Rosier cars were garaged in nearby Chelmsford and reportedly driven to the circuit on the public roads!

Conspicuous by its absence was the 'Thinwall Special' - a Ferrari run by bearing magnate Tony Vandervell. Generally, Vandervell's team, keen to build up Formula 1 experience, had willingly taken advantage of British organisers' wish to run Formula 1 or Formula Libre events. There was a feeling in the team of showing Alfred Owen's BRM team how to do it - a feeling fuelled by the popular press which lost no opportunity to stir up an imaginary feud between the two millionaire industrialists. However, on this occasion this 'feud' was temporarily suspended: Vandervell had apparently requested £1,000 starting money which the *Daily Mail* was unwilling to underwrite.

The Formula 2 section of the race was well supported and included ten runners from the previous month's World Championship event at Silverstone. Cooper-Bristols predominated with all seven of the extant Mark s in the race driven by Hawthorn, Brown, Brandon, Bryde, Barber, Loens and Sanderson. Other notable entries were a pair of the Maserati Platés (entered by Charles Platé), a variety of 2 litre Ferraris, two factory Connaughts, Moss in the advanced ERA G-type and the single-seater Rover - a product of Rover employees, Spen King and Peter Wilks in the company's experimental department.

The grid lined up in 5-4-5 formation. Alongside the two 100 mph qualifiers Villoresi and Gonzalez were Landi, Wharton and Rosier making a symmetrical Ferrari-BRM-Ferrari-BRM-Ferrari front row. Sharing the second row with the Talbot Lagos of Etancelin and Giraud Cabantous were the two fastest Formula 2 cars: Hawthorn (Cooper Bristol) in sixth slot and Poore (A-type Connaught) in eighth Moss with the Bristol-engined ERA headed the rest of the similarly engined Coopers by taking 10th place on the inside of 3.67 laps, 200 miles lay ahead of them.

L Rosier	K Wharton	F Landi		F Gonzalez	L Villoresi
(Ferrari 375)	(BRM 15)	(Ferrari 375)		(BRM 15)	(Ferrari 375)
Y G-Cabantous	D Poore	P Etancelin			M Hawthorn
(Talbot Lago T26C)	(Connaught A)	(Talbot Lago T26C-DA)			(Cooper 20)
R Willis	A Brown	A Crespo		K Downing	S Moss
(BMW)	(Cooper 20)	(Talbot Lago T26C)		(Connaught A)	(ERA G)
B Dobson	E Chaboud				
(Ferrari 12)	(Talbot Lago T26C)	etc.			

Source: *A Record of Grand Prix and Voiturette Racing, Vol 5* by Paul Sheldon

The whole scene, which must have gladdened the hearts of the hard working WECC members, was eloquently described for BBC Light Programme listeners by Raymond Baxter in the first ever radio commentary from the circuit.

At 3 p.m., by which time the rain had eased somewhat, Major H Cree dropped the Union Flag and the large field slithered into dramatic action. The three front row Ferraris left the BRM drivers fighting excessive wheelspin and gained an immediate advantage, initially in the order Landi, Rosier and Villoresi.

During the first frantic lap, poleman Villoresi soon asserted his expected authority at the head of the field and Rosier snatched second place from Landi. Gonzalez had got the difficult BRM really flying in fourth place with Hawthorn's little Cooper Bristol hanging on well in fifth. At the end of that first lap these five were followed by Etancelin, Moss, Brown, Poore, Crespo, Whitehead, Cabantous, Sanderson and - in a disappointing 15th place - the BRM of Ken Wharton. Gonzalez, throwing the BRM around in alarming slides, disposed of the wary Landi and began to close on second placed Rosier. Alas, as *Autosport* described, "Gonzalez is not using his head", and on the third lap he hurled the BRM into the right-hander Hangar Bend at impossible speed, lost control and in a flurry of straw and mud spun across the grass toward the scattering spectators on the outside of the bend. The BRM struck a spectator's car close to where the Ecurie Ecosse Jaguar had crashed earlier but fortunately, this time, damage was confined to the vehicles involved - and to Gonzalez' pride. It was by all accounts a stupid mistake and a great disappointment to the BRM team and its loyal supporters. The portly Argentinean 'Pampas Bull' returned to the pits in a towering rage. His torrent of Spanish was reported in a local newspaper as "This is terrible. Just plain bad luck..." but which *Autosport* said was translated by a

No.26 Ken Wharton (B.R.M.) took 16th place in Formula 1 race (*photo: Les Downes*)

No.11 F Cortese (Ferrari) took 17th place in Formula 1 and 2 race

Spanish speaking onlooker as meaning "something we couldn't possibly print" - which was probably nearer the mark!

With three Ferraris at the head of the field, one BRM already out and the other struggling in midfield, the remaining 64 laps must have looked a daunting prospect for the partisan crowd. In the slippery conditions, however, Hawthorn was hanging on and was even giving Landi a difficult time, Moss (ERA) was sixth and Poore (Connaught) was recovering well after an early off-course excursion. There might be something to cheer after all.

For a while Landi managed to shake Hawthorn off his tail and tried to take second from Rosier at Orchard Corner but in the attempt slid badly and fell back again. As the rain worsened 2nd, 3rd and 4th positions closed up and Poore was waved past by Moss in the faltering ERA to take second place in the Formula 2 section. The complexion of the race changed dramatically on the 23rd lap. As the blue Ferrari of Rosier and Landi's yellow version battled for second, Hawthorn, in a superb display of wet weather driving, relieved them of the trouble to take the place himself! By this stage an unhappy Wharton (BRM) had already been lapped and BRM management must have cast envious eyes in the direction of the cheaper, unsophisticated little Cooper-Bristol battling with the Ferraris.

The crowd soon had more to make them forget the worsening conditions they were enduring; not only was Hawthorn leaving Rosier and Landi far behind, he was rapidly closing on Villoresi who just a few laps earlier had looked so comfortable in the lead. *Autosport*'s reporter captured the excitement:

"Then on lap 30 comes what causes the biggest outburst of cheering to be heard at Boreham. The quite fantastic Hawthorn catches and passes Villoresi at Orchard Corner and here one sees the red car sliding around for the first time, as the Italian tries desperately to regain his lead. However, with a cheeky tail-wag, the little Cooper Bristol streaks away, the crowd almost going delirious with excitement."

In the meantime, Etancelin in the leading Talbot Lago had inherited fourth position when Landi had called at the pits to replace a damaged tyre. In the Formula 2 section of the race Alan Brown had made it a Cooper Bristol 1-2 when Poore's Connaught had stopped for fuel and Bobby Baird (Ferrari) had moved ahead of Moss into third in class.

Villoresi, recovering from a recent accident and troubled by steaming up goggles, was no match for Hawthorn in the dreadful conditions and fell back by up to five seconds each lap. By lap 36 Hawthorn was an amazing 49 seconds ahead. But soon the rain eased. Boreham seemed to suffer from more than its fair share of wet meetings but as one observer noted "if that was not enough... when the rain stopped, it stopped at the wrong time!"

The nimble Cooper Bristol was ideal for the streaming wet track but as the surface began to dry, so the Ferraris speeded up, Landi having regained fourth

The trophy being presented to Luigi Villoresi by Hon. Mrs Gerald Lascelles
Mike Hawthorn with his mother and father after winning the race (*photos: Autosport*)

position after his enforced stop. Hawthorn could not respond in the improving conditions and by lap 53 - with just 14 remaining - Villoresi had regained those lost 49 seconds and taken his Ferrari passed the Cooper Bristol back into the lead. Hawthorn did not relinquish the position easily and immediately retook the lead but it could not last and he had to give best to the superior power of the 4.5-litre cars. Within another six laps, Landi, having passed Rosier, took his Ferrari past the young Englishman.

Hawthorn, though, was experiencing trouble with his car. In his own account of the race he explained that it was not simply the drying track which disadvantaged him and that the crowd could not appreciate that he was also experiencing engine trouble. What was later diagnosed as a loose flywheel led him to cut engine revs dramatically in an attempt to keep going. He was convinced that without this problem he may well have been able to hang on for outright victory.

As this exciting race entered its final stages, Landi set off in hot pursuit of Villoresi. *Autosport*: "Landi's whirlwind driving gives the crowd a great kick. He comes out of Railway Corner in a series of power-slides, and does a tremendous looking full drift through the fast Hangar Bend". Pit signals warned Villoresi of the threat and, despite a scare on the last lap when Ken Downing's Connaught almost tripped him up, he ran out the winner by just 10 seconds, in a race lasting about two-and-a-half hours. Ironically the last few laps were run in bright sunshine.

Hawthorn coaxed his car over the line in third place, winning the Formula 2 section by more than a lap, with Etancelin bringing his Talbot home fourth a lap adrift of the leaders; Rosier had slipped to fifth. Formula 2 cars occupied the next four positions, Alan Brown beating Moss to sixth by just 0.4 second, Baird was eighth and Brown's Ecurie Richmond team-mate, Brandon, ninth.

Almost unnoticed, Wharton's BRM which had never been higher than ninth and had been lapped twice retired with gearbox problems after an undistinguished display - although he was eventually classified 16th.

"It was a big and pleasant surprise that after the race the Hon. Gerald Lascelles, the Queen's cousin, and his bride stepped out from the flower-decked grandstand and walked across the track to congratulate Villoresi," reported the *Essex Chronicle*. It went on, "The distinguished couple are just back from their honeymoon in the South of France. The crowd gave both visitors an ovation and they cheered again when the Hon. Mrs Lascelles, after placing a chaplet of laurel leaves around Villoresi's neck, rewarded him with a kiss on the cheek. This was their first public function since their St Margaret's, Westminster, wedding".

The victorious, prematurely grey, 42-year-old Villoresi was elated by the reception and stood up in his Ferrari waving his hands. In his broken English he exclaimed, "It ees splendid. I'm most proud. I shall race here more."

The crowd's biggest cheers, however, had been reserved for the magnificent Hawthorn - "a prodigiously praiseworthy drive" was *Motor Sport*'s verdict. It was a race that emphasized Hawthorn's huge potential and within two weeks, at the Dutch Grand Prix, he learnt that the Ferrari team were interested in his services. He stood on the verge of a glittering international career.

At the other end of the scale, the BRM had again not impressed. *Motor Sport* reported the BRM being "pushed away from what could be its last public engagement, its record disgraceful ... BRM must now be quietly disbanded".

The big crowd dispersed swiftly after the meeting. Despite the weather it had been an, exciting and enjoyable meeting. Few, if any, could have envisaged that they would not be returning to watch motor racing at Boreham again. BRM survived to fight another day but, astonishingly, for motor racing at Boreham it was the end of the line. The season's two remaining motor cycle meetings went ahead as planned but, after that, all circuit racing at the venue ceased.

INTERNATIONAL *DAILY MAIL* 100 MILE SPORTS CAR RACE   34 laps
Class E (1500-2000 cc)
K Wharton	Frazer-Nash	84.49 mph
R Salvadori	Frazer-Nash	
T A D Crook	Frazer-Nash	

Class F (1100-1500 cc)
J C C Mayers	Lester MG	79.39 mph
F C Davis	Cooper MG	
P Griffith	Lester MG	

Class G (up to 1100 cc)
C le S Metcalfe	Fiat	67.85 mph
A Baker	MG	
E Heath	MG	

Fastest lap: K Wharton, Frazer-Nash: 87.95 mph

INTERNATIONAL *DAILY MAIL* FORMULA 3 10 laps
A Brown	Cooper-Norton	83.84 mph
D Parker	Kieft-Norton	
S Moss	Cooper-Norton	

Fastest lap : A Brown, Cooper-Norton: 90.30 mph

Ken Wharton

INTERNATIONAL *DAILY MAIL* 100 MILE SPORTS CAR RACE   34 laps
Class C (over 3000 cc)
S Moss	Jaguar	88.09 mph
D Hamilton	Jaguar	
W A Dobson	Jaguar	

Class D (2000-3000 cc)

R Parnell	Aston Martin	86.35 mph
R Salvadori	Ferrari	
T L Cole	Ferrari	

Fastest lap: S Moss, Jaguar: 90.00 mph

INTERNATIONAL *DAILY MAIL* TROPHY for FORMULA 1 and FORMULA-1 2 67 laps

Formula 1

L Villoresi	4.5 Ferrari	82.83 mph
F Landi	4.5 Ferrari	
P Etancelin	4.5 Talbot	

Formula 2

M Hawthorn	Cooper-Bristol	82.21 mph
A Brown	Cooper Bristol	
S Moss	ERA G type	

SATURDAY, AUGUST 2nd
INTERNATIONAL
MOTOR RACE
MEETING
SPONSORED BY THE
Daily Mail
OFFICIAL PROGRAMME 1/6

ORGANISED BY THE WEST ESSEX CAR CLUB

Overall finishing positions

1st	L Villoresi	Ferrari
2nd	F Landi	Ferrari
3rd	M Hawthorn	Cooper Bristol (F2)
4th	P Etancelin	Talbot
5th	L Rosier	Ferrari
6th	A Brown	Cooper-Bristol (F2)
7th	S Moss	ERA (F2)
8th	R Baird	Ferrari (F2)
9th	E Brandon	Cooper-Bristol (F2)
10th	A Crespo	Talbot
11th	P Whitehead	Ferrari (F2)
12th	Y Giraud-Cabantous	Talbot
13th	N Sanderson	Cooper-Bristol (F2)
14th	J Kelly	Alta
15th	D Poore	Connaught (F2)
16th	K Wharton	BRM
17th	F Cortese	Ferrari (F2)
18th	K Downing	Connaught (F2)
19th	W Dobson	Ferrari (F2)
20th	E Chaboud	Talbot

No other classified finishers

Fastest laps: Formula 1 L Villoresi, Ferrari: 90.15 mph
Formula 2 E Brandon, Cooper-Bristol; 86.81 mph

MOTOR CYCLE RACE MEETING 'THE CHELMSFORD 100' - 2nd
SEPTEMBER, 1950

The Chelmsford & District Auto Club who were the organisers of motor cycle
meetings invited members of various other clubs to compete in their first ever
meeting on 2 September, 1950, announced as The Chelmsford 100.

Clerk of the Course that day was Alan B Mullee, a stalwart member of the
Club, and prime instigator in obtaining the use of the airfield for motor cycle
racing. In the race programme, he offered 'best thanks' to St John Ambulance
Brigade, British Red Cross, Marconi's and Military for their attendance at the
meeting. He also thanked the owners of Boreham Airfield, Co-Partnership Farms
Ltd, who with the Soldiers', Sailors' & Airmen's Families' Association had made
the meeting possible, he also thanked other clubs and their officials who were
giving help that day. Thanks were also due he said to club members for their
tireless work in preparing the course for the meeting.

The programme showed the total number of entrants for the meeting to be 81.

Prize money ranged from £15 for first place in the Junior events; £10 for
second place; £5 for third place; fourth to seventh places £1-10-0 (£1.50) each.
The biggest prize for the day was in the Chelmsford 100 race. First place £30,
second £15, third £10 and fourth £5; fifth to eighth place £2-10-0 (£2.50).

Practice for the day's racing was allowed between 9 a.m. and 12 noon.
Spectators numbered some 10,000 and at 1 o'clock the first race was under way
with a deafening roar and flurry of speed. Thousands of programmes fluttered as
machines tore into the first bend. Everyone was surprised at the speeds at which
the machines were travelling, but this was what they had come to see.

Ron Pike, who won two events, completed 24 miles in the Lightweight class
race in just over 20 minutes at 71.9 mph. In the eight lap scratch race, on a 348
A.J.S., he fought with J P E Hodgkin on the last lap at 79.4 mph. Speeds
increased in the Senior race with Hodgkin racing away from the start to win with
an average speed of 83.4 mph.

The Chelmsford 100 was won by the well-known rider, George Brown. His
fastest lap was at 87.9 mph, although it was thought his speed on the long
straights were in the region of 120 mph.

One of the wildest moments of the day's racing occurred when four side-car
machines in a mix up at one of the bends, refused to give way for each other, and
sent a dozen or so bales of straw flying in all directions as they crashed at around
70 mph: no one was hurt but the Surtees team, father and son, (John Jr. was to
become World Champion in cars and on motor cycles) lost a lap as their machine
overturned.

The worst moment in the racing took place on one of the corners, when
Monty Lockwood went into a slide, from which he recovered only to get into a

speed wobble, hit a straw bale at 60 mph, somersault and land on his head. His machine followed and crashed upside down only feet away. He was taken to hospital where it was found he had fractured his skull. On a less serious note, the laugh of the day occurred when a hare became mixed up in the Vintage race. It passed the crowd at the finish to the accompaniment of cheers and applause; it was officially timed at 35 mph. The animal half lapped the course before disappearing into the stubble.

It was said by one spectator who had watched racing of various types all over the country, that it was the best organised and most enjoyable he had ever attended.

Mr Eric N Boswell, the managing director of Co-Partnership Farms Ltd. was 'one of the happiest men on the course'. "I am delighted with the success of the meeting," he said. "Now we must go all out to build this track into something really big for both cars and motor cycles."

So ended the only race meeting in 1950, which according to all reports, had been a great success.

200 - 250 cc LIGHTWEIGHT SOLO RACE   8 laps
R H Pike (248 cc Rudge)   Winner's speed: 71.9 mph
H T Bostock (248 cc Springbok)
F Telfer (250 cc Velocette)

251 - 350 cc SOLO SCRATCH RACE   8 laps
R H Pike (348 cc.AJS)   Winner's speed: 79.4 mph
J P E Hodgkin (350 cc Velocette)
Max Klein (348 cc AJS)

351 - 500 cc SENIOR SOLO RACE
J P E Hodgkin (500 cc Vincent) Winner's speed: 83.4 mph
G Brown (498 cc Vincent)
A J Dudley-Ward (498 cc D.W.Special)

VINTAGE RACE   4 laps   'Pip' Harris (Norton)
F D Booth (497 cc Ariel)   Winner's speed: 66.3 mph
C E Allen (998 cc Brough)
F Booth (497 cc Ariel)

SIDECAR RACE   10 laps
P V Harris & C Billingham (598 cc Norton) Winners' speed: 71.3 mph
C S Smith & B Clements (499 cc Norton)
J Surtees Snr & Jnr (998 cc. Ariel)

CHELMSFORD '100' RACE   33 laps
G Brown (998 cc Vincent)   Winner's speed: 83.8 mph
Max Klein (348 cc AJS)
H T Bostock (498 cc Triumph)

George Brown (Vincent) being presented with 'Chelmsford 100' cup by Lord Perry. Eric Boswell in centre of picture

R H Pike (*photo: P Eaves*)

MOTOR CYCLE RACE MEETING - 28th APRIL, 1951

During 1951 three motor cycle race meetings were held; the first on 28 April was watched by an estimated crowd of 9,000. The meeting was in competition with the Football Association Cup Final of that year, local visiting circuses and a bitter wind.

Those who did attend the meeting, with 178 riders taking part, were to see an afternoon of exciting racing at high speeds and thrilling duels between the star riders and lesser known competitors.

Amongst the better known riders were George Brown, winner of the previous year's 'Chelmsford 100' race; Ron Pike, a winner of two races at Boreham in 1950; Robin Sherry, the well-known Essex rider; and John Surtees, Senior & Junior.

In the first race Ron Pike (248 Rudge) won the Lightweight (200-250 cc) race comfortably, but in the 251-350 cc Final, he was beaten into third place with Robin Sherry the winner and Les Dear second.

The second event, a 4 lap Vintage Solo Race, took less than ten minutes to run and, although so short, the first three to finish changed places numerous times up to the final lap, with Bullard the winner, two seconds ahead of Wiffen, with Fisher third.

In the first of the side-car races, C S Smith and B Clements (Norton-Watsonian) won easily with John Surtees Senior and Junior in second place, followed by L W Taylor in third.

The great event of the meeting was the Solo Scratch race 351-500 cc. George Brown (Vincent), the Boreham favourite, took on S T Barnett (Norton). There was nothing to choose between them as they drew clear of the field. Brown had the edge over Barnett on the straights, but Barnett showed more daring and skill at the corners, overtaking one straggler on the outside at Railway Corner, just missing the bales of straw, and again when he overtook Brown and two stragglers with a lightning change of direction coming out of a corner. By the 13th of 16 laps, Barnett had a lead of some 10 yards which he held to win the race, receiving a great ovation from the crowd.

In the second side-car race, the favourite P V (Pip) Harris, faded on the third lap, allowing B Boddice and passenger to easily take first place. After a keen struggle between Smith and Slate, first one and then the other took the lead 'like a yo-yo', said commentator Vic Hughes. Neck and neck they came towards the finish line at about 100 mph, with Slate taking second place with C Smith and B Clements third.

Revenge came to George Brown in the unlimited event however. Riding his Vincent machine in the last event, he left the field far behind winning by three quarters of a lap with J P E Hodgkin in second place and a little-known rider at

Heat 1 Junior 8 lap scratch race (251-350 cc solo). No.12 R H Pike (348 AJS) [3rd], No.110 R Alderslade (348 BSA), No.102 F A Faulkner (350 AJS), No.62 M P O'Rourke (348 AJS), ? (Norton), No.48 G Monty (348 AJS), No.142 T Baxter (348 BSA), No.53 S T Barnett (348 Norton), No.55 K J Faulkner (348 Velocette), No.42 A D Bassett (348 AJS), No.139 J R F Butolph (Royal Enfield)

No.53 S T Barnett (Norton), winner Solo scratch race

Event 8. Sidecar 8 lap scratch race (unlimited up to 1200 cc). No.180 unlisted competitors, No.59 J Surtees, Snr & Jnr (998 Vincent), No.177 S & G Burrage (596 Norton), No.134 D T Slate & A Bascombe (596 Norton), No.182 unlisted competitors, No.178 G E Harris & passenger (596 Norton), No.9 T W Bounds & L J Tate (600 BSA)

that time John Surtees, Jr, third on a Vincent.

Facilities at the course had greatly improved since the 1950 season, the Sound Relay System by the Marconi Company was said to be almost a complete success considering the blustery wind and roar of the engines. The commentaries were also said to have been excellent.

Casualties in the race had been few. In the final of the junior class race, T Baxter (348 B.S.A.) collided with one of the straw bales and was taken to hospital.

200-250 cc SOLO SCRATCH RACE   8 laps
R H Pike (249 cc Rudge)   Winner's speed 72.5 mph
B W T Rood (248 cc Velocette)
J C McCubbin (249 cc Rudge)

251-350 cc SOLO FINAL   16 laps
R H Sherry (348 cc AJS),   Winner's speed 81.56 mph
L A Dear (348 cc AJS)
R H Pike (348 cc AJS)

Up to 1000 cc - VINTAGE SOLO RACE   4 laps
C Bullard (499 cc Norton)   Winner's speed. 72.81 mph
A J Wiffen (499 cc Rudge)
D Fisher (348 cc Velocette)

Up to 1200 cc - SIDECAR SCRATCH RACE   8 laps
C S Smith & B Clements (499 cc Norton S.C.) Winners' speed 72.8 mph
J Surtees Snr.& Jnr.(998 cc Vincent S.C.)
L W Taylor & A Yates (596 cc Norton S.C.)

351-500 cc SOLO SCRATCH RACE   16 laps
S T Barnett (499 cc Norton)   Winner's speed 83.6 mph
G Brown (499 cc Norton)
F P Heath (499 cc Vincent)

Up to 1200 cc SIDECAR SCRATCH RACE   8 laps
W Boddice & passenger (596 cc Norton S.C.) Winners' speed 76.00 mph
D T Slate & A Bascombe (596 cc Norton S.C.)
C S Smith & B Clements (499 cc Norton S.C.)

Up to 1000 cc - SOLO SCRATCH RACE   16 laps
G Brown (998 cc Vincent)   Winner's speed 86.4 mph
J P E Hodgkin (998 cc Vincent)
J Surtees Jnr (499 cc Vincent)

MOTOR CYCLE RACE MEETING - 21st JULY, 1951

The second motor cycle meeting of the season attracted about 8,000 spectators, and a record entry of nearly 200 riders. It was reported that the crowd saw "some of the fastest and most interesting races of its kind yet seen at the track."

In the twelve lap junior race, the Essex rider, Robin Sherry, had a good win over the Australian, Ken Kavanagh. On lap two, no fewer than 14 riders were bunched together, but it then became a contest between Sherry, with Cecil Sandford in hot pursuit.

On lap five, Sherry was fifteen yards ahead of Kavanagh and although the Australian put in a great effort to clinch it, Sherry was the winner. K R Campbell, another Australian rider, ran out of petrol some 120 yards from the line, to be robbed of a place.

In the Lightweight 200-250 cc Scratch Race, C C Sandford made up for only third place in the first race of the day by winning this, with R H Pike second, H A Pierce third, and J C McCubbin fourth.

In the Senior Championship 351-500 cc final, Ken Kavanagh riding his 499 cc Norton, lapped the circuit at 88.5 mph, and was well ahead from the start with the young up and coming John Surtees, Jnr. close behind. With only one lap gone, it appeared Kavanagh was set to win, but George Brown was making a challenge for second place, however, Jim Crow and Sid Barnett, both on Nortons, were too good for him. Such was the lead after a flying start by Kavanagh, no-one was to catch him and he won easily. Crow took second place, and a duel for third place went to Barnett with Brown fourth.

The four lap Vintage Race was won by the local rider Albert J Wiffen, riding a 499 cc Rudge with an average speed of 72.12 mph.

The final event of this meeting with 40 riders taking part was the twelve lap Invitation Solo race for 251-1000 cc machines. Riding his famous 998 cc Vincent 'Gunga Din' was the ace Australian rider Tony McAlpine, who broke the lap record with a speed of 89.3 mph.

   A non-starter in the race was the well known Boreham favourite, George Brown, and this robbed the event of a possible stern test for the Australian. It was McAlpine who dominated the race from the start and became the winner, so the duel was between other riders as to who should take the other places. It was the other Australian Ken Kavanagh and J P E Hodgkin, who were neck and neck for most of the race with Kavanagh just ahead at the finish to take second place and Hodgkin third.

The meeting had been another great success with everything going off according to plan. Only two mishaps took place, but nothing serious. One rider went to hospital with cuts and bruises, and the machine of S T Barnett caught fire in one race, near Railway Corner.

No.172 Albert J Wiffen (499 cc Rudge), winner Vintage race (up to 1000 cc)

No.112 Ken Kavanagh (Norton), winner
Senior Championship race (351-500 cc)
(*photo: via Pam Ellwood*)

No.159 C C Sandford (Velocette), winner
200-250 cc Lightweight race
(*photo: Reg Watts*)

251-350 cc JUNIOR FINAL RACE   12 laps
R H Sherry (348 cc AJS)   Winner's speed 85.07 mph
K T Kavanagh (350 cc Norton)
C C Sandford (350 cc Velocette)

200-250 cc LIGHTWEIGHT RACE   8 laps
C C Sandford (250 cc Velocette) Winner's speed 75.94 mph
R H Pike (248 cc Rudge)
H A Pierce (249 cc Triumph)

351-500 cc SENIOR CHAMPIONSHIP RACE   17 laps
K T Kavanagh (499 cc Norton) Winner's speed 87.15 mph
J M Crow (499 cc Norton)
S T Barnett (499 cc Norton)

Up to 1000 cc VINTAGE SOLO RACE (over 20 years)   4 laps
A J Wiffen (499 cc Rudge)   Winner's speed 72.12 mph
F J Williams (499 cc Cotton-Blackburn)
J Catchpole (498 cc Scott)

251-1000 cc INVITATION SOLO RACE   12 Laps
T McAlpine (499 cc Vincent)   Winner's speed 87.78 mph
K T Kavanagh (499 cc Norton)
J P E Hodgkin (998 cc Vincent)

Junior scratch race final (251-350 cc) won by Robin Sherry (AJS) (*photo: via Pam Ellwood*)

MOTOR CYCLE RACE MEETING - 'THE CHELMSFORD 100' - 1st SEPTEMBER, 1951

Rain was a problem at motor cycling's third and final race meeting of the 1951 season, although a crowd estimated at 8,000 attended. The rain starting as a drizzle and ending as a total downpour, affected the upward trend of lap records being broken, as had been the case at previous meetings.

The famous TT rider Maurice Cann, and the up-and-coming star rider, John Surtees Jnr., provided the crowd with some excellent riding in very difficult conditions.

M O'Rourke (348 A.J.S.) won his heat in the opening event, the eight lap Junior Race easily, and also won the 12 lap Final at 81.52 mph average speed.

Ron Pike, a frequent competitor and winner at Boreham, on his 250 cc machine, was not taking part at this meeting, but it was not thought he would have changed the results. In the Lightweight Scratch Race for 200-250 cc machines over eight laps, Maurice Cann won easily in a field of 22 riders at 76.35 mph, The main interest was to see who would take second place to the winner. It was it was R E Geeson (248 R.E.G.), with D G Lashmar (249 L.E.F.) third.

In the Side-car Scratch Race (up to 1200 cc) 8 laps, C Smith and passenger B Clements, had a runaway win. The father and son team - John Surtees, Snr. & Jnr., riding their 998 cc Vincent, gave another impressive performance, whilst the team of T W Bounds and J Lawson Taite (BSA Golden Flash 642) seemed to have a gear arrangement causing the requirement to change up at the corners, (not down) which produced strange front wheel functions. With the Surtees men taking second place on their Vincent, the team of Bill Boddice and L Kelly on a Norton, rode steadily to take third place.

The big race of the day, the 'Chelmsford 100', took place under cloudy skies and rain, although the conditions were described as not too bad.

Several well-known riders did not take part, due to mechanical problems during practice. After great efforts, John Surtees Jnr. overtook H T Bostock (Triumph) who became dismounted at Railway Corner on the 14th lap of a 20 lap race. The rain continued and during the l9th lap it was clear that the weather was affecting the speeds, as the leader on the final lap clocked 65.8 mph on a course where speeds up to 90 mph were quite easily achieved when the track was dry.

Surtees, described by the local press as "a menace to the stars", won the race, George Brown (Norton), who had competed well with P E S Webb (J.A.B.S.), came second with the latter taking third place.

The Side-car Handicap Race which took place in worsening weather conditions, became an event of misfiring engines, although this nor the weather seemed to affect the eventual winners, C Smith and B Clements (499 Norton), but the speed was noticeably slower than the previous scratch race.

The weather conditions may have been the cause of only 22 of the 52 competitors named in the programme actually taking part in the Invitation Scratch race for solo machines (251-1000 cc). The race for these machines was usually the most exciting and fastest of the Boreham races.

J P E Hodgkin (998 Vincent), however, showed his skill and daring and although pressed by Webb, they both were lapping at around 70 mph. John Surtees, Jnr., who had been pressed constantly by Bostock, weaved his way through the field although both were passed eventually by Carter (499 Norton), before he and Lockwood (348 A.J.S.) retired on the eighth lap. Hodgkin (998 Vincent) eventually won the race with Webb (499 J.A.B.S.) second and Carter (499 Norton) third.

At the end of this race, the final meeting of a successful season, the curtain came down on the 1951 season and the heavens opened with a deluge of rain.

250-350 cc JUNIOR SCRATCH RACE   12 laps
M P O'Rourke (348 cc AJS)   Winner's speed 81.52 mph
C A Stevens (348 cc AJS)
J Surtees Jnr.(348 cc Norton)

200-250 cc LIGHTWEIGHT SCRATCH RACE   8 laps
M Cann (248 cc Moto-Gussi)   Winner's speed 76.35 mph
R E Geeson (248 cc R.E.G.)
D G Lashmer (249 cc L.E.F.)

Up to 1200 cc SIDECAR SCRATCH RACE   8 laps
C Smith & B Clements (499 cc Norton)   Winners' speed 72.30 mph
J Surtees Snr & Jnr (998 cc Vincent)
W Boddice & L Kelly (499 cc Norton)

351-500 cc CHELMSFORD '100' SENIOR CHAMPIONSHIP RACE   20 laps
J Surtees Jnr (499 cc Vincent)   Winner's speed 76.7 mph
G Brown (499 cc Norton)
P E S Webb (499 cc J.A.B.S.)

Up to 1200 cc SIDECAR HANDICAP RACE   8 laps
C Smith & B Clements (499 cc Norton) Winners' speed 64.47 mph
J Beeton & L Nutt (596 cc Norton)
L W Taylor & J Storr (596 cc Norton

251-1000 cc INVITATION SCRATCH RACE   12 laps
J P E Hodgkin (998 cc Vincent)   Winner's speed 70.25 mph
P E S Webb (499 cc J.A.B.S.)
P H Carter (499 cc Norton)

MOTOR CYCLE RACE MEETING - 26th APRIL, 1952

The first meeting of the 1952 season took place in brilliant sunshine, and a good crowd was in attendance to see over 200 competitors take part and the lap record broken by an Essex rider. The existing record of 89.26 mph had been held by the Australian, Tony McAlpine, since the previous July.

Robin Sherry (499 Norton) set the new record in the Senior Scratch race final, with a lap time of 1min.59 secs - 90.3 mph. The opinion of the riders on the airfield circuit when asked after the races was "excellent, and better than Silverstone, much higher speeds can be expected at the forthcoming International meeting in August."

In the Lightweight-Scratch Race (8 laps) the winner Maurice Cann (248 Motto Guzzi) got off to a bad start, but by lap five was in front and won easily. The engine of his machine refused to start initially, but when he did get going, he made an impressive dash through the field to overtake B W T Rood (248 Velocette) who took second place, and E Barrett (248 Motto Guzzi) third.

The start of the six lap Side-car race was described as indecisive but 'Pip' Harris and passenger C Billingham drew away in impressive style to win, with the last pair to finish more than a lap behind.

The main interest after the lead taken by Harris was, who were to take the other places G Stuart (596 Norton) with passenger R Moore, was sometimes sandwiched or overtaken by F W Johnson (998 Vincent) and passenger J Cahill, or J Beeton 499 Norton) and passenger L Nutt, but none of the trio caught E J Davis (998 Vincent) and passenger E G Allen, who took second place, with Bill Boddice (499 Norton) and passenger B Storr third.

J A Storr (348 Norton), the Birmingham rider, put on a notable display of riding when winning the Junior Scratch race final (251-350 cc) 12 laps. It was he and E Ring (348 AJS), the Australian rider, who dominated the race. Although he was last but one to get away at the start, he raced through the field, and by the sixth lap was in the lead, but was held up at Railway Corner in his attempts to pass the stragglers and just failed to win by the smallest of margins from Storr who was the winner. W R Fletcher (Velocette) was a long way back on his own, but took third place.

The Side-Car Handicap Race of 6 Laps was won easily by T W Bounds and L J Taite (643 B.S.A.) who were given an over-generous one and a half laps start. They were never overtaken, and finished half a lap ahead of Harris and Billingham (998 Vincent), second, with Boddice and Storr (596 Norton) third.

John Surtees, Jnr., was amongst the fifteen finalists in the Senior Scratch Race (351-500 cc), but it was the Essex star Robin Sherry who took an early lead from E Barrett (499 Norton) with J McArdle in second place, and Surtees in third place for a few laps, and Storr fourth.

No.29 M Cann
(Motto Guzzi),
winner 200-250 cc
Lightweight
scratch race

No.55 P Harris &
C Billingham
(Vincent), winners
up to 1200 cc
Sidecar scratch
race

No.43 J A Storr (Norton), winner 251-350 cc Scratch race final (*photos: Reg Watts*)

Some keen competition was going on amongst the other competitors, notably, Bostock, Brand, Webb, Reed, Rood and Stevens to name but a few. Sherry appeared to lose some ground, then Storr overtook McArdle and was looking to overtake the leader Sherry, but then Sherry set up the lap record of 90.3 mph and with speed and skill went on to win with Storr second, and McArdle third.

200-250 cc LIGHTWEIGHT SCRATCH RACE   8 laps
M Cann (248 cc Motto Gussi)   Winner's speed 76.04 mph
B W T.Rood (250 cc Velocette)
E Barrett (248 cc Motto Gussi)

Up to 1200 cc SIDECAR SCRATCH RACE   6 laps
P V Harris & C Billingham (998 cc Vincent S.C.) Winners' speed 79.91 mph
E J Davis & E G Allen (998 cc Vincent S.C.)
W Boddice & B Storr (499 cc Norton S.C.)

251-350 cc SCRATCH RACE   12 Laps
J A Storr (348 cc Norton)   Winner's speed 83.67 mph
E Ring (348 cc AJS)
W R Fletcher (348 cc Velocette)

Up to 1200 cc SIDECAR HANDICAP RACE   6 Laps
T W Bounds & L J Taite (643 cc BSA). 3min.12 secs. Winners' speed 70.81 mph
P V Harris & C Billingham (998 cc Vincent) Scratch.
W Boddice & B Storr (596 cc Norton) 2min 45 secs.

351-500 cc SENIOR SCRATCH RACE   15 Laps
R H Sherry (499 cc Norton)   Winner's speed 86.91 mph
J A Storr (499 cc Norton)
J McArdle (499 cc Norton)

93

MOTOR CYCLE RACE MEETING - 26th JULY, 1952

The second motor cycle meeting of the 1952 season was sponsored by the *Evening News* and was the first motor cycle event to be held on the refurbished track. A crowd estimated at 25,000 were in attendance to watch the races.

The commentators were Murray Walker, now with ITV Television as a Formula 1 Grand Prix Motor Racing commentator, his father, Graham Walker, and E W Fitch.

The starting area was bedecked with banners and flags adding to the occasion of record breaking performances.

The first event, Heat 1 Junior Race (under 350 cc) 6 laps, was won by Kavanagh, after Sherry had been in the lead up to half way.

In the three lap Ultra-Lightweight Race (up to 125 cc), S W C Cook (123 B.S.A.) led all the way to win.

John Hagan (E.M.C.Puch) failed to produce his usual speed, due to a quick repair to a piston which had given trouble during practice. He made up for things after stopping, and finished fourth.

Heat One of the Senior Race (351-500 cc) saw Robin Sherry (500 Norton) give a fine display on the "Porcupine" and led from the start to win.

Ken Kavanagh won Heat 2 of the Senior Race, although Les Graham on the incredible M.V. 'Four' soon recovered after a bad start to finish second, and broke the lap record in the process.

The final of the Senior Race (up to 500 cc) 15 laps, produced an impressive start with Kavanagh, Sherry and Graham, out in front and numerous other riders alongside and behind.

After some delay before the flag dropped, with riders in a state of some irritation, they got away. Graham could be seen and heard in the leading bunch, but Kavanagh was in some sort of trouble, and almost last to start. At Tower Bend on the first lap Graham was behind Sherry and slowing down. Coming out of Railway Corner to start the second lap, Graham was nowhere in the hunt, and the leaders were in the following order - Sherry (498 A.J.S.), Webb (499 Norton) and Keeler (498 Triumph), then Graham and George Brown (499 Norton). A little way behind was Kavanagh who had fought his way through the field. At lap four, such was the pace of Kavanagh, that he was in second place, behind Sherry with Brown third. Graham then stopped to refit the jet well on the offside carburettor which had fallen off. Kavanagh was now in the lead with Graham mobile again and set off on the impossible to try and recover two laps. He did in fact catch up with the leaders and overtook Sherry, but failed to hold the position and Sherry took second place with the flying Norton with Kavanagh on board taking the winners flag and setting a new lap record, with George Brown third unchallenged.

It was unfortunate that the Essex rider Robin Sherry was to compete against the Australian Ken Kavanagh at his brilliant best. He broke the lap record raising the speed to 95.24 mph, which had been set by Robin Sherry at the April meeting only three months before. Kavanagh had increased the speed by nearly five mph.

Les Graham had already broken the lap record, set up by Sherry, in Heat 2 of the Senior Race, with a speed of 92.14 mph. The new record beat the lap record of 94.41 mph for cars which had been set up in June by Dennis Poore.

Kavanagh took the lead from the start in the Junior 350 cc Final, with Sherry trying everything in an attempt to catch him. Towards the end of the race, Sherry had not reached the straight coming out of Railway Corner when Kavanagh was beyond Hangar Bend. With Kavanagh winning with ease, Sherry took second place, and J A Storr (348 Norton) third.

Up to 125 cc ULTRA LIGHTWEIGHT RACE   3 laps
S W C Cook (123 cc BSA)   Winner's speed 58.05 mph
N R Jones (123 cc BSA)
W H Aldridge (123 cc BSA)

Up to 1200 cc SIDECAR SCRATCH RACE   6 laps
E J Davis & E G Allen (998 cc Vincent s.c.) Winners' speed 79.59 mph
W Boddice & B Storr (499 cc Norton s.c.)
P V Harris & C Billingham (499 cc Norton s.c.)

SENIOR SCRATCH RACE up to 500 cc   15 laps
K T Kavanagh (499 cc Norton)   Winner's speed 90.91 mph
R H Sherry (498 cc AJS)
G Brown (499 cc Norton)

Up to 250 cc LIGHTWEIGHT RACE   8 laps
M Cann (248 cc Moto Guzzi)   Winner's speed 80.09 mph
B W T Rood (248 cc Velocette)
E Barrett (248 cc Moto Guzzi)

Up to 1200 cc SIDECAR HANDICAP RACE   6 laps
B Beevers & F Woodward (499 cc Norton s.c.) Winners' speed 69.53 mph
E Summers & A Summers (499 cc Norton s.c.)
L Taylor & P Glover (499 cc Norton s.c.)

JUNIOR SCRATCH RACE   12 laps
K T Kavanagh (348 cc Norton)   Winner's speed 87.4 mph
R H Sherry (348 cc AJS)
J A Storr (348 cc Norton)

MOTOR CYCLE RACE MEETING - 4th AUGUST 1952 - INTERNATIONAL FESTIVAL OF MOTOR SPORT - BRITISH CHAMPIONSHIPS

This motor cycle race meeting, at which no fewer than four British Championship races were run, and with 134 riders taking part, was the biggest motor cycle meeting to take place at Boreham.

It was organised by the Auto Cycle Union, with the co-operation of the Chelmsford & District Auto Club, and sponsored by *Daily Mail* Newspapers.

This meeting concluded the *Daily Mail* International Festival of Motor Sport which had been held over the weekend, with the International Motor car racing event having taken place two days before on the Saturday.

The BBC Radio Light Programme broadcast commentaries during the day by Graham and Murray Walker and E W Fitch.

Racing took place during spells of heavy rain and intermittent sunshine, and as a result only one record was broken, by the outstanding rider taking part, the Australian K T (Ken) Kavanagh.

Racing started at 1.15 p.m., in front of what was described as 'another big crowd' and on a circuit said to be 'the fastest of its kind in the country.'

The first event, Heat 1 of the British Championship Junior Race, (350 cc) which was won by Ken Kavanagh raising the 350 cc lap record to 89.71 mph, with Robin Sherry second and Les Graham third.

The second Heat of the race, although keenly fought out, was slower than Heat 1, and was won by Rod Coleman, with an average speed of 87.92 mph, followed by Geoff Monty in second place and George Brown third.

At the start of the six lap Sidecar Scratch Race (up to 1200 cc) a squally period of heavy rain began. One of the eight riders taking part from overseas countries in various events was Hans Haldemann the Swiss Champion on his 718 cc Norton Special with passenger J Albisser. The Haldemann machine had an elaborate triangulated all in one sidecar, built in his own workshop. He almost managed to hold off E J (Ted) Davis (998 Vincent) with passenger E G Allen, but finally took third place with P V (Pip) Harris and C Billingham (499 Norton S.C.) who won with an average speed of 73.03 mph despite unfavourable weather.

Les Graham (125 M.V.Agusta) had an easy victory in the first of the British Championship races, in the Ultra Lightweight race (machines up to 125 cc) second place went to John Hogan (E.M.C. Puch) very narrowly from H Williams.

The rain had stopped for the second of the British Championship races, the Junior event for machines 251-350 cc, but there was no sign of the track drying out, and the drivers were warned that oil and rubber left by the racing cars from the Saturday events had made the surface very slippery, now that rain had fallen.

After a good start in difficult conditions, J McArdle (Norton) was leading, followed by D Farrant (A.J.S.), Sandford and W R Fletcher (both Velocettes).

P V ('Pip') Harris & C Billingham (499 Norton), winners Sidecar scratch race
W Boddice & W G Storr (499 Norton), winners Sidecar handicap race (*photos: Reg Watts*)

At the only real left hand bend on the circuit, Tower Bend, Sandford was leading, but at the end of the lap it was Kavanagh who was leading by the shortest of distances from Sandford and Graham, with the others trailing. After another lap Graham was second but Kavanagh was pulling further away in the lead.

At half way, Kavanagh had more than 10 seconds lead, with Graham second followed by Sherry and Sandford. Coleman's machine was suffering from problems with the front wheel, and began to lose ground. George Brown (A.J.S.) was now in eighth from twentieth place on the first lap. On lap nine, the leading four were spaced out and it was Kavanagh who took the winners flag on a wet track to win, with an average speed of 80.85 mph.

The start of the Sidecar Handicap Race was held up due to torrential rain and although it was still raining when the race finally started, the worst of the weather had passed over, but inches of water still lay on the circuit in places. From the halfway point in the race, Bill Boddice and passenger W G Storr (499 Norton) were in the lead, and won with P V ('Pip') Harris and C Billingham (499 Norton), racing from scratch, second and G Stuart and D Coombes (590 Norton) third.

The third of the British Championship Races was the Senior race for machines up to 500 cc. Harry Bostock (498 Triumph) made a good start, but soon Graham and Kavanagh had passed him. Then Kavanagh overtook Graham on the inside at Orchard Corner, then on the straight to Railway Corner, Graham took the lead again but lost it to Kavanagh again on the bend. At the end of the exciting first lap, it was Kavanagh in the lead which he held for 14 laps to win the race. From the eighth lap to the end of the race it rained continuously, and by half way Kavanagh was 30 seconds ahead of Graham, which he held to the end of the race. In the third lap George Brown was in third place which he held to the end.

Fourth place was a great duel through many laps between Sherry, Sandford, and Ernie Ring, but then Sherry moved between Sandford and Ring, then Sandford began to slip back. Then it was a race between Ring and Sherry until something went wrong with Ring's engine, to let Sherry in for the fourth place.

The eighth and final race of the meeting was the British Championship Lightweight Race (126-250 cc). It was over eight laps and was won by Fergus Anderson on a factory entered Moto Guzzi machine. Les Graham, also riding a works entered Velocette was no match for Anderson. Cecil Sandford, on a modified Velocette, led on the first lap but ended in third place ahead of the German rider, Heinrich Thorn-Prikker (250 cc Moto Guzzi).

The prizes at the end of the meeting were presented by The Rt. Hon. Lord Brabazon of Tara PC, MC, President of the Auto Cycling Union.

BRITISH CHAMPIONSHIP ULTRA LIGHTWEIGHT RACE up to 125 cc 3 laps
R L Graham (M.V.Agusta)   Winner's speed 66.8 mph
J A Hogan (E.M.C. Puch)
H Williams (BSA)

BRITISH CHAMPIONSHIP LIGHTWEIGHT RACE, 126-250 cc   8 laps
F Anderson (Moto Gussi)   Winner's speed 72.57 mph
R L Graham (Velocette)
C C Sandford (Velocette)

BRITISH CHAMPIONSHIP JUNIOR RACE, 251-350 cc   12 laps
K T Kavanagh (Norton)   Winner's speed 80.85 mph
R L Graham (Velocette)
R H Sherry (AJS)

BRITISH CHAMPIONSHIP SENIOR RACE, up to 500 cc   15 laps
K T Kavanagh (Norton)   Winner's speed 79.49 mph
R L Graham (MV Agusta)
G Brown (Norton)

SIDECAR SCRATCH RACE, up to 1200 cc   6 laps
P V Harris & C Billingham (499 cc Norton s.c.) Winners' speed 73.03 mph
E J Davis & E G Allen (998 cc Vincent s.c.)
H Haldemann & J Albisser (718 cc Norton s.c.)

SIDECAR HANDICAP RACE   6 laps
W Boddice & W G Storr (499 cc Norton s.c.) Winners' speed 69.6 mph
P V Harris & C Billingham (490 cc Norton s.c.)
G Stuart & D Coombes (596 cc Norton s.c.)

Daily Mail British Championship Senior Race Trophy -
won by Ken Kavanagh (Norton)

MOTOR CYCLE RACE MEETING (NATIONAL MEETING) - 23rd AUGUST, 1952

The star of this meeting, as things turned out, was the same as had been at the previous meeting a few weeks before - the Australian, K T (Ken) Kavanagh.

He had raced at four of the eight meetings held here and had won no fewer than eleven races in that time, four of which had been Heat wins. He also held the track record for motor cycles at 95.24 mph (faster than the record for cars) and also the track record for a Junior event (machines up to 359 cc), with 92.31 mph. which was set up at this meeting.

The season had been a momentous one for the organisers, the Chelmsford & District Auto Club. Two important ambitions had been achieved, firstly, it made the circuit second to none in the country, this statement was reinforced after this meeting, when Ken Kavanagh said, "This is one of the best courses I have raced over. Boreham has definitely become Britain's fastest Track. I hope to race regularly here and will not be satisfied until I have lapped the Boreham course at 100 mph."

The second achievement had been to attract riders of International fame to compete here, on a circuit set amongst the cornfields of Essex.

Racing started at 1.15 p.m. in sunny weather with Heat 1 of six laps in the Junior Scratch Race (251-350 cc). It was won by none other than Ken Kavanagh (350 Norton) at an average speed of 86.93 mph. Robin Sherry was second (350 Norton) 85.06 mph, and third was Rod Coleman (348 A.J.S.), 84.53 mph.

In the Ultra Lightweight 3 lap race, (up to 125 cc), John Hogan and F H Burman rode almost side by side for the three laps, with the remaining ten riders way behind. Hogan (125 E.M.C.Puch) won with an average speed of 66.89 mph. But for a bad start by H Williams, who was riding a 125 M.V.Agusta belonging to Les Graham, he may have given the first three riders more competition.

Ken Kavanagh, riding a 499 Norton previously owned by Ray Amm, won the first Heat of the 6 lap Senior Scratch Race (352-500 cc), this was his second win of the day. Ernie Ring (498 Matchless) was second.

In Heat 2 of this race, Rod Coleman beat Les Graham (500 M.V.Agusta) with an average speed of 89.78 mph, a little down on that of Ken Kavanagh at 92.26 mph.

E J Davis and passenger, E G Allen, (998 Vincent Watsonian) easily won the Sidecar Scratch race with P V Harris and passenger, C Billingham, (499 Norton) second and Bill Boddice with passenger, E Storr, (499 Norton) third.

The lap record for the Junior Scratch Race (251-350 cc) over twelve laps, was broken by Ken Kavanagh in this event. He finished 51 seconds ahead of Coleman who was second, with Ernie Ring third, 10 seconds behind. Robin Sherry, in second place for eight laps, retired when his gear pedal came off.

Maurice Cann (248 Moto Guzzi) won the Lightweight Scratch Race over 8 laps, at an average speed of 79.75 mph, not matched by B W T Rood (248 Velocette), who came second; Les Graham, also on a Velocette, finished third.

The Sidecar Handicap Race (up to 1200 cc) over 6 laps was a first class race. First away was E Walker and passenger, D G Roberts (499 Norton), and D Yorke with passenger, E J Green (497 Rudge J.A.P.). Yorke won by just about two yards from Walker. Just about as close were E J Davis and passenger, E G Allen (998 Vincent), who were third.

The eleventh and final event of the day was the 15 lap final Senior Scratch Race (351-500 cc). For just half a lap, the Essex star Robin Sherry challenged the skill, daring and speed of Ken Kavanagh, but the Australian got clean away lapping at over 90 mph to build up a big lead. Les Graham on his noisy 498 cc M.V.Agusta was behind Kavanagh and chasing along in third place was Sherry.

After a bad start, Coleman made good progress to gain fourth place. John Surtees (499 Norton) rode a steady race to take fifth. But it was Kavanagh's race, his fourth win of the day. He had undoubtedly been the star in the years 1951 and 1952 at this circuit, where he had thrilled the crowds with his skill, speed and daring, and on a course which had been very much to his liking.

This was the last race meeting of the 1952 season at Boreham, and, although arrangements were already in hand for the 1953 season, no further race meetings ever took place here.

ULTRA-LIGHTWEIGHT RACE, up to 125 cc   3 laps
J A Hogan (E.M.C.Puch)   Winner's speed 66.89 mph
F H Burman E.M.C.Puch)
D Bell (E.M.C.Puch)

SIDECAR SCRATCH RACE, Up to 1200 cc   6 laps
E J Davis & E G Allen (998 cc Vincent s.c.)   Winners' speed 80.52 mph
P V Harris & C Billingham (499 cc Norton)
W Boddice & E Storr (499 cc Norton s.c.)

SCRATCH RACE FINAL, 251-350 cc   12 laps
K T Kavanagh (348 cc Norton)   Winner's speed 90.16 mph
R Coleman (348 cc A.J.S.)
E Ring (348 cc A.J.S.)

LIGHTWEIGHT SCRATCH RACE, 250 cc   8 laps
M Cann (248 cc Moto Gussi)   Winner's speed 79.75 mph
B W T Rood (248 cc Velocette)
R L Graham (248 cc Velocette)

SIDECAR HANDICAP RACE, up to 1200 cc   6 laps

D Yorke & E J Green (497 cc Rudge) no handicap Winners' speed 72.34 mph

E Walker & D G Roberts (499 cc Norton s.c.) no handicap

E J Davis & E G Allen (998 cc Vincent s.c.) 2 mins.

SCRATCH RACE FINAL, 500 cc   15 laps

K T Kavanagh (499 cc Norton)   Winner's speed 93.32 mph

R L Graham (498 cc M.V.Agusta)

R H Sherry (498 cc A.J.S.)

No.70 Derek Yorke &
E J Green (497 Rudge),
winners Sidecar handicap race

(photos: Reg Watts)

No.1 Ken Kavanagh
(499 Norton), winner
Scratch race Final

THE END OF RACING AT BOREHAM

For the second year in succession, the West Essex Car Club's final meeting of the year, due to have been held on 18th October, was cancelled. Planned as a Closed Club Meeting, it attracted a very poor entry and the Club had no real alternative but to cancel the event. The Club reported that a regulation governing the use of retread tyres in competition "was the main deterring factor and was directly responsible for the paucity of the entry list."

This disappointment apart, the 1952 season had ended on a high note certainly so far as motor racing was concerned. The West Essex Car Club was clearly ambitious: late in the season, and at very short notice, it had even offered to run the RAC's prestigious Tourist Trophy race at Boreham when the Ulster Automobile Club was forced to cancel its 1952 running of the event at Dundrod. "Alas," the WECC reported to its members, "this could not be, and the whole affair will remain a 'what-might-have-been' and just a wonderful thought." Although this particular idea did not bear fruit there seemed to be every prospect of the organising clubs building on the success of their first two full seasons as they looked forward to 1953. The West Essex Car Club showed its serious intentions when it applied for permission to run the 1953 British Grand Prix at Boreham as well as that year's Tourist Trophy. Dates eventually allocated to Boreham in the motor racing calendar for 1953 were perhaps rather more realistic and included the then traditional opening event of a speed trial on the main runway and another International meeting on August Bank Holiday weekend. May and June meetings were planned, together with another attempt at a late season event in October. Four motor cycle meetings, two national and two international, were also allocated dates at the circuit. However, just two months before the first meeting was due to take place, the motoring press announced that racing at Boreham was finished.

Exactly why the circuit closed has proved difficult to determine. It is clear that it was not a case of just fading away. Both the organising clubs were ambitious, considerable investment had taken place and the venue looked set to become established as one of the finest tracks in the country.

The end came as a shock to the West Essex Car Club and was a bitter disappointment. "It seems fantastic," the Club's first bulletin of 1953 reported, "that Boreham is no more (for 1953 at least) for as a name it was inextricably bound up with ourselves as a Club. The news came as a very sudden and sharp shock to the Committee in general, and to our Competition Secretary in particular, for there had been no intimation of the impending loss of the circuit... "

The brief press reports about the closure of Boreham which were carried in motoring journals in February, 1953, are slightly ambiguous statements. The substance does not differ between journals and reads:

"The Motor Racing Co. Ltd., which was formed to sponsor racing at Boreham has decided to withdraw support and to terminate its lease of the circuit. Although the company had no objection to the continued use of the circuit by the West Essex Car Club which had always been the organizing body concerned with race meetings there, the owners of the circuit have refused to allow any form of motor sport to take place there this year - so that is that."

This statement does not mention the *Daily Mail* but, bearing in mind that newspaper's involvement, does support the view that the Motor Racing Company was established by the *Daily Mail* to manage the newspaper's financial interests in the circuit. It is regrettable that the *Daily Mail*'s own records do not appear to contain anything about the relationship with the circuit nor its withdrawal of support. After a tentative involvement in 1951 the newspaper made a big commitment to racing in 1952. We do not know exactly what the level of that commitment was but references to the paper's unwillingness to meet Tony Vandervell's starting money demands at the International meeting suggests a considerable input and control at that meeting at least. In December, 1952, as the Chelmsford Auto Club - organisers of motor cycle meetings - considered prospects for the next year, competitions secretary, Alan Mullee, said, "We hope, naturally, to run again at Boreham but we do not know exactly what the situation is, the *Daily Mail* have got the track on lease and at the moment we cannot get a decision from them whether they are going to carry on with it or not". Whilst, as mentioned earlier, it was probably a mistake on Mullee's part to state that the *Daily Mail* itself held a lease, if a leading figure in one of the organising clubs thought this to be the case, it points to a high level of interest on the part of the newspaper and a close involvement with the Motor Racing Company.

Records of the Motor Racing Company itself have not survived although the company was not actually dissolved until June, 1967, long after it had apparently ceased to carry out the task for which it had been set up. Only a small sample of companies' records are retained by the Public Record Office, and Companies House has confirmed that records relating to the Motor Racing Company Limited were destroyed during a sift of old records which it carried out in conjunction with the Public Record Office. In the absence of such records the reasons for the company's and newspaper's withdrawal must remain a matter of conjecture.

Financial problems may well have been a determining factor although, if so, one might have expected these to have become apparent rather earlier in the close season. The sums of money invested would not have been small and it is likely that return on this investment fell below expectations. It seems likely that official crowd figures did not reach the levels envisaged certainly insofar as the August, 1952, International was concerned where a crowd of 100,000 or more was predicted. *Autocar* reckoned that actual figures on the day were half this number and this would have represented a considerable shortfall in anticipated income.

Mike Hawthorn, in his book *Challenge Me the Race*, felt that the weather played a part in the circuit's downfall. Referring to Boreham he wrote that the poor weather at the International meeting was one of the things that helped to defeat the project. Boreham was indeed unfortunate to suffer from a high proportion of wet meetings and it is easy to get the impression that the Essex summers of 1951 and 1952 were particularly wet. In fact, they were not notably wetter than average, it was just unfortunate that wet days happened to coincide with race days.

The suggestion that spectators circumvented the admission payments referred to in an earlier chapter may indeed have created a leakage of potential funds, but organisers did face the much more serious leakage of funds in the form of the Entertainments Tax. This tax undoubtedly placed a very heavy burden on race organisers taking between a third and a half of gate receipts. Silverstone, of course, suffered from the same tax but, from the Midlands circuit's very first meeting - the RAC Grand Prix - it did at least have a much larger initial purse. Grand Prix crowds of 100,000 could be relied upon on an annual basis. Silverstone reckoned to lose £8,500 of the £24,000 gate receipts to the tax and that for each 25/- [£1.25] grandstand seat, 11/10d [59p] went to the government.

From the financial point of view, of particular concern might have been the recognition that, notwithstanding the investment already undertaken, much still needed to be done. In this respect, spectator safety was an issue which would have needed to be addressed before too long. Even today, spectators who attended events can recall being concerned about the adequacy of the straw bales separating them from the action. *Motor Sport* was not alone in expressing the view that this aspect needed attention: "straw bales are rather too much in evidence" Bill Boddy wrote in his September 1952 Editorial, "nor did we like the proximity of the spectators to the racers, with but a rope protection". Silverstone, by comparison, had devised a far more effective system of ditches and earth banks, but to provide these around Boreham's perimeter would have been a costly undertaking. The West Essex Car Club maintained that safety precautions taken at the 1952 meetings had been well in excess of those prescribed by the RAC, but there must have been some concern. The repercussions of the accident that befell Ian Stewart's Jaguar at the International meeting rumbled on for many months. One elderly lady had been critically injured and, although she was making satisfactory progress, there remained the possibility of legal action. A sum of £1,000 from the Club's insurers and £1,000 from the *Daily Mail* was made available for distribution to injured parties and it must have been with some relief that the Club heard in February 1953 that "the injured parties have no animosity towards the Club and were in no way interested in going to law".

The surface-only access to the centre paddock was a further aspect of the track layout which required improvement. Chelmsford driver, Alan Rippon, writing in a local newspaper, highlighted this particular weakness that caused excessive delays and inevitably extended the gaps between races. A vehicle bridge or the earlier suggested tunnel would have been a requirement before too long.

Some or all of these matters would have weighed heavily on those responsible for the financial control of the *Daily Mail*'s interests in the circuit. Perhaps the head-to-head confrontation which had been engineered between the *Daily Mail*-supported Boreham circuit and the *Daily Express*-supported Silverstone circuit had reached the stage where the *Daily Mail*, faced with the need for further investment, had decided to withdraw from the contest and to accept defeat.

The position of the landowner, Co-Partnership Farms Ltd, in the events leading to the circuit's closure also remain somewhat obscure. The press statement announcing the end of racing at Boreham stated that the owners of the circuit had refused to allow any form of motor sport to take place which suggests that, even if the organising clubs had been able to find an alternative backer, this would not have made any difference. If this truly reflects Co-Partnership Farms' position it would denote a marked change in attitude on that company's part. Disappointingly the surviving company records of Co-Partnership Farms Ltd do not mention any matters relating to Boreham circuit and we are left to speculate on how a company, praised in 1951 for its co-operation and helpfulness, changed its attitude so dramatically. It has been suggested that adjoining landowners did not like what was happening at Boreham, that perhaps the whole thing had become too big and disruptive, and wanted it stopped. It may be that they brought pressure to bear but in trying to chart the demise of the circuit it seems that for every view expressed there is a counter-view. An alternative interviewee stated just as strongly that this was not the case: neighbouring landowners - Lord Rayleigh and the Seabrook family - were keen motoring families and would not have campaigned against the project. There was, it is claimed, general support for the venture in the locality.

If, then, Co-Partnership Farms did not have its collective mind changed by outside pressure, was it from within that change came about? Henry Ford had a passionate interest in farming and in 1930 he had purchased 2,000 acres of land at Boreham for an experiment in collective farming. Financial connection with Ford ceased in 1946 when Co-Partnership Farms was formed with funds from Ford's friend, Lord Perry of Stock. Financial involvement may well have ceased, but influence, even after the death of Henry Ford in 1947, may well have still been quite strong. It was, after all, Ford's inspiration and money that had started the project.

In post-war years the Ford Motor Company had enjoyed the use of another Essex airfield, Matching Green, for testing its vehicles. This airfield was not owned by Ford and became unavailable for use. The presence of another suitable airfield on land with Ford connections may have led to the need to rid Boreham of its erstwhile motor sporting tenants. The motives could well have existed and there are those who, today, are quite ready to lay the blame at Ford's door, but the dates do not tie in too well. The Ford Motor Company did not actually buy the site, initially for heavy goods testing, until 1955 (followed by Ford Motorsport in 1963), so there was no real urgency for the circuit to cease operations when it did.

Contemporary sources seem to suggest that the landowner was not blameless in the matter of the circuit's closure and that negotiations between Co-Partnership Farms and the Motor Racing Company simply failed to reach a successful conclusion. Whether the disagreement between these two organisations related to finance or to matters of overall control cannot be determined but it appears that through their lack of vision, and their lack of courage to build on what had already been achieved, the opportunity to create a first class circuit in Essex slipped away. Under the heading 'The Brevity of Boreham' the Editorial of the February, 1953, edition of *Iota* - the official organ of the club which catered for 500 cc F3 cars - read, "There is an old adage which suggests that one should learn to walk before trying to run. Whilst motor racing in Great Britain has progressed well into the running stage, it may be that from time to time progress may falter. The news... that there will be no more meetings at Boreham may be regarded as one of those setbacks, one which comes from trying to run just a little too fast". Such criticism, which a subsequent letter from *Iota*'s Associate Editor to an understandably aggrieved WECC clarified, was not referring in any way to inefficiency on the part of the West Essex Car Club. "Our reference to 'walking before running,'" the response continued "was levelled at your sponsors and the landowners who, it would seem, have a great deal to learn".

The same source darkly intimated that other forces may have been at work. The date for the West Essex Car Club's International meeting planned for 1953 clashed - as it had done in 1952 - with the weekend of the German Grand Prix. This was perhaps simply the inevitable result of an over-crowded calendar with too many organisers wanting to hold prestigious events featuring well-known drivers, but some people - including *Iota*'s Associate Editor - clearly thought otherwise. "We won't deny that to get your international dates clashing with the German Grand Prix two years running is a pretty sickening business, and should never have happened. We have heard some pretty rotten rumours in connection with this business, but that of course cannot be discussed in this letter, and in any case does not reflect on your Club's good name. It would seem that sport and big business just don't mix." It is a tantalising snippet which seems to suggest that someone, somewhere, did not want Boreham to survive...

Initially the West Essex Car Club had hoped that the loss of Boreham might be temporary and although the question of regaining the use of the circuit was pursued by the Club's Competition Secretary towards the end of 1953, his efforts came to nothing. The Club found itself on a stage where forces far more powerful than itself were pulling the strings. Racing at Boreham Circuit really had come to an end.

"It is a loss," the WECC Competition Secretary wrote, "not only to ourselves, but to motor sport as a whole, make no mistake. It had every prospect of proving the best and fastest circuit in the country..."

The high point of motor sport at Boreham: the Ferrari of Francisco Landi leads the field away at the start of the race for Formula 1 and 2 cars, 2nd August, 1952 (*photo: Autocar/Quadrant Picture Library*)

FORD MOTOR COMPANY AT THE AIRFIELD

Although Boreham has always been associated with the preparation and development of the company's motor rally cars at its Motorsport centre which has been based at the airfield since 1963, it was in 1955 that the company first moved to the site and the airfield became a proving ground for the development of the company's commercial vehicles.

The development of both commercial vehicles and rally cars was carried on here until 1986, when the Iveco-Ford truck business came into being and truck development work began to slowly wind down; in the following year it was officially discontinued, leaving Motorsport on their own at Boreham.

Ford Competitions Department (as it was then known, later to be Motorsport) until the summer of 1963 had been located at Lincoln Cars Limited in Middlesex, but the potential to expand and acquire better facilities was thought to be at the quiet and secluded site in rural Essex at the old wartime airfield at Boreham.

Previous to the move, Ford had relied on V8 Pilots, Zephyrs, Anglias, and Cortinas for rallying. At the time of considering release of funds to build the Competitions Department at Boreham, ex-rally manager, Bill Barnett, with the Public Affairs Manager of Ford, Walter Hayes (later to become Vice-Chairman of Ford of Europe) became involved and persuaded the Board of Directors that if Ford were to remain in motor sport and be competitive, it would have to reorganise and the job should be carried out properly.

As a result of this, Alan Platt, who had a good reputation for organisational flair was appointed Competitions Manager.

"The beauty of Boreham," said Bill Barnett, "was its motor racing circuit. We could build a car, and 100 yards later we were on a test track."

It was from this start that the company's successes in motor rallying really began to take off.

In 1964 a Cortina G.T., driven by Peter Hughes and Billy Young, won the East African Safari Rally; the previous year they had come second in an Anglia.

In the years to follow a fleet of successful rally cars were developed at Boreham, including the Lotus Cortina, Escorts, including the famous twin cam, RS1600, RS1800, Sierra Cosworth, and the Escort World Rally car. The host of drivers who joined the company included Roger Clark, Hannu Mikkola, Gunnar Palm, Øve Andersson, Timo Makinen, Bjorn Waldegard, François Delecour, and Carlos Sainz.

In 1968 the Escort Twin-Cam rally version was developed and used as the company rally car. It was to commence a run of great successes for Ford over the next thirty years. The rally car, requiring extensive modifications to a production version family model, together with development work, was carried out at Boreham. No fewer than 46 World Class Rally wins, 3 World Manufacturer's titles and 2 World Drivers' Championships were won Eight consecutive wins were achieved in the British R.A.C. Rally between 1972 and 1979.

The 1,000 Lakes Rally in Finland in 1968 was won by Hannu Mikkola, his first ever World Rally win driving an Escort.

In the London to Mexico World Cup Rally in 1970, one of the toughest rallies ever held, six Boreham prepared cars were entered and five finished, taking first, third, fifth, sixth and eighth places, the winning car being driven by Hannu Mikkola and Gunnar Palm almost an hour ahead of the second placed car.

In 1972 Roger Clark became the first Briton to win a World Championship Rally driving a Mark 1 Escort. Three years in succession - 1973-5 - the British R.A.C. Rally was won by Timo Makinen, a feat that has never been equalled.

The World Drivers' Championship in 1981 was won by Ari Vatanen, driving an Escort - the first time a privately-entered car driver had won the World title.

Farewell to the now-legendary Ford Escorts took place in the November, 1998, Network Q Rally of Great Britain for the F.I.A. World Rally Championship. Juha Kankkunen achieved second place, just three minutes behind the winner; Bruno Thiry, a minute behind, took third.

In 1995 T.M.C. Pioneer Aggregates, Ltd., began their operation of gravel extraction from the airfield site and, at the end of 1996, a change in policy at Motorsport came about, together with management changes. The Ford Rally Championship programme of operations was relocated away from Essex and Boreham was left to concentrate on serving customer requirements, with other testing and development work on the Ford rally Ka. So ended a major part of the Ford Motorsport operations at Boreham.

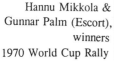

Hannu Mikkola & Gunnar Palm (Escort), winners 1970 World Cup Rally

STIRLING MOSS RETURNS TO BOREHAM

The following report was written by Stirling Moss, following his appraisal of two cars at Boreham in January, 1964. One of the cars, (owned at the time by Mr Hugh Bergel), was a 1926 2.3 litre G.P. Bugatti Type 35T. The other car (owned at the time by Mr Peter Waller), was a 1935 1.5 litre supercharged E.R.A. R9B. The article was first published by the Vintage Sports Car Club (V.S.C.C.) in their Bulletin No. 82 - Summer 1964, it is published here by permission of Mr Neil Murray (V.S.C.C) and Mr Stirling Moss, O.B.E..

"I've always wanted to drive those two motor racing classics, the Bugatti and the E.R.A., somehow the opportunity had never presented itself - until now. Earlier this year I was invited to try a 1926 2.3 litre Bugatti G.P. car and a 1935 1.5 litre super-charged E.R.A. on a private circuit outside London. I was very happy to do this because, in addition to driving two greats, it also got me behind the wheel of a racing car again - even if it wasn't the type of vehicle I'd been used to.

It is rather ironic that these drives should have to come after my retirement from racing. At the beginning of my career, I would have given anything for this experience. Most of my boyhood rivals were connected with one or other and I remember casting envious glances at Raymond Mays' 2 - litre E.R.A. at my first hill climbs.

It was lightly snowing, windy day when I drove to the test circuit at Boreham Essex. There I met Hugh Bergel, owner of the Bugatti, and Peter Waller with his E.R.A.. Bergel's car, driven by his son, Richard, has raced regularly with many successes since 1959, while Waller has been conducting a series of fights with Bira's Remus (driven by its owner, Patrick Lindsay) for the past five years.

Afterwards, Peter Waller told me that no one else had been allowed to drive his car in the six years he'd owned it.

Before driving the Bugatti, Hugh Bergel gave me some background information. The Type 35 Bugatti first appeared at the French Grand Prix in 1924. It was a 2-litre (60 mm bore x 80 mm stroke) unblown straight-eight single O.H.C. engine built with built up crank shaft running on three ball and two roller main bearings, with one piece con-rods and roller big-ends. Later, by fitting crankshafts of different strokes, it was also available in 1.5 litre and 2.3 litre versions, all three with or without blowers.

The same chassis and body could be had with a plain bearing four cylinder 1.5 litre engine. There was also a model called the imitation G.P. with a 'cooking' version of the eight cylinder engine, which was used in two touring cars.

In 1931, the bottom end of the roller bearing engine was fitted with a double O.H.C. block and head and this continued as a G.P. car for several years. Both single cam and twin cam 2.3 blown engines were used in high performance sports cars with very attractive body-work.

The Type 35, in its many variations, was put into production; several hundred were built and could be bought off the shelf. The latest Bugatti register lists 110 Type 35s still known to exist. There are 21 of these straight-eights in Britain but about eight or ten are in the 'cooking model'. The car I drove is one of only five or six full G.P. cars regularly raced here.

On getting into the Bugatti, I was a little apprehensive to hear that the gearbox was back to front (first gear was backwards to the left; second straight forwards; third away from me and backwards while fourth was forward again).

Luckily, all pedals were in conventional positions but I was told that first gear was a little difficult to get into and I had to snatch it. I did this, cautiously, let in the clutch and the Bugatti drew slowly away. After reaching 60 mph, I realised that the brakes needed a longish movement of my right foot and I approached the first corner.

It was obvious that the steering was more direct than I'd been used to and that the car had nowhere near the adhesion of the semi modern G.P. car. Even though I went through the corner with considerable caution, I found the back end tended to swing out. This was easily corrected, but at the same time, I found I was likely to give too much correction to the steering. I was quite impressed with the power of the car, though it was missing on two or more cylinders.

After I had done a couple of laps, Hugh Bergel waved me in to replace the fouled up plugs. I needed him to tell me this - because not being accustomed to the sound of the engine, I would have continued without realising that the car was giving only two-thirds of its possible performance.

I reached speeds of 100 mph with the Bugatti without pressing myself or the car. There were three reasons for this: I felt the weather conditions were bad, it was not my car - also I was out of practice. I liked the Bug's immediate responsiveness and the lack of play in the steering.

Once one got the hang of the gearbox, there was no difficulty with it, but I found the windscreen almost useless. Obviously one is more in the air stream than in the modern G.P. car but it was difficult to get the angle of the screen correct so that I could look over it and not get my head blown off, it was a hard drive though. It proved one thing - that the drivers must have been very fit to have lasted in long distance races. Today's cars owe a lot to the Bugatti, yet it struck me how far the modern designer has developed engine performance, road holding, suspension and tyre adhesion.

I liked the look of the car but its lack of comfort makes me wonder if our G.P. drivers match the speeds of their predecessors in cars of this era. I found the E.R.A easier to drive and it definitely had a softer seat, (in fact it was one of the most comfortable seats I've ever been in, although I would have preferred it a little further back and inclined at a much greater angle).

Stirling Moss in the Bugatti Type 35T (*photo: Ford Motor Co., Ltd.*)

No.30 Stirling Moss (Cooper), No. 2 Eric Brandon (Cooper) 100 miles Sports Car Race (*photo: Les Downes*)

I was told that the car had about 150 hp and I would not contest this. It was most responsive to the throttle and had extremely good brakes. These are not hydraulic and the secret of getting them to work properly rests with the drums as well as other adjustments. Once again, it was a longer movement of the pedal than I'd been used to, but it was extremely light.

After being shown the controls of the pre-selector gearbox, I took off in the car, which sounded - and felt - more conventional. This was to be expected, because the E.R.A. is about ten years younger than the Bug (in fact, it was in a similar car that Bob Gerard won so many races in post-war years).

The car was fitted with quite a low axle ratio - 4.5 - and had 650 x 16 in. wheels fitted on the back. The top speed was about 120/125 m.p.h. at 6000 r.p.m. certainly the car was willing to reach this even in the bad weather conditions, on the short Boreham straight.

The driving position was nearly as difficult as the Bugatti but, of course, the gearbox was far easier. The brakes were as light but more powerful and the steering was as responsive and nearly as highly geared.

The E.R.A. did not seem quite so prone to sliding on the wet track - but this could have been due to its larger section tyres. I was asked not to exceed 6,000 revs. which was quite comfortable - because the power came in about 4,000 and, therefore there was quite a large rev. range to use.

There was plenty of wind blowing around me but the windscreen seemed slightly more effective. Sitting as high as one does in the E.R.A., one can certainly see what's ahead. The maximum speed I reached was around 120 m.p.h. and my lap time around the circuit was therefore considerably faster than in the Bug, but I felt, in both cases , I could have gone faster even under the bad conditions, if I had learnt more about the cars, used more of the machine - been prepared to stick my neck out a bit further. The latter I never reckon to do, incidentally, I was told that of the 17A and B type E.R.A.s made, 16 still exist and at least 12 are - or could easily be - in racing condition. The E.R.A. must surely be one of the few single seaters of world class to have been built around a push-rod engine.

Both the Bugatti and the E.R.A. were in tip-top condition and looked as if they had only just been produced - a pretty fantastic achievement when you consider their age. But the tremendous amount of work and enthusiasm spent on them by their owners is well worthwhile when one realises the interest and fun to be had with these great vintage racing cars on modern circuits".

The following in an extract from an article written by George Beare for the Ford Times *of March, 1964, on the Stirling Moss appraisal of the same two cars.*

"It rolled and reverberated across the frozen flats of Essex - a sound like tearing calico amplified ten thousand times. The sound of great exhausts that rocked the major circuits of Europe during Nuvolari's time. The sound echoing

1934 Frazer-Nash (Brian Mather) (*photo by John Lock*)

Austin 7, Bard FF2000

Riley Special, Lister Jaguar, XK120 Jaguar

overtones of motoring history. Two of motordom's car gods were on the track again - the Type 35-T Bugatti and the Type 'B' E.R.A. And driving them, an abdicated monarch of the wheel - Stirling Moss.

"I remember these old racers when I was a kid down at Brooklands," said Moss, "Ever since, I have wanted to drive one."

Conditions were far from ideal for dicing with a strange racing car on an unfamiliar track. It was snowing; the circuit was iced up; there was a howling east wind; and visibility was downright bad even for normal speeds.

The E.R.A. had an iced-up carburettor and, while it was being worked on, they opened up the Bugatti which was big and sky-blue and 37 years old. They opened it up and exposed its beautiful straight-eight innards (it wasn't the engine though, Harry Bergel said, which had made the Bug's name. It was the rigidly-engineered chassis which had allowed drivers like Chiron to fling them round cruelly difficult corners at more than 90 mph).

Harry Bergel, who has had the car for four years, drove around the track to give it a 'warm.' Then Moss took it. As the volume of sound from the Bugatti's engine rose from the Haydnesque to the Wagnerian, one could almost feel Moss calling up all his remembered skills.

Cold, and blue of face, Moss extricated himself from behind the wheel. "What a wonderful sound he said". He had trouble changing down. Up changes went through very smoothly but downwards they were difficult to judge because of the extremely rapid engine acceleration in neutral.

"But that doesn't mean a thing," said Moss. "This is my fault, not the car's. I found it marvellously impressive."

Waller now had the E.R.A. ready. This was a little younger than the Bugatti, class of '34. Moss gave it about five years. "It was perishing cold going round in that Bug," Moss said. And to cheer him, Waller said; "In the E.R.A. you will get all the heat, from the engine on your lower half and the sleet on top."

"Well," said Moss, "If you don't see me when I come past, you will know I am under the seat." And he took the E.R.A. off like a Boeing 707.

Apart from the down-changes, he had been a bit doubtful of the Bugatti's brakes and this had limited his best lap speed to a little over 60 mph But in the E.R.A. he went up to something in the region of 80. And when one remembers that the best lap speed on this particular circuit for a Lotus modified Cortina is 74.5 mph no one could say that the E.R.A. (or Moss) wasn't pulling out the stops. Down the straight watchers had their ears assaulted by an almost unbearable noise each time the car hurtled past at well over the ton.

Apart from the cold, Moss suffered the additional hardship of having absolutely no room to move in the car. Until he thawed out, words failed him. They virtually had to lift him out, half frozen. "How in heaven's name did Eddie Hall get in and out of them?" he gasped.

H.R.H. Princess Anne tries out the driver's seat of a Tyrrell Ford racing car during her visit to Motorsport in 1972 (*photos: Ford Motor Co., Ltd.*)

Alan Jones, World Champion Grand Prix racing driver in 1980 (left) and Patrick Tambay, the French Grand Prix driver (white overalls) at Boreham, early 1986. The occasion was 'shake down' tests on the Ford-Beatrice racing car prior to its introduction to the 1986 racing scene

"I don't know about Eddie Hall," said Waller, "but I had a big bloke driving this the other day and I had to dismantle the steering wheel to get him out."

The following is an extract from an article first published in the Ferrari Magazine, *Issue 72, 1986, the in-house magazine of the Ferrari Owners Club, and published here with their permission.*

Although the title of the event suggests only Ford and Ferrari cars took part, it was decided by the organisers that, to add variety to the occasion, other makes of car, together with their drivers, were invited to take part.

FORD FERRARI LE MANS DAY AT BOREHAM by RICHARD ALLEN

Inevitably in a company the size of Ford, there are many unblinkered car bulls, some of whom own Ferraris. A couple of years ago an idea germinated on staging a special event to celebrate the G.T.40s Le Mans victories. Boreham seemed like the ideal place with the theme to be 'Ford versus Ferrari at le Mans'. Some discussion took place at director level between Bill Camplisson, a previous Ferrari owner whilst in the States, Stuart Turner and John Southgate, Directors of Motorsport and Public Affairs respectively, and approval was given. Ironically, the event would be a private affair to be organised by Ford Public Affairs man, David Burgess-Wise.

Well known as a motoring writer, David has a penchant for old machinery, and it was decided to extend the scope of the event by inviting Le Mans associated histories by other manufacturers than Ford and Ferrari. Bryan Wingfield took on the task of GT40 recruitment, with Ferrari competition cars being the responsibility of FOC member Terry Hoyle. In addition to these the Essex Ferraristi were eager to join in with their road cars, and understandably Ford fancied running the RS200 and Sierra Cosworth in this sort of company.

Sunday, 15th June, this year was the chosen date, and the weather was perfect. Specially decked out with flags, banners and bunting, with refreshment marquees and tasteful Ford product display, the Boreham facility looked surprisingly attractive in brilliant sunshine. Several hundred people came along to watch. The majority being Ford personnel from the Boreham and Dunton locations with their families.

A walk through the paddock areas revealed an impressive line up of some nine GT40s with derivatives as far apart as the Bell and Colvill Gulf liveried racer and a MK5 Safir Engineering recently built targa top version. Included were the Ford France and ex-Colonel Ronnie Hoare cars, both of which ran in this year's Le Mans historic parade. From before the war there were Lagondas, Astons, Frazer-Nashes, Bentleys, Bugattis, an Alfa P3, and a Scuderia Ferrari Alfa Romeo 8C, reputed to be the car that Enzo Ferrari drove to his last victory. Moving on to the

Control Point
Ferrari 250 SWB (Terry Hoyle)

Ferrari 250 LM (David Piper)`
Ford GT 40

Dukes Straight, looking towards Railway Corner from Control Point
Dukes Straight, looking towards Orchard Corner: Control Point on right (*photos: Ford Motor Co., Ltd.*)

later period, there were three Ferrari 250 SWBs of Stuart Passey, Clive Beecham and Bryn Williams, John Godfrey with the diminutive Ferrari 196P, and David Piper with a choice of 275LM or P2/3. Not to mention his Porsche 917. Sprinkled amongst this mouth-watering collection, were A.C.Cobra, Jaguar C and D Types, Richard Attwood's Ford F3L, and two big Lola sports racers. About 20 road-going Ferraris included 275GTBs, Daytonas, Boxers, a Lusso, Testarossa, 246GT, and most 308 variants.

These cars were to be split into batches taking account of age and category, before being let loose on the ultra fast 3.9 miles Boreham circuit. There was a drivers briefing and we were requested to "refrain from unseemly behaviour of furious driving"! In other words racing would be discouraged. A pace car would lead for a couple of laps to enable cars to be spread out whilst warming up.

For the road-going Ferraris the Sierra Cosworth pace car would stay for the whole twenty minute session. Everybody feared this to be a deliberate attempt to restrain the pace. Subsequent events proved otherwise.

Amongst the historic racers Martin Colvill in the Gulf GT40 was devastatingly quick, with only the Lola Aston providing brief resistance. John Godfrey was also going very well in the beautiful 196SP, passing many cars of much greater engine capacity with ease. The 250 SWBs were impressive too with Stuart Passey and Clive Beecham enjoying this opportunity to exercise these beautifully restored machines, both of which have excellent sixties racing pedigrees. The two Martins, McGlone and Emmison in the two 275GTBs pounded round in close company. Maybe they were not racing or even driving furiously but they were certainly teasing each other! Terry Hoyle was also out in his well known Lusso, reporting afterwards that whilst pressing on through an 80 mph corner he was overtaken round the outside by a Sierra Cosworth four up, with passengers taking photos out of the rear window!

"That's progress," remarked Terry ruefully.

The last batch of cars out on the circuit were the more up-to-date road going Ferraris. After the two lap warm up everybody got moving fairly swiftly. However the undermentioned pace car driven by Ford's development Engineer John Hitchins disappeared into the distance, and was soon passing some of the Ferraris and not just 308s either! Obviously Mr Hitchins had been round Boreham before, and he was driving an uncherished company car! In the midst of all this Martin Colvill was let loose taking passengers round in the GT40. Unfortunately a fair amount of stones had been lifted from the paddock area by the slick-shod racers on the circuit. As the GT40 blasted past the Ferraris, several windscreens were cracked and a stone peck epidemic broke out. Happily though there were no serious incidents, although Geoff Dark had a near thing when a tyre blew out spun his 308GTB into a cornfield.

During the day our hosts provided a lunch and any amount of non-alcoholic refreshments. The atmosphere was delightfully relaxed and informal and everyone thought it proved a really memorable occasion. Not only a fitting tribute to the GT40, but also a farewell to Boreham. Ford Motor Company are to be congratulated and thanked by all who attended.

The following article was written by Brian K Joscelyne and Alan Wheatley in 1987 and first published in the Aston Martin Owners' Club journal at that time. It is re-published here with their permission. The story gives the background to the Aston Martin re-union held at Boreham on 29th July, 1987.

ASTON MARTIN - TEAM DB2 - REUNION (1987)

On July 29 this year, there took place a rather special reunion of five rather special DB2 Aston Martins - the works team cars of 1950 and 1951. As far as we know they had not been seen all together as a group since they were being raced as a factory team some 37 years ago. Just why these five cars hold a special place in Aston Martin's competition history can be realised if you look at the major results achieved by them over just two seasons.

At the Le Mans 24 Hours (the world's top endurance race) they finished 3rd, 5th (twice) 6th and 7th overall and lst in class (twice) 2nd in class (twice) and third in class as well as winning the Index of Performance. In the Mille Miglia (then the worlds top road race) they finished llth, 12th, and 13th overall, winning the class twice and second once in the course of taking the Grand Touring Category.

In the Tourist Trophy races at the fearsome Dundrod road circuit they clocked up overall placing of 4th, 5th, 7th & 8th, with a class win, two seconds and two thirds.

At the Silverstone one hour race (the top U.K. event for production cars) class positions ran through lst, 2nd, 3rd and 4th and included a 6th overall. Just for good measure Alpine cups (for completing unpenalised runs) were won in the Alpine Rally then Europe's premier road rally. And all this with virtually standard production cars ! No wonder these particular Astons are still regarded as something special.

But results such as these could never have been achieved without having a determined manager behind the team. John Wyer describes how he came to be involved:

When David Brown invited me, in March, 1950, to manage his Aston Martin racing team, I think we must both have wondered what the hell we were getting into. I asked David if he regarded it as a permanent position and he said, "Certainly not, only one season." I felt that made his position fairly clear. For my part I had some doubts about committing to even one season. I had never managed a racing team before. There were no schools to go to, no books to read. I had managed one car owned and driven by friendly associates in endurance races as the 24-Hours of Spa and the Paris 12 hours at Montlhery, where we had attracted certain favourable comment by the efficiency of our operation. I think this is where David Brown may first have noticed me. We also attempted Le Mans where, at least, I observed Wyer's 'First Rule of Le Mans' - If you are not going to be there for the whole 24-hours, make quite sure you get back to the hotel for dinner on Saturday night and bed by midnight.

Perhaps fortunately the official Aston Martin team had problems of its own, so we escaped notice.

In truth, I had absolutely no idea what I was taking on. If I had expected the racing team to be a going concern I could not have been more wrong. David Brown told me, "We have made reservations at the Hotel Moderne at Le Mans. We have renewed the contracts of Macklin and Brackenbury, who drove for us last year. The other drivers and everything else are your concern." I asked, "What about the cars?" and David replied, "The cars are not started; you will have to do something about that".

With the Le Mans race less than three months away, desperate measures were called for. The Aston Martin DB2, a great concept design, had been prematurely announced and displayed, long before there were any cars available for sale. There were at least fifty customers for every car we could hope to make. The production and sales people were naturally reluctant to part with one of their precious cars for what seemed to them to be a frivolous purpose.

But by devious means, and with a lot of support from David Brown, I extracted three cars from the line. It is a measure of our position that they were the seventh, eighth, and ninth production cars to be built.

This was a start, but there was a long way to go. Starting from a production car is not the best way to build a race car, because so much work has already gone in which cannot be checked, short of a complete rebuild, for which there was no time. Inevitably the car is too heavy and the weight is in inaccessible places. A further small difficulty was that there was space in the racing department to work on only two cars with reasonable efficiency. Frequently I took one car home and kept it in my own garage to provide more room.

I had a staff of six - Percy Kemish, the superintendent, and, originally four mechanics, to which I added a fifth. None of us had much sleep. Between these and other distractions I had to engage the other four drivers, which involved 'selling' my choices to David Brown, make all the travel and transportation arrangements, and work out all the detail administration and staff work without which nobody would arrive at Le Mans on the right day.

Unbelievably, the cars were finished and I even succeeded in giving each of them a settling down test of about 100 miles on public roads. Serious race testing

Drivers and cars have a rest near the Control Tower. L to r: Eric Thompson, George Abecassis, Hon. Gerald Lascelles, Harold Beach, Jack Fairman (*photo: Phil Rudge*)

Aston Martin DB2 works team (1950-1) about to start motoring at the Boreham re-union

there was none, and the cars we sent to Le Mans were an unknown quantity.

Even more incredibly, after all these tribulations the race was a minor triumph. After yet one more disaster when one car was inexcusably crashed on the way to the race - at that point I began seriously to wonder if my future really lay with Aston Martin - the other two cars behaved impeccably. They finished first and second in the three ~ litre class, broke the class record for the 24-Hours and finished fifth and sixth overall. By any standard it was a remarkable performance for a close to standard DB2 and did a great deal to establish the name. The finest hour of the DB2 was to come the following year when, with better prepared cars - because we had a year to do it - we secured the first three places in the class, broke all our own records and finished a very close third overall. But 1950 had to come first to show the way."

From John Wyer's comments above it can be seen he had quite a soft spot for the DB2.

The results he obtained in 1950 and 1951 were out of all proportion to what might have been expected with just five cars genuinely off the production line. No wonder people were clamouring to buy the DB2 once it had been released to the public. In the end 411 examples were built over a three year period.

But the five team cars are the ones that carry the glory and are rightly prized today. Alan Wheatley owns one of them, XMC77, and it was his idea to get them all together again. Let him tell the story:

"It was Charlie Williams' fault - and very grateful I am to him. You see, it all started in 1985 with the club's Jubilee celebrations. Charles who lives in Victoria decided he would like to do the European Tour in his DB2 team car, XMC76, so nothing daunted he arranged to transport himself and his car from Australia to England. In the end the car made it (see our 1985 yearbook) but Charles was delayed; by about two years!"

"How Charles Williams finally got to do the European Tour in 1987 is another story, which he may tell us one day. What particularly interested me was that all but one of the surviving DB2 team cars were now within about 150 miles of each other in the south of England. So, wouldn't it be a good idea to try and get them all together. But where and how? I put this idea to Chris Nixon who was immediately enthusiastic and offered to help. He thought that *Classic and Sports Car* magazine would be interested in doing an article on a DB2 team car reunion, in return for which they would support the event and provide a venue. And so that is what we did. But where should we hold it?

"The first choice was to hold the reunion at Goodwood as the cars had raced there. Certainly we wanted a circuit where we could exercise the cars in the way that David Brown and John Wyer had intended. This was to be an action fun day; no standing around 'posing' Unfortunately it was not possible to use Goodwood and in the end we settled for Boreham near Chelmsford, in Essex. Ford have owned the circuit for many years, kindly gave us exclusive use of the track for the day. They also put the canteen at our disposal which turned out to be welcome."

Next was the question of who would come. Of the three 1949 team cars, one was written off, one is in America and one is being rebuilt; so we scored blank here. However Derek Durst, who now owns UMC66 the first Lagonda engined car contrived to be in England on the correct day and brought many interesting photographs of his and the other early cars. (Derek promises us the story for a future magazine - *Editor*)."

"The three 1950 cars are all hale and hearty. Gerald Lascelles brought VMF64 accompanied by his wife. This is the most famous and most successful of the DB2s (see the Register for details) and has been owned by Gerald since the works sold it to him after he left Feltham. Eric Thompson brought VMF65, a car he used to race in the fifties when owned by Rob Walker. Eric was the first private owner of VMF63, and this car was brought by its current owner Richard Forshaw. Richard had to rearrange a business trip abroad to make it to Boreham, which is typical of the enthusiasm shown by everyone for the event and for which Chris and I were most grateful.

"Of the 1951 cars, clearly I had to have my own car XMC77 there as the instigator of the event, though the saga of the work involved could fill an article all on its own. Anyway, with the help of Martin Cheetham and his team the car was ready, just. XMC76 was an interesting problem, as although Charles Williams finally made it to England in 1987, he could not stay long enough to be at Boreham. However, he was keen for his car to be there, even if he couldn't be. I thought' for a while about driving both the lightweight DB2 there together, but decided eventually that this was beyond even this ultimate DB2 enthusiast, (perhaps if one of them had been left hand drive I might have managed it.)

Charles and I agreed to ask Andy Hodgeton to drive XMC76 and he readily agreed, roping in Geoffrey Harris to help. Little did they know what they were letting themselves in for."

"Finally we invited as many of the personalities as we could find who were involved when the cars raced from 1949 to 1953. The event was topped off by three supporting MKIII (one from AML belonging to Victor Gauntlet) which came along to enjoy the fun. Victor very kindly provided lunch at a local hostelry for all participants - a very generous gesture and typical of the Company Chairman. Thank you Victor, from all of us".

"So all the plans were laid and all we needed now was the weather. And we got it, but not in the way we had hoped for. July 29th, 1987, will be remembered as the day of 'the storm'. It would seem that we chose the wettest part of the country on the wettest day of the wettest summer for years. The newspaper headlines next day spoke of nine foot floods, chaos on the roads and Terry Wogan marooned. (Who? *Ed.*) Traffic on the M25 motorway round London was at first moving very slowly in poor visibility, and was then blocked by a landslide causing some of us to take a lengthy diversion. But everyone made it, five cars in all. The time remaining before lunch was taken up by static photography of the cars and the personalities present and then it was down to the pub for lunch. It was memorable."

George Abecassis and Brian Shawe-Taylor, who shared XMC77 at Le Mans in 1951, met again for the first time in many years. Jack Fairman, who was in the Le Mans team in 1950, was telling increasingly tall stories to Eric Thompson, who no doubt replied with a few good yarns of his own. Gerald Lascelles was reminiscing, while Brian Joscelyne listened avidly. Gerald was also trying to decide if he was going to have another drink and let his wife drive home, while she was having the similar, reverse, thoughts! At least, I think that was the gist of it. Harold Beach was smiling at the thought that the cars he helped to design were still going strong over thirty five years later."

Lola Aston Martin

Alan Wheatley splashes through (*photo: Roger Stowers*)

'TYRELL 017' RACING CAR VISIT (MARCH, 1989)

Michele Alboreto, the Italian driver, and Jonathan Palmer, Formula I drivers for the Tyrell team in 1989, were at Boreham in March of that year to carry out shakedown tests on the car's systems, particularly amongst which was the new 6 speed longitudinal gearbox, located in front of the axle.

The two drivers took it in turns during some 60 laps around the circuit running through the gearbox up and down.

The car had a number of design changes from the previous year including a new suspension. The team were due to take the car to Rio, but the new 018 car, designed by Harvey Postlethwaite, was planned to be ready for the San Marino Grand Prix at Imola on 23 April, 1989.

Tyrrell Formula 1 Grand Prix racing car at Boreham for shakedown tests, 1989 (*photo: Ford Motor Co., Ltd.*)

DRIVING A £2 MILLION CAR

The following article by Brian K Joscelyne tells of a sales film made at Boreham of three interesting and valuable cars, one of which he drove.

Boreham has been many things in its time, including a little known venue for filming some of the world's most valuable cars in action.

A particular occasion of this kind took place during 1989 at the height of the boom in the value of classic cars.   Christies, the fine art auctioneers had developed a department specialising in the sales of vintage, veteran, and classic cars at the time, when prices were escalating rapidly.

Competition cars with a history attached were the most sought after, and three of these, two Aston Martin's and a Ferrari, had been consigned to their sale in May that year at Monte Carlo, held to coincide with the Monaco Grand Prix.

Wealthy collectors would be present and could of course inspect the cars being offered prior to the auction.   But to show bidders the cars were in full running order, short video films were made so that brief clips could be seen in the sale room immediately prior to bidding commencing.

Christies engaged a professional video production company and Boreham was secured with Ford Motor Company permission for the filming to take place.

Wednesday, 5th April, 1989, was the day selected and all concerned assembled there, myself included as I had been requested to drive the Ferrari. Unfortunately the weather was simply awful and it rained all day.   This did not matter too much for one of the Aston Martins, which was a closed coupe and a prototype DB2, and only the second built with the six cylinder engine, designed by W O Bentley for his post war Lagonda saloon.   It was a 1949 works development car.   As part of that development, it was raced in 1950 at Monza in Italy, and at the Targa Florio road race in Sicily, driven by Lance Macklin.   It had been registered UMC272 in 1949, and retains the number to this day.   For some twenty years prior to the auction, this car was owned by Peter Lee, and he had extensively restored the car over the years 1977-1987.

The filming went ahead in spite of the weather and the film crew seemed reasonably satisfied.   At the Monaco auction, this interesting prototype sold for a good price and passed into the collection of Simon Draper who at that time was just starting to build up his unique collection of historic Aston Martin cars.

The second Aston Martin was really special, being one of only two DBR2 sports racing cars built for the factory racing team in 1957.   Known as DBR2/1 this was built for the 24 hour Le Mans race that year and was later raced by Tony Brooks and Stirling Moss who had two victories with it.   Halfway through the 1958 season, it was shipped to America where its successes continued.   With such a provenance this car was to be the star of the auction according to Christies. The owner at the time was Victor Gauntlett, then boss of Aston Martin, and he acquired the services of Rex Woodgate to drive it from Newport Pagnell to

Aston Martin BD 2/1 (built 1957)
later sold for £2.2 million

Ferrari 196 SP (built 1962)
later sold for £1.87 million

Aston Martin DB2 prototype
(built 1949) later sold
for an undisclosed sum

Boreham. This was most appropriate as Rex maintained the car throughout its racing career in 1957 and 1958, both in Europe and the U.S.A. He had a wet run to Boreham but duly hustled the car round the track splashing through huge areas of standing water but with lots of filming taking place. Because the conditions were so unfavourable, a re-shoot of filming took place at Chobham a few days later. The filming must have been effective and satisfactory, because at the auction, £2.2 Million pounds was paid for it by Paul Vesty. This was a record price at that time for a single car at a public auction.

The Ferrari which was to be filmed and later sold at Monaco, was another rare sports/racer with a racing pedigree, and a price near that of the DBR2 Aston Martin was expected to be paid for it at the Monaco auction. It was owned by John Godfrey for some twenty years, and had been built in 1962 as part of the factory team to compete in long distance World Championship sports car events. Known as the 196SP, it was amongst the first mid-engined sports cars built by Ferrari, and had been successful at the Nurburgring and the Targa Florio. It had also won the European Mountain Championship, and had a fine pedigree having been driven by Pedro Rodriguez, Lorenzo Bandini, and Ludovico Scarfiotti. The chassis number was 0804 and it had a rear mounted 2 litre V6 engine which would rev. at 7,000 rprm driving through a five speed transaxle with beautifully close ratios. It had an all independent suspension, disc brakes, and was of advanced design for its time.

Bodywork featured a divided shark nose, with air intakes along the sides of the body. The all red body carried the famous Ferrari team badge. The cockpit was spacious and the driver sat close to the car's centreline.

John Godfrey insisted that I should drive the car for him on this occasion of the filming, as I had raced it for him in the mid-seventies at Silverstone. But when we assembled at Boreham, that Wednesday, the weather was so bad that John would not let the car run as it was in concours condition ready for sale, so it was arranged to meet the following Monday, and this time the weather was fine.

The camera was set up for the high speed runs at one of the corners on the circuit. After a few laps I was revelling in the performance of the car's superb engine and gearbox. I had been timed at an average speed of 90 mph per lap.

After the high speed runs, a further filming session was carried out at a much reduced speed with the camera car running alongside and in front of the car for various other shots to be taken. For this I was wearing racing overalls, crash helmet and vizor of the correct racing period.

All the filming went off well and to the satisfaction of John Godfrey, who was pleased that the car was unblemished. It was then consigned for the sale.

About three weeks later, I was informed by John that the auction had been a huge success, and that the car had been sold for £1.87 Million; he sounded rather pleased!

WEST ESSEX CAR CLUB 50th ANNIVERSARY CELEBRATIONS
BOREHAM AIRFIELD - 20th SEPTEMBER, 1998

On a sunny September afternoon, members of the West Essex Car Club gathered to celebrate the club's 50th anniversary. It was fitting that, by courtesy of the airfield's owners, the Ford Motor Company, that historic Boreham Airfield, the scene of the club's earliest motor sporting activities, should be chosen as the venue of this important milestone in the life of the club.

After welcoming speeches and a toast, members and guests enjoyed a buffet lunch and participated in a number of activities - a photo quiz, a foot rally, a video show and a low-speed test of driving accuracy.

A collection of cars ranging from a gorgeous Ferrari F40 to a rallying Ford Ka was on display and included a representative vehicle - appropriately enough a Ford in each case - from each of the five decades of the club's existence. For those visitors interested in the historical associations of the venue, the highlight of the afternoon was a guided bus ride around the remains of the old circuit from Tower Bend through Waltham Corner, Hangar Bend - the scene of Gonzalez' celebrated error in the 1952 International - and the notorious Railway Corner before returning along the main runway (the original sprint course) and past the old airfield control tower.

In a special issue of the club's long-running magazine *Wheelspin*, the club's Chairman, Chris Rees, referred to the importance of club-level motorsport, which the "West Essex Car Club has, throughout its history, pioneered and will hopefully continue to do so for the next 50 years as without it we will never have our Damon Hills and Colin McRaes". The structure of modern motor sport no longer sees regional clubs organising important international events like the WECC did for one momentous day at Boreham in the summer of 1952, but the club continues to play a vital grass-roots rôle in motor sport today.

A collection of cars at the West Essex Car Club's 50th anniversary celebrations

SAND, GRAVEL, AND AN ANCIENT WINDMILL

During the last Ice Age, a great ice sheet, estimated at perhaps 1,000 metres thick, covered the North Pole, Scandinavia, the North Sea, and most of Britain.

The approximate edge of the ice cap in this area of the country was north of a line running from Brentwood, through Boreham to Harwich.

The resultant geological reaction to this enormous weight and movement of ice, together with climatic changes, resulted in very large deposits of high grade sand and gravel under the airfield, Park Farm, and Bulls Lodge at Boreham. The quantities were to amount to about 33 Million Tonnes of workable reserves.

As this type of material is used for the production of concrete for the civil engineering and construction industries, it was inevitable that one day this basic material would be extracted from the sites at Boreham.

In 1990, after a long period of negotiations, permission was granted to TMC Pioneer Aggregates Ltd to set up a quarry at Bulls Lodge and to commence extraction and processing of the deposits. The systematic removal of gravel commenced during 1995 in the north-east area of the airfield and will proceed for a number of years until all the quality deposits are exhausted.

It is required of TMC Pioneer Aggregates Ltd, that the land is to be restored after the removal of the deposits. The topsoil, removed from the site before extraction, is to be replaced, many thousands of new trees are to be planted - many already have. A 125 acre lake is to be created with the surrounding area being used for agricultural purposes in the medium term. In the long term recreational uses will be promoted.

During 1996 the Essex County Council Archæological Group, who had already in recent years been involved in archæological work in the area of the airfield at Bulls Lodge, and Great Holts Farm, carried out field work in the north east area of the airfield where initial extraction of gravel was to take place.

An evaluation of these results showed that archæological features were widespread in the area, which promoted the removal of earth at the intersection of two runways, (09-21 and 03-21). Outstanding archæological results were achieved. What was thought to be the remains of a 12th or 13th century post type windmill was found in the corner of an early ditched field, or possibly a moated enclosure.

Two associated buildings were also found, one of which was thought to be a granary.

So this was to be the demise of one of the last of East Anglian wartime airfields, said to be the best preserved. It had certainly given many thousands of people, in post-war years, some exciting times, watching the stars of yesteryear racing in motor-car and motor cycle racing events, and for which it will long be remembered.

GOOD-BYE BOREHAM

AUTHORS' ACKNOWLEDGEMENTS

In preparing a book of this nature, which contains so many photographs, some taken about 55 years ago, it was a task of some proportion in trying to find them.

As the authors, in those distant days, were living many miles from the Boreham venue, and employed in other things, only a few of the photographs in the book were taken by either of us.

When research began in 1984, the project was purely a hobby and little was thought of it ever being published. As a result of this quite a number of photographs collected at that time were not labelled with the supplier's name. When publication seemed a possibility, we had problems deciding who had supplied which photographs.

We have done our best to correct this situation, and where we are sure who supplied certain photos we have added their name near the caption, where we were not sure we left the name off and placed it in the acknowledgements. We apologise for this and hope that certain contributors will accept this.

We have done our best to make the book as error-free as possible, but cannot guarantee this and apologise in advance for any mistakes.

We offer special thanks to Les Downes for allowing us to reproduce a large number of photos from his large and outstanding collection, all of which he took at race meetings.

Our thanks also are extended to the following who in many ways have given help towards the successful completion of the book.

Richard Allen
Sophia Appleton
Nigel Barnes
William Barnett
William C Baskett
Raymond Baxter
George Beare
Derek Bircher
Ian Bond
Michael Bowyer
The British Library (Newspapers)
Alan Brown
David Burgess-Wise
Paul Carlier
Annice Collet
Derek W Cooper
Hugh Conway
David Copp
Norman Cottee
John Cowtey (*In Absentia*)
Michael Deekes
Kenneth Denyer
Leslie Downes
Peter Eaves
Pamela Ellwood
Peter Ellwood (*In absentia*)

Essex County Council
Essex Chronicle Series
  Newspapers Ltd.
Peter & Suzane Everingham
Ford Motor Co. Ltd.
Derek Gunn
Ann Harris
Malcolm Heywood
Peter Higham.
David R Holland
John Holmes
Brian K Joscelyne
Ken Keeble
T C (Terry) Kruger
Nick Lavender
Bob Light
John Lock
Cheryl Lynch
Don McHugh
Sylvia Mitchell
Charles H Martin
D Moore (*in absentia*)
Stirling Moss, O.B.E.
Neil Murray
Patrick Murrell
Gary Nicholls

Christopher G Nottage
Donald A Osborn
J B Palmer
Tracy Palmer
Martin Phillips
Bruce Preble (*In absentia*)
The Printing Place Ltd.(Raymond
Barron & Denis Colverson)
Eric D Probert
Llewllyn B Ranson
Arthur J Rickett
Meryl Rippon
Phil Rudge
Peter A Russell
Roy Salvadori
Pamela & Anthony Skingley
Ray Spearman
Bruce Spollon
Roger Stowers
Ron Taylor
Marie Tieche
Norman A Toms
Stuart Toms
Chris Tooley
Murray Walker O.B.E.
Reginald Watts (*In absentia*)

Alan Wheatley   Albert J Wiffen   Colin Wilson
Hilary White   T C W Wigg (*in absentia*)   James Woodmason
James Whyman   Jost Wildbolz   Derek R Yorke

We offer our apologies to anyone we may have forgotten, but to whom we also offer our sincere thanks.

Bryan Jones and John Frankland

Bryan Jones

John Frankland

BRYAN JONES

Bryan Jones was born at Halesowen, Worcestershire. After an engineering apprenticeship he completed his National Service with Royal Electrical & Mechanical Engineers. In 1966 he came to live in Essex, when he took up employment with Ford Motor Company as a Design Engineer at its Research and Engineering Centre at Dunton. This is the fourth book he has been a contributing author to, the others being *Boreham - History Tales and memories of an Essex village, volumes 1 & 2,* and *Wings and Wheels - the history of Boreham Airfield.* His other interests include local, military & family history, golf and choral singing. He is married, has two married daughters and lives at Boreham.

JOHN FRANKLAND

John Frankland's childhood years were spent in his birthplace Harpole, Northamptonshire, and Greenock in Scotland. In his early teens his family moved to South London where, after completing his secondary education, he earned a degree in Town Planning at South Bank Polytechnic. He is now employed as a planner by Essex County Council. This is his second book, his first being an illustrated account of the history of South Woodham Ferrers, the Essex town where he now lives with his wife, Janet, and two children Rebecca and Timothy. Within the local community he is a member of the town's Evangelical Church, is a founder member of the Local History Society and, for six years, was editor of the town's community magazine. His interest in motor sport began more than 35 years ago when Crystal Palace was just a short bus ride from his home and when Brands Hatch, Goodwood and Silverstone were all within a reasonable cycling distance.

Track Marshall Stuart Wood brings the day to an end

Bibliography

Barker, J R W ERA: a concise history, Transport Bookman
Boddy, W The History of Brooklands Motor Course, Grenville, 1957
Boddy, W Four Wheel Drift, Grenville Publishing, 1994
Carrick, P Silverstone: the story of Britain's fastest circuit, Pelham, 1974
Gauld, C Ecurie Ecosse, Gauld, 1992
Hamilton, D Touch Wood!, Barrie & Rockcliff,1960
Hawthorn, M Challenge Me the Race, Kimber,1958
Henry, A Ferrari: the Grand Prix cars, Hazelton, 1984
Nixon, C Mon Ami Mate, Transport Bookman, 1991
Nixon, C Racing the David Brown Aston Martins, Transport Bookman, 1980
Nye, D BRM Volume 1, MRP, 1994
Nye, D The Classic Single Seaters, Macmillan, 1995
Nye, D Cooper Cars, Osprey , 1983
Nye, D *and* Moss, S Stirling Moss: my cars my career,   Patrick Stevens, 1987
Parfitt, P Racing at Crystal Palace, MRP, 1991
Salvadori, R *and* Pritchard, A Roy Salvadori, Racing Driver, Patrick Stevens, 1985
Walkerley, R Brooklands to Goodwood, Foulis, 1961
Weguelin, D The History of English Racing Automobiles Limited, White Mouse Editions, 1980
Whyte, A Jaguar Sports Racing and Works Competition Cars to 1953, Haynes, 1982

Autocar
Autosport
Essex Chronicle Series Ltd.
Ford News

The Motor
Motor Cycling
Motor Sport

Stirling Moss

iJesus

The Culture of God in our Digital Culture

— NADIM NASSAR —

FOREWORDS BY

RAYMOND, LORD HYLTON
ALAN SCOTLAND

Sacristy
Press

Sacristy Press
PO Box 612, Durham, DH1 9HT

www.sacristy.co.uk

First published in 2023 by Sacristy Press, Durham

Copyright © Nadim Nassar 2023
The moral rights of the author have been asserted.

Sacristy Limited, registered in England & Wales, number 7565667

British Library Cataloguing-in-Publication Data
A catalogue record for the book is available from the British Library

ISBN 978-1-78959-255-9

I dedicate this book to the candles of light and love in my life, my family—to my mother and my siblings: Mona, Maha, Nassar, Noha and Huda

Contents

Foreword

Raymond, Lord Hylton

Dr Nadim Nassar is unique. As far as I know, he is the only Anglican priest in England who originates from Syria, indeed from the port city of Latakia. We became friends in London because of my concern for, and visits to, war-torn Syria and Iraq, where violence has driven so many into exile. Some remain near their former homes, for example in Lebanon, Turkey, Jordan, etc. Others are scattered throughout Europe and the world.

Dr Nassar's personal experience is also unique, since his Bible and theology studies began in Beirut, in the midst of the worst fighting of the Lebanese civil war back in the 1980s. He reflected later on this experience in Germany and at Cambridge. The result of this was his previous book, *The Culture of God*, published by Hodder & Stoughton in 2018. This new book, entitled *iJesus: The Culture of God in Our Digital World*, builds on the earlier one. It considers how the internet and communication technology have already affected the general culture and the state of minds of many societies in our global village.

For me, as a Roman Catholic layman, the first book was valuable theology, reflecting fresh light on the mystery of the Holy Trinity. By expounding passages from the Old and New Testaments, the sequel develops these thoughts and relates them to Jesus Christ, our Saviour, and to his incarnation and mission to his own early culture and to the World. It seems to me wholly orthodox and yet stimulating and challenging. Fr Nadim states: "According to the Christian faith, God the Father, God the Son and God the Holy Spirit and one God, in communion with himself. In the community of the Trinity, there is no domination and there is no separation . . . We talk about the Trinity as being distinct but united (persons) . . . based on love." He goes on to say: "Jesus Christ gave us access to the culture of God. Only through the Incarnation can we have access to the heart and mind of God, as well as the revelation that God is Trinity."

There is ample discussion of the new phenomenon of globalization, which is accelerated by information and communication technology. We need open and critical minds to assess the merits and demerits of these, with their opportunities for good and temptations to evil. A well-developed faith helps one to make moral judgements and informed choices, with a humble spirit.

Following and knowing Christ is not a religion but a pilgrimage of faith, inspired by love—his love for us and our love for him, for our neighbour and even our enemy. Jesus showed us the way, by loving Judas as he betrayed him, and Peter as he denied him.

My friend Nadim Nassar concludes, saying: "The only way to free ourselves from bitterness and hate is to hold on to the value of forgiveness. We can face the digital transformation of ourselves and our world, through the love that Jesus lived and taught, through the power of the risen Jesus, not the digital Jesus."

I pray that this book will be a blessing to many, enabling and empowering them to cope with the modern world, with all its crises and conflicts.

Raymond, Lord Hylton
December 2022

Foreword

Alan Scotland

I have known my dear friend Father Nadim for a good number of years, and I travelled with him and his sister Huda throughout Syria just before the latest war broke out. He has always remained zealous in rescuing the hurting and engaging with compassion towards the disenfranchised.

This book is without question a "Tour de Force". Nadim writes with intrigue, beginning with the title, *iJesus*, and continuing throughout the book. He takes the reader on a journey of discovery through the cycles of times past to the current digital age in which we live.

Father Nadim traces the positive impact of such cycles of globalization and at the same time exposes the disruptive forces that are inevitably at work. He takes time to highlight the current trends and the need for the Church to discover the true culture of God in the modern world. He draws the reader's attention to the benefits and to the dangers. He arouses interest, surprising the reader with divine inspiration throughout. Nadim warmly explains in an engaging manner lessons that ought to be learned from history and the scriptures as he introduces the true culture of God towards humankind. I found myself fascinated by such nuances and compelling insights.

Highlighting, as my friend does, the three different roles that Jesus revealed to help his followers understand the culture of God in the context of his Kingdom:

- the true nature of God and his interaction with his followers;
- his empowerment of the believer in relationship;
- Christ being our compass that leads us to the heart of the Divine Trinity.

The heartfelt appeal is for Christians to return to their roots which are the Scriptures.

The insight into the story of the disciples with Jesus in the storm in Mark 4:35–41 is surprising, yet so warming and satisfying. It is told with brilliance, in style and depth. It is not only skilfully cited, but it also helps the reader to adjusts the lens that they see through in life and in their own trials in their day-to-day living. Nadim throughout acts as our guide, providing us with a road map to the culture of God.

Uncompromisingly, the challenge is brought to the reader, in how we relate to our own identity, in this current digital culture. He gives a heartfelt critique of the obsessive nature of the emphasis on the new "I": "we have lost a sense of belonging to each other ... our digital culture feeds our ego and helps us to forget our debt of gratitude to those around us. . ."

This prophetic voice is powerfully running throughout the text of this book. It haunts us with the reality that the true redeemer of fallen and lost humanity is the risen Christ, and we ought not to sleepwalk into the digital world.

It is precisely why, in such a digital culture Nadim highlights the need for us to return to the basics, to Jesus Christ himself, in the worlds of sci-fi and fantasy.

We are reminded where we ought to abide, in Christ: "He is our home, we must put down our roots in community and be able to feel a sense of belonging." With no holds barred, we are warned, that "the marriage between a corrupted ideology and a highly sophisticated technology has given birth to a new age of terror". The evidence as such is all around the world.

It with this in mind we are encouraged to abide in Christ: "Being in Christ, abiding in Christ means being a citizen of the Divine culture."

In a profound way, having read the book I am deeply moved by the insights that are recorded. None less so than the closing chapter highlighting the reality, that online, in our digital world is a lonely world. It can never replace the physical: "God desires the physical world, that is what we are reminded about—in the incarnation." Having read this book, it has deepened my faith and caused me to value the God given relationships and friendships.

This journey that I have travelled on through the catching of the heart of my dear friend Nadim has painted on the canvas of my heart colours that will never fade. For this I am truly grateful.

Alan Scotland
Founder of Global Horizons

Preface

It took me almost ten years of deliberation and prayerful thinking to write my first book, *The Culture of God*, that talks about the culture of the Trinity—Father, Son and Holy Spirit—revealed in our earthly culture through Jesus Christ, the eternal Son who became one of us. I was overwhelmed with joy by the positive reactions and feedback I received from so many people, many of whom came from different denominations within the Church and some from within other religious communities who used the book as a teaching aid to help enlarge their understanding of the Christian faith.

Before the pandemic, I was invited to preach about the culture of God at a conference in Oxford. The discussion following my talk inspired me to write this book, taking the idea of the culture of God further by engaging with our digital culture today. This book is not an academic book, although a lot of research went into it. It is a reflection on how to live our Christian faith in today's digital culture. I feel that I should also make clear that in calling God "he", I don't in any way intend to attribute a gender to him as we commonly perceive it.

I started the process with the help of my late friend and brother, St John Wright, whom I sadly lost to Covid in early 2020. St John had also helped me to write the first book, and his sudden death left a gaping hole in our lives. After that I was not left alone in this endeavour as my dearest friend, Carina Dingemans, who is the daughter of the late founding chairman of the Awareness Foundation, my friend and mentor, Charles Longbottom. Carina offered to help me on the journey, and I am deeply grateful for her as she faithfully remained with me until the end of the book. Immense thanks to her family, who put up with the many hours that we worked together. I am also incredibly grateful and thankful to my own family, who have encouraged me every step of the way to write this book. On a journey like this, we feel the meaning of family and friends who accompany us through the highs and lows of life with patience and self-giving love.

During the difficult time of the pandemic and its aftermath, many people felt the pressure of not having fellowship with their loved ones. We all became increasingly aware of the importance of our personal encounters and the importance of expressing our love more to each other. Although the pandemic gave us the opportunity to appreciate the advanced technology that enables us to keep in touch with each other, it also taught us that nothing replaces looking at each other in person while we talk or touching the skin of someone we love with a handshake or a kiss.

We are enriched and blessed by the faithful friends around us. I want to express my warmest thanks to my beloved friend Father Roberto Vecchi for his insight and deep and loving engagement with me every step of the way while writing this book. Yet again I am so grateful to my friend Anthony Whittingham for his comments and encouragement. In a digital world, we can't ignore the input from the younger generation who are immersed in this technological culture, and I would like to thank my niece Alexandra Barbar and her brother George for their enthusiasm and input, especially with the social media and sci-fi and fantasy chapters. I would also like to thank wholeheartedly Natalie Watson and Richard Rutherford Hilton at Sacristy Press for their care and support. Finally, I am deeply grateful to my Lord and Saviour Jesus Christ, who blessed me with the gift of communicating his message so that we can reflect his unconditional love for humanity.

1

The "Global Village" and
the quest to find God

Jesus Christ is the same yesterday and today
and for ever (Hebrews 13:8).

This verse from the letter to the Hebrews brings Jesus Christ into the centre of human existence and makes him the cornerstone of life uniting humanity in him. In him, humanity becomes one family with no distinctions of race, culture, religion, sexual orientation or gender. As St Paul says in his letter to the Galatians, "There is neither Jew nor Gentile, neither slave nor free, nor is there male and female, for you are all one in Christ Jesus" (Galatians 3:28). This does not mean, however, removing that which makes us different; on the contrary, it is a celebration of diversity, making it a blessing instead of a source of conflict. We live in an age of so-called globalization, which is an attempt to make the world a global village by means of advanced technology, an open market and a kind of homogenization of experience where, for instance, you can get the same type of burger in New York, Tokyo and Beirut.

What we today call globalization is not the invention of the twentieth century, as this idea has captured the imagination of many emperors and empires throughout history, such as the Roman, Byzantine and Persian empires in ancient and even medieval times. Their globalization was always partial and temporary, although they left us a huge heritage.

We have also seen what it means when one country rules another country or one people dominates another country, and this has not stopped even today. We have seen that clearly in the twentieth century with the obsession of the Nazi Party under Adolf Hitler to dominate or subjugate the world under one ideology, including dangerous ideas about the supremacy of one race or group. This has cost the world millions of lives and devastated cultures, cities and countries. Even in the twenty-first century, we have seen countries trying to dominate and invade other countries, causing the same effects of devastation, destruction and bloodshed as if we are failing again and again to learn from history.

The most dominant version of globalization is an economic and cultural one, where companies rather than armies compete to gain global advantages. This has only been possible because of technological advancements in communication and transportation. This globalization was greatly accelerated by the rise of the internet and the use of digital technology. There are three aspects to transportation; the first is the speed and the ease of transportation, the second is the rapidly reducing cost of transportation, and the third is a new freedom of trade due to the work of organizations such as the World Trade Organization. In the second half of the twentieth century, there was rapid progress in the development of ships, planes and trains; this development decreased the cost of moving goods and made it far easier and more convenient.

In reaction to the seemingly unstoppable dominance of giant, global entities, a kind of resistance has emerged. Small businesses, local interests and community action have sprung up in response and are, in some areas, flourishing. For example, in the UK, the Welsh language that had almost died out has seen an exponential growth in recent years and is now an inspiration for communities around the world seeking to protect and revive their own minority tongues.

There is a lot of talk about the rights of minorities within the wider community. The suffering of minorities around the world brings us to the heart of the Culture of God. Human communities are made in the image of God, because they reflect the image of the Trinity. According to the Christian faith, God the Father, God the Son and God the Holy Spirit are one God in communion with himself. In the community of the Trinity, there is no domination and there is no separation; but at the same time, no one person is consumed or subsumed with the other. We talk about the Trinity as being distinct but united. This is the source of harmony based on love because love is the essence of that community.

In the human community, when people interact with one another they produce what we call culture. The visible signs of any culture are, for example, its language, religion, art, cuisine and so on. That applies also to the Trinity as the Father, Son and Holy Spirit are in permanent interaction and therefore produce culture. This culture was totally inaccessible to us, so we needed someone from that culture to tell us about it. That someone was Jesus Christ, who gave us access to this culture. He revealed to us that God is the Trinity. He also revealed to us that God is love. In my first book, *The Culture of God*, I talked about how Jesus revealed the culture of God in his own Syrian earthly culture. In this book, I want to explore the role and the meaning of this culture that Jesus revealed within the context of our highly digital and technologically sophisticated cultures.

Many Christians find it difficult to deal with the subject of the Trinity, and we therefore often avoid exploring one of the most exciting and inspiring areas of the Christian faith. I do not believe that the Trinity is an intellectual or theological exercise, but rather is the reality of God. Even after thousands of books and papers have been written on this subject, I feel that we have only touched the surface of this magnificent divine revelation. We must be careful to recognize that only through the Trinity can we engage with the reality of the incarnation. Only through the incarnation can we have access to the heart and mind of God, as well as the revelation that God is Trinity.

God himself communicated with us directly through Jesus Christ and that should revolutionize the way that we communicate with God and with each other. Faith without communication is dead, exactly like community without communication. God in Christ has taught us that the entire human family is called and invited into a new relationship based on love and love alone; and certainly not based on merit or on how good we are. In our present digital and increasingly complex individual and international relationships, we need to revisit the topic of communication that prepares the way for what we today call globalization.

Communication revolutionized the economies of the world, from small businesses to global corporations. The dot-com boom of the late 1990s and early 2000s showed just how this sector grew exponentially. Satellites have given us pin-point navigation whether we are on foot, in a car or steering a massive oil tanker. Open markets and ease of communication and transportation gave global companies the opportunity to invest in cheaper and less regulated labour in less economically developed countries, saving themselves a fortune while exploiting the new globalization. As much as communication has always been vital in the development of our world, we must also recognize that most conflict around the world has been caused or enabled by the lack of communication, or through miscommunication.When we look at different texts in the Bible, we see how people misunderstood God's communication. They even killed prophets and messengers from God and rejected the many ways in which God tried to build a relationship with humanity, until he decided to communicate with us in a way that had never happened before in our human history. He wanted us to learn how safe communication could transform our lives and our communities. Today, we still wage wars destroying each other's societies and countries due to either intentional or unintentional miscommunication, through media and social media attacks. We have seen most recently in Iraq, Yemen, Syria, Libya and Ukraine how the communication war is as important as the military attacks themselves.

Global communication has another crucial aspect, which is the cultural and intellectual. As goods became easier to make and to move, so did ideas and information. Today, people have unlimited and unrestricted access to information. This is both a good and a terrible thing. Let's start with the "good". It is amazing to be able to buy any book instantly and start reading it on your device in seconds, or to identify a piece of music through an app and be playing it on your own device straight away. We can talk to friends and family all around the world, and even see them while we are talking. Less than a generation ago, this would have been impossible. Anything can be found online, whether it's how to make a table, plant a tree or cook a meal, or name the population of Ireland or the identity of an actor in an old TV show. Information is really at our fingertips.

Like anything in life, global communication has a dark side. Some people have challenged governments with the news that the internet can teach you how to build a nuclear bomb. Hackers and computer viruses commit acts of theft, blackmail or virtual vandalism, and our electronic identities can be stolen and cloned. Many people have become addicted through global communications, whether through online gambling, computer games or pornography. While many wonderful, inspiring messages are spread through the internet, there are also poisonous, false messages of extremism and fanaticism, as well as abuse and harassment. We will look at some of these later.

I grew up in a religiously and denominationally diverse society. Unfortunately, since I was six years old, Syria has been ruled by a single totalitarian ideological party. My personal experience of diversity did not include cultural and racial diversity, which I only encountered when I travelled outside Syria. In Syria, there are indeed different cultural and national identities, such as Armenian, Assyrian, Syriac, Kurdish and Arabic, and all of these groups have formed the rich social and cultural fabric of Syrian society. Each have tried to maintain their own distinct identity, but within a totalitarian system that could only achieve limited results. During the war in Syria, these identities were unleashed as the government lost control of much of the country.

Syria still embraces a rich diversity of religions, and this diversity has changed throughout history. For example, the present Sunni Muslim majority in Syria was not a majority until the twelfth century. We should not forget that the followers of Christ were first called Christians (Acts 11:26) in the city of Antioch in Syria, the third most important city in the Roman Empire after Rome and Alexandria. At that time, Syria was the meeting place between the West and the East. Although the majority of the population would have been Syriac, Syria had embraced Hellenistic and Roman cultures and had engaged with Egyptian and Mesopotamian (Iraqi) cultures. We know from Luke that the church in Antioch, which was served by Paul and Barnabas, flourished to become the most important church since the ascension of the Lord. Antioch was an important city in Syria until 1939, when the French army withdrew and a Turkish army occupied the city.

My upbringing in Syria, from the perspective of globalization, was far from the fever of technological and economic changes that were happening in the West. It was very difficult to import goods into Syria, so the economy was local rather than global. We had no connection to international brands. Although Lattakia was an important Mediterranean port and a connection to the world, we were not that different from the rest of the country. We did have an advantage in communications because we could pick up TV channels from Egypt, Greece, Cyprus and Lebanon. Most of Syria, away from the coast, was not treated to such luxuries. Communication with the outside world was extremely limited due to the political situation. I left Syria in 1981 to go to Lebanon and live in the capital, Beirut, an amazing cosmopolitan city with great cultural richness despite the civil war. Whatever was rejected in the Arab world would still be available in Lebanon. Books which had been banned across the Middle East were freely on sale in Beirut. Lebanon and especially Beirut were known for their openness and freedom of expression—especially journalism. Only in Beirut could you buy complete magazines; in the rest of the Near East, government censors would cut out anything they felt was "wrong" for their people to see.

Beirut was in touch with the most important and recent music and film. For instance, movies were released in cinemas in Beirut before Europe. I was transported into the world of globalization, albeit one mixed with violence and horror. For decades, Lebanon had been a gateway between West and East. The country had many universities, many languages were spoken. Being in this climate gave me a lot to think about, and it challenged me as I moved from local/national to global/international. This journey was very important for me as it gave me the opportunity to re-evaluate what I had been going through in Syria in my childhood and youth.

I remember visiting the United States for the first time and encountering the widest form of globalization. The conference that I attended there included delegations from many countries, and this was the first time I encountered people from Africa, Europe and South America. This was my first and most eye-opening encounter with globalization. Unlike other people at the conference, I had never experienced Coca-Cola or McDonald's in my life. On the other hand, I discovered that only a handful of global corporations dominated the world.

In the 1980s the Iron Curtain still cut across Europe, dividing the Warsaw Pact countries from the West, and we had two understandings of globalization: one believed that communism was the best system for the peoples of the world, while the other favoured democratic capitalism as the best for everyone. The communist camp always accused the capitalists of greed, individualism and creating huge inequalities between rich and poor. The Western camp, of course, accused the communists of leading totalitarian regimes which lacked freedoms and human dignity.

If we look at both camps from the perspective of the Culture of God, through the dynamic relationship between the persons of the Trinity, how would we see the world at that time? If we look at the socialist and the capitalist camps, we see that both were influenced, directly or indirectly, by the teachings of Jesus Christ. For example, some of those Christian principles that influenced both camps were the freedom of expression, of belief and of movement, and the fair distribution of wealth. We also have human principles that not only Christianity, but all religions, call for, including justice, forgiveness and peace.

But neither the capitalists nor the socialists could apply those principles which both claimed they believed in.

I grew up in a socialist satellite of the communist camp; Syria had a strong relationship with the Soviet Union, although Syria was never a communist country—religion, which illuminates every part of Syrian life, would not have been tolerated under communism. When I moved to Germany in the 1990s, and then afterwards to Britain, I experienced the capitalist system. I also had the opportunity to experience for many years the collapse of the communist camp, in Europe and especially in Germany, which had reunited less than two years before I arrived. I remember travelling with a group of international students to Berlin; we saw East Berlin first, then West Berlin and of course the remnants of the infamous wall. We walked along a street in East Berlin, and I noticed that the lowest floors of the buildings were painted and elegant, while the upper stories were in a state of decay. I learned that this was so that the high communist officials in their cars would see everything was well maintained. The difference between East and West Berlin was painfully obvious. The newly reunited Germany was still groaning under the enormous economic pressure to rebuild a collapsed, bankrupt country. The people of East Germany suffered the evils of persecution, oppression, imprisonment and censorship. I am not saying that life in West Germany was ideal, but the West Germans lived with advanced personal freedoms.

The greatest lesson I learned in my travels is that the more we talk about certain principles, the less they are practised in real life. For example, the three major pillars of the Ba'ath Party in Syria are unity, freedom and socialism. In fact, since the Ba'ath Party took over, Syria has never been further from all three principles. Before the fall of the Iron Curtain, communist East Germany called itself the German Democratic Republic—although there was no democracy. In reunited Germany, one of the parties is called the Christian Democratic Union of Germany, and in the eight years I spent in Germany I saw nothing Christian about it whatsoever. Going back to my time in Lebanon during the bloody civil war there, I remember hearing from heads of the militias, murderers and thieves, the most brilliant rhetoric about heroism and sacrifice for freedom. Even Isis and similar ideological organizations manipulate and exploit so much of religion to recruit young people to help them in their pursuit of worldly, not godly, power.

Every human empire attempted in its own way to export its own culture in an attempt to dominate the world. Those empires pursued their own interests, and today we witness the struggle between global corporations, governments and global causes (such as environmentalism) to dominate resources and peoples. Where is the Culture of God in all this? We do not see the Culture of God in politics or in the clash of economic giants. We see the Culture of God in faithful people who would give their lives in serving their own local communities. An Italian priest told me that Giorgio La Pira, the Mayor of Florence in the 1950s and 60s, went to the Soviet Union, and he said that the future of humanity is not to be found in national governments talking but in mayors of cities talking: the world should be a network of cities. In other words, what matters is the local community, which is the way that Jesus lived.

The Universal Christ, today facing the culture of globalization, starts from a poor, humble man engaging with his society and challenging his entire religious establishment. He dedicated himself to serve the poor, the sick and the needy where he lived. He succeeded in living and implementing the culture of the most powerful, most holy God in his little community. This is what I believe to be the true global thinking, which is the true Culture of God which can be lived in every community in the world, giving people dignity and value whether in a village in the Himalayas, in a city in civil war, or in a huge metropolis like London or New York.

The quest to find God

Many scholars, theologians and philosophers agree with the hypothesis that humans have a natural tendency to search for something beyond them, something bigger than them. Most often, this is linked with the desire to find the meaning of life—why things happen—alongside the journey of understanding the dynamics of the world—how things happen. For many people those two concepts clash, and this is what we find in the apparent dilemma of science or faith; the quest to understand the world is in itself the quest to find a meaning for life. In this case, in the popular culture, we say that science works to understand how things happen as well as why things happen; for many, though, the two quests are separate: understanding how things happen (science) can never answer the question "why". The meaning of life—why?—cannot be found in a laboratory. Understanding physics tells us nothing about life's meaning.

When we talk about religious institutions, including the Church, we mostly talk about a man-made system which could easily be misguided and even, in the worst scenario, become corrupt. The human spiritual quest is as old as human existence. This should not be confused with the rise of religion, of temples and priests. Faith is, in its essence, a trust that we have that there is something beyond us; that "something" can take a variety of shapes—it might be a force that orders our universe, the consciousness of the universe—which we join when we die, and of course for others it is more personal, in the sense that we can develop a genuine relationship with that "something". The monotheistic faiths certainly see the latter version as truth.

Out of this faith in a creator and sustainer of the universe, humans established institutions to teach about that faith and to offer a place of worship. Many societies developed magnificent mythologies which tried hard to explain the world around humanity, to give them meaning and purpose. They included what they called Gods, Demigods and Heroes to represent the elements around them, such as the Sun, the Moon and the Sea; they wove stories around those personalities, putting them in intimate relationships with humanity and with each other. The rise of mythology is the journey to connect the spiritual quest and the scientific quest. We read rich and highly imaginative stories around the phenomena that human beings could not understand. A strong example would be the rising and the setting of the sun, and we can read different stories in different cultures trying to make sense of this all-important event and connecting it to their lives. Mythology was also concerned with the origin of things, like fire or time. In mythology, the "why" and the "how" are intertwined. We have the curiosity not only to find out the technicalities of life and the world around us, but also their purpose, and this leads us to respect both quests.

Later, those two quests separated, and the priest stopped being the medicine man or the astronomer and instead became more concerned with the meaning of life and the relationship between humans and the godly realm. Even today, we have religions that believe in multitudes of gods, and others that believe in only one God, and we have a spiritual system that believes in no deities. Looking at this rich and exciting tapestry of human spirituality, we can see that faith and religion exercised some kind of globalization way before the economic globalization that we know today.

Many military conquests and acts of colonization carried with them the spread of a particular religion, initially for the benefit of the invaders. In the time of Christ, we see that the Roman emperor was often deified and worshipped right across the Empire. Much more recently, when the British and the French apportioned the Near East between them after the fall of the Ottoman Empire, they brought with them their own churches. So, we find Anglican (or Episcopal) churches in Palestine and Jordan (which became British territories), while in Syria and Lebanon we find that the Roman Catholic Church benefited from French rule.

During the long period of the exploration and colonization of North and South America, the explorers took their home church with them. Immigration, without military power, can do the same, bringing a particular denomination to the forefront to meet the needs of large immigrant populations; we can see this in the United States, where the Catholic Church has benefited from the influx of Irish, Italian and Spanish immigrants.

Equally, cultural and civic movement within a country can influence the spiritual life there. For example, following the Renaissance, Europe went into what we call the Enlightenment or the Age of Reason. That influenced not only the political, cultural and ethical side of society but also the religious or spiritual one. The Enlightenment had positive and negative aspects, many of which are with us even today. One of the Enlightenment's positive influences was that it challenged the authority of the Church and the way that religion understood many aspects of life; before the Enlightenment, there were many things which people accepted were "acts of God", such as natural disasters and the weather. With the Enlightenment, people realized that not everything we cannot understand should be labelled as God's. Exploration and scientific experimentation, and the use of logic and reason, inevitably reduced the power of the Church and the grip of the Church on society.

A negative influence of the Enlightenment was that the Church retreated from the public square to the extent that people's understanding of faith changed; no longer did faith have a place in the public world, becoming a "private matter". You can't ask someone about their faith, and the consequence of that is that people with faith have come to be seen as "weird" in some way. Secularism, originally just the separation of Church and State, became anti-religious or anti-faith. At the end of the twentieth century, people thought that religion was on its way out, especially in Europe. But that didn't happen.

After the impact of the Enlightenment, the West was further convulsed by the Industrial Revolution that brought new manufacturing processes to Europe and the United States and led to the rise of mass production and the growth of cities. This was followed by the Nuclear Age in the twentieth century that culminated in the use of the atomic bomb that brought an end to the Second World War. After this came the feverish space race and the rise of digital technology. Since the Enlightenment, we can see how secularism has become more and more ingrained in society. I would argue, however, that digital technology has allowed faith to re-emerge within society and enabled people of faith, as well as those who are curious about their spirituality, to engage with themselves and others in a way that removes barriers and feelings of shame about their religion.

Digital technology has reconciled the how and the why. Technology can help us to explore wider issues like the meaning of life as well as improving our material comfort without the shadow of the Church as an institution. We don't need the Church in the same way anymore. We are free to explore any number of initiatives that bring faith and technology together and help us on our spiritual journey.

St John says in his narrative of the Gospel, "The Word became flesh and made his dwelling among us" (John 1:14). We see here a transformation of the eternal Word to embrace our humanity in order to emphasize the personal dimension of God's relationship with us and to reveal to us that the culture of the Trinity is intimate and personal. We are on a quest to find God and God is on a quest to find us. These quests meet in the person of Jesus Christ. The ultimate quest to find God in Christianity is in finding God among us (and not in an abstract way). Jesus Christ was, and is, the embodiment of the Culture of God among us. The more we know him, the more we understand and value that culture.

In our lives today, I can say metaphorically, and in a way literally, that the Word has been transformed into a gadget that gives us an image and/or a sound. The question is how do we take this transformation and use it in a way that makes our lives more intimate and personal rather than erecting barriers between us? If we want to live the Culture of God in the digital culture, we need to make a serious effort to look critically at the impact and the role of technology in our lives and relationships. Many people, especially young people, think that Christianity can be old-fashioned and boring, but I am very excited to challenge that perception in this book and prove that our Lord could be revolutionary even in our digital age, exactly as he was in his time.

Impact and understanding

In Genesis, we see that after God created life he gave an order to Adam and Eve not to eat from the tree of knowledge: "And the Lord God commanded the man, 'You are free to eat from any tree in the garden; but you must not eat from the tree of the knowledge of good and evil, for when you eat from it you will certainly die'" (Genesis 2:16–17). The story describes the temptations that God created within this perfect life in order to give value to their freedom of choice. If they had no choices, their freedom would have had no value. Also, if there were no consequences to their choices, their freedom would be empty and unreal. Human reality always presents us with choices and consequences, and we are constantly choosing and responding to what life puts in our way.

We are therefore constantly facing the consequences of our choices, which reappear at different stages in our lives. When I arrived in Germany, I didn't think that I would stay in Europe, but choices that I made, including visiting Cambridge for research, opened up to me the possibility of choosing to move from Germany to the UK. The consequences of different choices over seven years resulted in my staying and working in London, which was a completely new option in my life that I decided to seize upon. The point I wish to make is that choices belong to the very essence of our lives and the story of Adam and Eve explores this truth about our existence. Whatever our perspective on the story itself, we must admit that God created us and wanted us to have choices and face everything that life throws at us on our journey of meeting those choices.

Every choice is promoted in our lives in a different way. Some choices look more attractive to us than others. In a way, life has its own marketing strategy. It's up to us to go beyond the promotion and try to see the truth beneath the surface. Another interesting character in the Garden of Eden worth looking at in our process of understanding this section of the book is the serpent. We can say that the serpent was the first marketing agent whose nature it was to present the other side of the equation in order to test the value of freedom. We understand today that the serpent was the first to present fake news. It was a lie to say that eating from the forbidden tree would make Adam and Eve like God.

Let's see how Adam and Eve regarded the scene. First of all, they were forbidden from eating from a tree with properties that they couldn't understand. How could they make a choice without understanding what was meant by good and evil? The serpent took advantage of their ignorance and explained the situation in the light of its own interest. Adam and Eve had three options: to believe the serpent and eat; not to believe the serpent and keep the status quo; or to go to God for more information about the tree. The most attractive option to them in the story was to eat because they wanted to be like God. They depended on the serpent's information and nothing else. As we know, they decided to eat and face the consequences. This story, like all mythological stories, deals with the truth, and it's up to us to learn from the characters, the plot and the ending. Regardless of the historical accuracy of the story, it provokes our thinking and urges us to study new dimensions relevant to each generation.

Today, as we live with increasing digital influence, the question of the influence and accuracy of communication has never been more relevant or important. We are hammered every day with an enormous number of news items coming to us wherever we turn our heads, trying to inform us of what is happening around us from a specific point of view. We all remember, for example, the news we received when 9/11 happened in New York and the amount of interpretation and analysis provided by so many people around the world from every media outlet that we had at that time. Similarly, we recall the incredible wave of news about the Covid-19 pandemic, which hit every part of the globe in 2020. We were overwhelmed with information and analysis despite the huge ignorance we had in the early stages about the virus and the endless possibilities for its mutation.

Communication has been vitally important throughout the history of humanity; even the resurrection of our Lord Jesus Christ was announced to a few women, who took the news and had the responsibility to communicate it to the disciples of the Lord. We see that Peter and John, although they were overwhelmed with the news that the women carried to them, decided to run and see the empty tomb for themselves. I wouldn't describe this action as meaning that they didn't believe the women, but rather that the news was so important that they found themselves running without thinking to the tomb. In today's world, we are surrounded by endless sources of information that can often be contradictory. That puts us under enormous pressure to check the credibility of those sources before we build our choices on them. We must consider that any choice we make has consequences, not only on our own lives but often on the lives of many people around us.

In today's technological world, every one of us has become a distributor of news because of the open platforms that we have. One of the important factors that we must consider is that space and time have shrunk in a way and that news has become so instant that I may know about something that has happened in my home town in Syria before my sister who lives in that town. The vast development in communication technology took place alongside the advancement of transportation. The simultaneous development of both created what we call globalization. Unfortunately, the leaps in developing both sectors did not result in an increase in peaceful living around the world. We still see war zones in many countries, whether in the Middle East, Africa or even Europe. The combination of these two effects created a demographic movement that is unprecedented in terms of scale and volume of people who are either displaced within their country or forced to emigrate entirely.

2

The impact of the rise of digital technology on our life in a multicultural society

At present, the world has more than 70 million refugees, mostly as a result of religious or sectarian conflicts. From the second half of the twentieth century, there have been different waves of immigration caused either by economic hardship or political unrest and wars. If we look at the Near East, we see huge demographic movements that have shaken the region since the civil war in Lebanon in the mid-1970s, then the Iran-Iraq war in the 1980s, followed by the Gulf War in the 1990s that created a huge wave of refugees. Then came the Syrian war that has now raged for over twelve years. One of the biggest displacements in modern history has resulted from this conflict in Syria that forced half of the population (about 12 million people) to be on the move either within Syria or elsewhere. More recently, we have seen the conflict in Ukraine that has added more millions of refugees and displaced people fleeing to safety in the heart of Europe.

These dramatic developments have brought vastly different cultures into uncomfortable proximity in too short a space of time. There was no healthy encounter that allowed time for people to get acquainted and understand each other. As a result, these demographic changes have led to hostile reactions amongst some elements in the "host" population, even resulting in violence. People have been tempted to resort to extreme nationalist political parties and protest movements that seek to enforce what it is to be British, French or American. Such reactions are motivated primarily by fear. In countries where unemployment is high, this problem is exacerbated especially by radical religious ideologies that put people into categories, highlighting the differences and making these differences appear as threats rather than a source of richness and inspiration.

Many of these refugees are entirely capable of excelling in the host culture. Many charities have been formed in the West with the intention of helping refugees integrate and thrive. The refugee crisis in the West is a relatively recent phenomenon, while the issue of immigration is older than this recent wave of refugees. In Western Europe, minority immigrant communities have retreated into ghettos for safety and also to preserve their distinctive cultural identity. Religion, language, dress and traditions have tended to be reinforced over the majority culture. Consequently, second and third generation immigrants feel torn between their inherited cultural and religious identity and that of the host culture. At the same time, the host culture feels invaded and threatened by these foreign, alien "intruders".

I have a friend who is regularly challenged by the parents of an immigrant community over the health and sex education that she is responsible for offering by law to primary school children in her council area. Her biggest challenge is dealing with the anger of these parents who refuse to accept this education and would rather the sole responsibility lie with them. This conflict between cultures is still very real. Western culture has developed a professional way of educating young people in this field, which the immigrant community often continues to reject, preferring to stick with their own cultural norms. For many immigrants in such communities, religion often plays a dominant role in this narrative, even within health and sex education.

Jonathan Sacks, in his 2002 Templeton Lecture on "The Dignity of Difference: Avoiding the Clash of Civilizations", observes that identity is inevitably bound up with religion and is defined by setting "us" over "them"—Catholic against Protestant, Muslim against Jew, Hindu against Muslim. When people lived in relatively stable, homogeneous communities this was not such an issue, but today, through globalization and the sheer diversity of our multicultural societies, we live in conscious presence of difference. This awareness of difference and division has been further highlighted by recent global movements such as #MeToo and BlackLivesMatter. The real challenge for any religion today is to make space for "the other", the one whose stories and symbols, rituals and celebrations, values and sensibilities are radically different.

Social media has highlighted and embraced these challenges. The death of George Floyd, that ignited the flame of the BlackLivesMatter movement, was filmed on a mobile phone and then went viral on social media platforms. The issues around the #MeToo movement were also given voice through social media and encouraged others to express and share their own experiences. Digital technology has accentuated the need to deal with the problems of diversity. It has highlighted how mainstream media has failed to address many of these issues. The pressure that has come from the new ways of communication via the internet and social media has transformed the narrative and given rise to an unstoppable demand for change. Of course, the challenges of multiculturalism cannot be fixed overnight, but social media has made them impossible to ignore. It is now up to us to use these digital tools to find creative and effective solutions for these challenges of difference and communication. We have started along this road, and we now must continue.

After more than two thousand years of interpreting and meditating on the words of Christ and St Paul, we still find ourselves in the same dilemma of who is in and who is out. Who do we include and who do we exclude? How do we judge each other—according to gender, sexuality, identity, colour of skin? We make judgements against each other based on a shallow understanding and on what we perceive to be the truth of the other. Christ helps us to look at humanity from the divine perspective, through the perspective of the Son of Man. Christ chose this title for himself, despite knowing that he was the Son of God. He gave us this unique opportunity to re-evaluate everything based on a brand-new outlook and empowered us to have the ability to look at our lives through a divine perspective, which is the Culture of the Trinity.

Jesus himself was rejected, and St Peter in his first letter tells us: "As you come to him, the living Stone—rejected by humans but chosen by God and precious to him—you also, like living stones, are being built into a spiritual house to be a holy priesthood, offering spiritual sacrifices acceptable to God through Jesus Christ" (1 Peter 2:4–5). St Peter speaks here about humanity not in terms of certain groups, but in general. For God, we are all in and no one is out. It's not up to us to categorize people and reject them based on any kind of list. When we look at this from the perspective of the Culture of God, we hear very clearly the words of Jesus from Matthew's Gospel:

> Jesus said to them, "Have you never read in the Scriptures:
> 'The stone the builders rejected
>   has become the cornerstone;
> the Lord has done this,
>   and it is marvellous in our eyes'"? (Matthew 21:42)

Jesus here repeats the words of Psalm 118, but this time, as usual, he puts himself in the centre of the Scriptures. The cornerstone that was rejected by the builders was himself, the cornerstone of life and the new cornerstone between himself and God. He is telling us that, through him, we have a new way of interpreting the Scriptures, life, humanity, our existence and everything. In this book, we are trying to repeat this process, looking at the digital world around us empowered by the perspective of that cornerstone.

Our reality is rapidly changing. As our understanding of our faith and this cornerstone that sacrificed himself that we might have life and have it abundantly grows, we must reflect on our lives today from his perspective, looking at the impact of the technological age on our existence. Every era in human history has influenced our lives positively and negatively. Likewise, we need to reflect on the sea change that this technological advance has had on our lives and on the different communities within society. We do this armed and empowered by the Culture of the Trinity that was revealed to us by the Son of Man, Jesus Christ.

The mind and other gifts in the digital age

It is easy to indulge in a long reflection on the negative side of technology. We can see all around us the disadvantages. But let us first reflect upon the positive effects that such a dramatic revolution has had on our lives in the last twenty-five years. Most importantly, we should pause and give thanks for the gift of the mind that we have received from God, the mind that has the ability to reject even God himself but is also empowered to reveal the glory of the Creator. Even the most vehement atheist stands in awe before the magnificence of the human mind and what it can produce. We are where we are because of the productivity of our minds interacting, competing and wrestling with each other and with the world around us. Everything we enjoy today is the product of humanity seeking to progress and to grow in knowledge and also in creativity.

The digital culture that we find ourselves in today is no doubt a product of this creativity and shows how much we can change our existence if we dedicate our minds and our gifts to improving the quality of life while preserving human dignity. One of the most obvious and glorious influences that our digital culture gives us is in the medical field. Jesus Christ touched the hearts and minds of his society and many times revealed his identity and his love through words of healing. He wanted to tell us that God also loves our physical reality and created our bodies that we may look after them. Medical advances today can be seen through the prism of the healing acts of Jesus. When we look after our bodies and develop ways to improve our health, we are fulfilling God's will as the God of Life. The Culture of God is the Culture of Life and that is the source of the love of God flowing through us and inspiring us to help each other eradicate diseases, ease the sufferings of people and comfort those in physical pain.

When I look at a sophisticated apparatus to help diagnose illness, that touches my soul because I see that as a gift that is part of God's plan for humanity. Regardless of where and how the recent pandemic started, for example, we saw scientists around the world collaborating to preserve human life. We should look at this effort and praise God for the gifts of science and technology that can produce vaccines that save millions of lives. Being in the Culture of God is going beyond political gains to see the grace of God in the middle of tragedy. It is up to us how we look at science. Some people see it as the cross of salvation. Science is a replacement for God. Another view argues that science has an inflated ego and scientists have too much control over our lives and how we live. Another perspective looks at science as something that goes hand in hand with faith. Believing in God and embracing faith can inspire scientists to excel, seeing life as a precious gift from God.

The way I see this relationship is that the heart of the Culture of the Trinity is light, love and life. When we take these qualities and look at them on a human level, we see that when the mind is enlightened human beings can be creative. When we love life and love each other, we can dedicate this illuminated mind to improve the quality of our lives. In this case, those three qualities of light, love and life are in a continuous dynamic relationship that brings the two cultures of the divine and human closer and closer. When we look at science from that perspective, we see how both faith and science exist in an energetic relationship with one another. The love of God can flow through scientists to change and improve human life while maintaining its sanctity and integrity.

We must consider this dynamic between faith and science while exploring the ever-expanding world of digital technology. It is important for us to look at the balance in our lives between God who is in the world and the massive change that is shaking our world. Exploring this connection between science and faith reminds me of Jesus Christ at the Garden of Gethsemane. Finding his disciples asleep, he said: "Watch and pray so that you will not fall into temptation. The spirit is willing, but the flesh is weak" (Mark 14:38). In other words, although we have the desire to be with God, the temptation to immerse ourselves in the world around us often means that we drift away from his presence.

Another major advantage of the digital revolution that has transformed the world took place in the field of human communication. Advances in communications technology and easy access to international travel have been major contributing factors in this aspect of globalization. The Western culture of modernity (using the most up-to-date techniques and equipment) has infiltrated indigenous civilizations through the export of European-style education and latterly mass entertainment via satellite TV and so on. Global communication supported by modern transportation has rendered geographical distance irrelevant and my closest "neighbours" may not live next door or even in my locality.

In Europe and the United States, people do not appreciate the impact of almost instant technological revolution on society, because the advance from industrialization to "high tech" in their nations has been gradual and spread over several generations. The situation in the Middle East and in developing countries is very different. Within one generation, email, the internet, satellite TV and mobile telephones have become part and parcel of daily life, especially for the young. In the Middle East, this is interpreted as a new form of cultural imperialism because there has been insufficient time for the indigenous culture to adapt to this sudden, radical change at the heart of everyday life. For example, in Aleppo, the second largest city in Syria, very few TV channels were available until 1990.

Within fifteen years, the population was able to access hundreds of channels from all over the world, in different languages, representing diverse cultures and by implication differing religions, social customs and ethical codes. Of course, after more than a decade of war, the situation has changed not just for the people of Aleppo but also those within Syria generally and the wider Near East region. Such a change didn't happen without consequences, social and religious. People were exposed to many different cultures and ideas and were able to freely access material and ways of thinking that weren't available before, such as pornography or acts of extreme violence. After the explosion of satellite channels on TV came the rise of personal computing, a development that has again been a blessing and also a challenge. The biggest challenge is in finding ways to integrate this new form of communication within our daily lives and finding a balance between the new technology and the essence of ourselves and our communities.

Relate and communicate

Communication has been one of the main arteries carrying the culture of science, knowledge and social interaction throughout the world. When we talk about communication, we mean the internet, mobile technology and the network of satellites that cover the whole earth in a tight web of data transfer. These days we take for granted the fruits of such development. Those who were born in the 1990s know nothing else but communication through the internet and digital technology. Some of them remember the shift from text messages to video chats and conferencing. I, however, cannot take this technology for granted having grown up with another reality with no phones or TVs. I remember vividly how life was at that time. I am careful not to be too nostalgic about life in those times as I cannot ignore or deny the amazing influence of digital communication on our lives. If someone had told me in the late 1970s that one day in my own lifetime I would be chatting to someone on the other side of the world audio-visually, I would have laughed as it would have sounded like science fiction. But science fiction has become reality.

During the Covid-19 pandemic from 2020 onwards, we experienced a new dimension to communication when most churches broadcast their services and spiritual activities live on YouTube or Facebook or other digital platforms. Businesses also reverted to visual communications to allow people to work remotely. Suddenly we found ourselves stuck at home but still open to the whole world through our communication devices. We also learned that, although such devices help economies around the world to keep going and people to remain in touch with one another, they can't replace face-to-face encounters and cannot save millions of people from feeling lonely and isolated. Communication devices and methods are extremely helpful and have become windows on the world, but we have come to realize that they cannot take precedence in our lives.

Schools and universities have also had to go through huge changes and offer education online. The whole education process cannot just depend on distance learning, however. Students of every age need the experience and personal interaction of being in the same place and doing things together. Advanced technology is only possible because of inspirational methods and ways of teaching. Schools and universities have in many countries made great leaps to give their students the opportunity to think freely and experiment creatively so that achievements in engineering, computer science and many other fields can flourish. High-tech methods of teaching have impacted the lives of students and influenced the ways they approach projects.

I remember when I was at school in Syria, teaching methods were archaic and based mostly on learning by rote. Nowadays it's not about the information that you transmit but how you help people to analyse and be creative with the information that is given to them. Technology has opened the doors for education much wider than the traditional idea of being a student. Today the sky's the limit as we are all invited to go on a non-stop journey of learning through online videos, podcasts, audio books and so on. The aim of education is not just limited to getting a degree or accessing a library to borrow a book, it is instead a life-enhancing journey that never ends. Thanks to technology, I have been delighted to join reading groups around the world to discuss my book *The Culture of God* and engage with them live. I have now talked to groups in Hong Kong, Canada and Europe.

We also need to acknowledge that the more technology advances the more it accelerates and the more our horizons open up. Although I am a priest, science is a hobby that allows me to engage in an exciting way with so many scientific enterprises around the world. Communication and education are inextricably linked. The better the communication, the better the understanding. Sometimes I wonder, if Jesus Christ was living in today's world, how would he communicate with people and what kind of parables would he use in order to teach and reveal his original culture, the Culture of the Trinity? And what method of education would he use?

Billions of people are concerned about the health of our planet. We have an interdependent environmental system. All the elements of earth are interlinked. We cannot improve the water quality, for example, without considering the atmosphere. God the Creator made us stewards to look after this magnificent ecosystem that needs to be sustained not just for our generation but for future generations to come. We follow the heated debates about the fragility of the environment and how much it is under strain because of our abuse of its natural resources. Technology, however, has offered us an important tool in diagnosing the damage and treating it. We are now better able to examine these problems and construct realistic solutions. Technology is offering opportunities to replace unrecyclable forms of plastic, responsible for destroying so much of our environment, with recyclable ones.

Most countries are now aware of the seriousness of air pollution. Many international initiatives and conferences have been held to encourage people and governments to reduce the world's carbon footprint, which is damaging the earth's atmosphere and consequently causing global temperature rises and melting ice caps. We can't ignore the progress we've made around the world in recycling garbage and using it to manufacture useful materials. As Christians, we have a major role to play in raising awareness about our responsibility to protect what God has given us and to value the world around us. There are of course a number of theological studies and initiatives devoted to this.

If we look at the mind of God and his passionate words, the first thing that comes to mind is the journey that God made to become one of us. This journey in Jesus Christ allowed God to experience our humanity and the limitations of space and time. At the same time, the divine journey reflects the deep love that God has for us and our fragile planet. Living simultaneously in the Culture of God and in human culture, we look at our planet through the eyes of the divine culture that made God decide to come and visit us from an outpouring of his love. This should be our motivation to love the earth and do everything to protect it. We as human beings and our planet lie at the heart of God and his culture. God is in his mind and heart passionate about life because he is life and the source of life. That life comes to us eternally and continuously out of God's love.

If we look at the Industrial Revolution, for example, we can recognize the excitement and massive change that came in the wake of this era of mass production and mechanization that opened up the market to an ever-widening variety of products. This changed the way we shopped and the way we worked. I remember growing up in Syria knowing all about London's smog, thinking how romantic that sounded. Later I realized that the fog was not a natural phenomenon but rather a by-product of the factories and burning of fossil fuels—a price that the city paid for being an industrial city. We can say the same about any revolution that changes our lives—excitement at the growth of possibilities followed by a growing realization of the consequences of this change. The digital revolution is no different.

Computers became a domestic product that anyone could have at home. The internet changed everything again—and continues to do so as we explore its full potential. One generation of technology follows closely on the next and filters into every corner of our lives, becoming cheaper and cheaper and therefore more and more accessible. This technology makes our lives easier, more comfortable, and often acts as a spur to further creativity and productivity. On the other hand, we must look at the challenges of technology. I remember when I was fairly young a heated discussion about machines taking the place of workers. That discussion opened my eyes to the flipside of technology. Can it really make people redundant? When I was in Germany, the German finance minister at the time argued that the way forward was to accelerate technology as every new generation of technology needed a new generation of people to run it. For him, technology wasn't a threat. Other experts, however, argue that millions of people have lost their jobs from machines taking their places, especially in manufacturing.

Since I bought my first computer until now (a period of about twenty-five years), I have been constantly thinking "what is next?" The process of innovation is unstoppable, and the ripple effect of each new invention flows through many different areas. This cascade of consequences brings with it fear of what this will mean. We are always on the threshold of something bigger and the change that brings with it, or promises, is constant. A friend told me once with amazement that the head teacher at her son's school had told her that the school was training its students for jobs that don't currently exist. On one hand, this is scary. At the time that my friend and I were at school, we would never have heard this growing up. In ten years, when those students finish higher education, who knows what kind of technology will be in place and how we will be working?

Having said that, did we ever imagine the situation we had in 2020 when the whole world was almost paralyzed by the coronavirus pandemic? Did we ever think that we would be stuck at home for months and months while witnessing one wave of the virus after another? So much has changed in that time, in the way we think, we work and most importantly in the way we communicate with each other. The way we pray, worship and support each other has been profoundly changed. When I think back, I feel heartbroken as I lost more than twenty people close to me in Syria, the United States and the UK. Having gone through the pain of losing so many dear ones, I was delighted to hear the news about the vaccine, although many people were sceptical about it, especially those that believed the conspiracy theories that the vaccine would change their DNA or in some way microchip the recipient.

Without the technology we have, it would have been impossible to develop vaccines in such a short time and save millions of lives. At the same time, we have seen how the vaccine has been manipulated for political purposes across the world and has become an international issue that highlights the divide between rich and poor countries. I feel that the challenges that our rapidly changing technological age brings are also an opportunity for us to think about our humanity. For this age more than ever, people's identity is at stake. The question for me is what makes us human? When we answer this question, we hold the key to answering more existential questions like our role on earth or the purpose of life.

I remember that, at the height of the pandemic, many people started asking themselves why they spent the money they did pre-pandemic on, for example, entertainment, sport or shopping. We never used to question the millions paid to stars in the sports and entertainment industry. Suddenly, an invisible virus grounded these highly paid individuals at home. The people who saved our lives and kept the world running were lowly paid workers like healthcare staff, delivery drivers and supermarket cashiers. They went to work despite the risks and without, at least initially, adequate protection. This totally changed my perspective of life along with, I'm sure, many others. One of the most prestigious magazines that always had celebrities and top models on its cover decided to feature instead the real heroes of the pandemic. The faces of famous people were replaced by nurses, hospital staff and cashiers who risked their lives to keep us safe.

Some pharmaceutical companies exploited the pandemic, making billions in profits. It seems that even the death of millions around the world doesn't change some ways of thinking. If technology falls into the hands of people who have lost their humanity, we will be facing demonic forces. Because of that, I am convinced more than ever that our identity as human beings should be re-examined. Jesus Christ wrestled with this question of his identity all his life, and especially on the cross. The Culture of God helps us to explore our identity and see our purpose in life through the life and teachings of Christ, who revealed to us the heart and mind of the Trinity. We cannot explore our identity separate from the identity of our Creator because, as the Scriptures say, we are created in his image. Living in the age of digital revolution, we bring the Culture of the Trinity to the heart of this exercise so that we can sense the meaning of our existence and our relationship with God and each other. In this time of desperate need, people must stand up to the power of darkness that preys on our humanity for financial reward, whether in the name of religion or science or any other mask it chooses to use.

Where is Jesus Christ in all this?

This section deals with the interaction of two powers: the rise of digital technology and the power of faith (in this case, in the person of Jesus Christ). We will look at how the former influences the latter. In order to do that, we must explore these two powers and analyse the resources and tools that they have to influence the other. In order to see this influence on our understanding of Jesus Christ, we need to also understand the power of Jesus Christ. The relationship between digital culture and the person of Jesus Christ can take many forms and can either work in dialogue with one another or in contrast.

The most important source that we have to explore the power of Jesus Christ is the Scriptures. These, for people of faith, are indeed the Word of God. In the case of Jews and Muslims, the fundamental authority on which all else is built is God's revelation enshrined in Scripture, whether in the Torah or the Quran. Muslims believe that the words of the Quran are Allah's eternal will for all humanity. This teaching was revealed to the prophet Muhammad through the angel Jibreel. The Prophet recited the words he heard (Quran means recitation), and his followers memorized, recorded and later compiled them in a book. The Arabic text of the Quran today is identical to the standardized version issued by Uthman, Muhammad's third successor. Since the words of the Quran come from Allah himself, they must be preserved exactly in Arabic, and translations are not regarded as "the real thing". Although the book is handled with great respect, it is Allah's teaching and not the book itself that is holy to Muslims.

It has always been necessary to interpret and apply the teaching in the Quran and the words and deeds of the Prophet in the Hadith to contemporary circumstances and problems in the life of the Muslim community. This interpretation is called Shari'ah, meaning "pathway". Shari'ah is the code of behaviour for a Muslim and determines whether an action is right (*halal*) or wrong (*haram*) for believers. The technique of working out Shari'ah law involves using human reason and judgement, tradition and the opinions of respected people, principles of justice etc. However, such principles of interpretation, based on human intelligence and knowledge, are not applied to the Quran. It is not acceptable, for example, to use historical critical methods like those employed by Christians to interpret the Bible, since this would appear to challenge the text of the Quran itself.

Similarly, the cornerstone of modern Judaism is sacred text—the Hebrew Bible—and more particularly the Pentateuch (the first five books of the Old Testament), which is considered to be the direct and most fundamental revelation as delivered to Moses on Mount Sinai. The books of the Torah (meaning teaching or instruction, rather than "law") show how God works in creation and in history, and how his people should live in relationship to each other, to other nations and to the world. Traditional Judaism has regarded not only the contents of the Torah, but every letter of the received text, as sacred. This makes it difficult for the Orthodox community to come to terms with modern biblical scholarship, but Liberal and Progressive Judaism is ready to use historical critical methods to understand the context in which the biblical tradition was formed as an aid to interpreting its meaning for today.

In its understanding of revelation and the authority of Scripture, Christianity is unique among the monotheistic religions of the world. For Christians, God's self-disclosure is primarily in a person, not a sacred book or tradition. Christianity is not knowledge about anything; Christianity is knowledge of somebody. It is the good news of God made known in Jesus the Christ, or in Paul's shorthand, nothing else matters except "to know Christ—yes, to know the power of his resurrection and participation in his sufferings" (Philippians 3:10). This does not exclude God's self-revelation in creation and in the story of human cultures and religions, but Christian revelation is not the transmission of a body of learning and law contained in a book; rather it is disclosed in a relationship between one person, the risen Christ, and another. So the fundamental authority for Christians is not trapped within a book, nor is it found within the institutional Church; on the contrary, it is revealed through Christ who is Lord both of the Scriptures and of the Church, yet who has chosen to reveal the Godhead through the Scriptures and the Church.

The Bible is the unique witness to the saving work of God; it directs our attention to the living Word of God in Jesus Christ, as John the Baptist pointed away from himself and to Jesus as the Son of God:

> The next day John saw Jesus coming toward him and said, "Look, the Lamb of God, who takes away the sin of the world! This is the one I meant when I said, 'A man who comes after me has surpassed me because he was before me.' I myself did not know him, but the reason I came baptizing with water was that he might be revealed to Israel." Then John gave this testimony: "I saw the Spirit come down from heaven as a dove and remain on him" (John 1:29–32).

Thus, the Bible is only God's word in a derivative sense. The implications are exciting and challenging. For example, revelation is both an objective occurrence involving particular people and particular places, and a subjective experience—it calls for our personal response and appropriation. Thus, Christianity is rescued from being the religion of the book and becomes a faith system relating to a Person. Furthermore, because Christianity is about knowing the risen, living Christ, the Church has the responsibility in every generation and in different cultures to reinterpret the timeless revelation in Christ for its time and place.

When the Word became flesh, God chose a particular culture, religion and location for that revelation. The first task of Gospel interpretation is to understand the original cultural context in which a passage was written, and to rediscover what the writers were seeking to tell us about Christ in his incarnate life. It is imperative to express this same message, the Word becoming flesh, in a way that speaks to our own culture and at this particular point in history. The authority for this enterprise is not based exclusively *in* the Scriptures or *in* the tradition of the Church, but rather *through* the ongoing interaction between the contemporary body of believers and the Risen Lord. Jesus warned the religious leaders: "You study the Scriptures diligently because you think that in them you have eternal life. These are the very Scriptures that testify about me, yet you refuse to come to me to have life" (John 5:39–40). This ongoing exercise of using the Scriptures as a signpost, rather than a finishing post, is an important and continuous task for the whole people of God in each generation.

In this way, the experience of the original Pentecost in which "a crowd came together in bewilderment, because each one heard their own language being spoken" (Acts 2:6) will be repeated for every culture and language to the end of time. In every generation and in every culture, people experience the Word made flesh through the Scriptures in a different way. This is because Christianity is a living, breathing relationship between the faithful and the crucified Risen Lord. The power of that person is alive in the faithful of that community, comforting and ultimately transforming the lives of people in that community. Living in an ever-changing and challenging digital age dynamically influences our interaction with Jesus Christ. We cannot ignore the power of the prevailing culture and its pressure on us. Instead, it is an opportunity for us to engage with today's digital and highly technological culture from the perspective of Jesus Christ. It is our responsibility as the disciples of Christ to create different ways for our faith to interact.

We need to remember that faith itself is not a product but a process. As we live in the kingdom of God, through our faith in Christ, and experience the culture of the Trinity through living the relationship with, and the teachings of, Jesus Christ, we remember that Jesus told us, "I have much more to say to you, more than you can now bear. But when he, the Spirit of truth, comes, he will guide you into all the truth. He will not speak on his own; he will speak only what he hears, and he will tell you what is yet to come" (John 16:12–13). These verses tell us that the revelation of Christ was not given as a finished product but is instead an ongoing process leading us through change to maturity. This prevailing digital culture is not different from earlier cultures, in the sense that we seek security rather than the adventure of journeying towards an authentic maturity. The problem arises when we resist change in a changing culture. In order for our faith to stay alive, it must keep changing to keep pace with our rapidly changing lives.

I am aware that in this fast-paced world, too much change fuels insecurity, which leads naturally to fear and an often hostile reaction against the forces of change. The person of Christ, however, remains the grounding force that provides us with continuity and a sense of security that is not afraid of change. Our faith in Christ should not make us reject the prevailing culture. On the contrary, it should help us understand our relationship with, and the teachings of, Jesus Christ in a way that is relevant to our lives today.

Understanding Christ afresh affirms the fact that the opposite of faith is not doubt but certainty. We, as Christians, should not seek false certainty. The person of Christ should give us certainty that is based on faith rather than surface understanding and objective proof. St Paul says, "For we live by faith, not by sight" (2 Corinthians 5:7). St Augustine says, "we go to God by love not by navigation." In our world today, there is increasing polarization between the fundamentalism of certainty and the extreme liberalism that can often become agnosticism. For me, both miss the point of Christianity. Christianity is neither black and white nor so insubstantial that nothing can be known and everything is open to question. I believe in a faith that seeks understanding rather than an understanding that may lead to faith.

The process of understanding our faith in today's culture does not in any way mean that we compromise or water down our faith. I believe strongly that today's culture could provide us with new vocabulary and new metaphors with which to express our faith and find a deeper connection with God. Understanding Jesus Christ today for me is exciting. The present culture provides compelling and thought-provoking tools that we can use in order to challenge ourselves in ways that we never could before. For example, the interaction between humanity and artificial intelligence in our digital culture widens the range of our understanding of what it means to be human and by extension our understanding of the humanity of Jesus Christ. When we say that God is the Creator and we are in the process of creating an artificial cell, this poses the question of what it means to create life. What implication does this then have for our understanding of Jesus Christ?

These questions and many more that emerge as the human mind expands in knowledge and in experience are essential in deepening our faith and spiritual life. These questions and issues should not pose a threat to our faith but rather an exciting opportunity to welcome a wider engagement with the changing culture around us and with the consequences that continue to emerge from the exciting human journey. The whole concept of the Culture of God came as a result of wrestling with human situations of war and peace, love and hate, science and knowledge, art and creativity and many more issues that form our dynamic human culture.

The Culture of the Trinity, which is the Culture of God the Creator who most creatively made space for us to exist in his infinite love, remains a mystery that fills us with wonder and awe and, at the same time, motivates us to live our lives creatively, expanding in every way with love and dignity while respecting the sanctity of life. The person of Jesus Christ, the perfect image of God and humanity, the Son of Man, opens the door for us to enter into infinite possibilities and opportunities to progress in every way and keep our hearts and minds transforming our lives and being transformed in turn by him. He gave us the freedom and the choice to be aided by his power in order to unfold the mystery of life in us and around us. This book offers us nothing but a glimpse of the infinite possibilities of what the risen Jesus Christ has given us.

3

Christianity facing the digital age

Throughout the ages, science and faith have found themselves at different periods at odds with one another. We all know that science has had its share of persecution from the Church. We all remember the condemnation that Galileo received from the Catholic Church in the first half of the seventeenth century. This formed a turning point in the history of humanity and still resonates today. It has become a symbol of the clash between science and religion. In this book, our subject is not faith and science, but we must bring it into focus when we consider the Culture of God and the rise of digital technology.

For many people of faith, whether Christian or non-Christian, this dilemma still exists, and the issue of reconciling faith and science remains a controversial hot topic. Throughout my life, I have met people who rejected faith because they wanted to be more scientific, but then I discovered that most of them did this because they had bad experiences with religion. I was excited to read, for example, *The God Delusion* by Richard Dawkins. When I read it, I felt deeply disappointed because I felt that, despite the author's denial that his atheism came from a bad experience of religion, I could see that the more he denied this, the more he confirmed it. Dawkins could not in any page of the book show me how science could show me any meaning for my life. The book, to me, reflected a deep bitterness about religion rather than faith. This applies to many atheists I have met in my life.

Atheism, I insist, is a position of faith whether we like it or not. Both the believer and non-believer have the same departure point, which is faith. One has the belief that God exists and the other that he doesn't. I am not convinced that any atheist can say that their position is totally objective and has nothing to do with their own personal experience with faith or religion. We need to be aware that faith in this context takes the form of an intellectual discussion. This is different from faith from the biblical perspective, which is building a living relationship with God who reveals himself as love in Christ. Theism and atheism are products of our intellect and philosophical discussion. Christian faith is being in love with God who became one of us in Christ.

For the younger generation, their psychological imperative is to belong. For young people in general in the West, the trend is not to go to church or to be otherwise associated with Christianity as a religion. Most young people feel that the Church is obsolete, and even the language the Church uses to talk about faith doesn't resonate with them. Many young people refuse faith because they think of God as yet another figure of authority that they have to please. We have failed in modern times, and especially in our digital age, to present God as God reveals himself as the one who sees us because he is in love with us. Many young people feel they are on a spiritual journey to seek out God, but we fail to present to them that God is the one who searches out humanity. The journey is to fall in love with God, who is already in love with us and who seeks to lift us up and enrich our lives.

On the other hand, the fashion in Islam is to be religious. Wearing the hijab, for example, has become a huge trend and often a political and cultural statement rather than just expressing a commitment to faith. Although the fashion is to be religious, we see that the biggest growth in atheism is in Egypt and the Near East, where people have experienced the dark side of religion and therefore more and more people are rejecting that and turning away from faith.

I remember sitting with a group of highly educated young people here in the West. They took the opportunity of sitting with a member of the clergy to ask me about faith. At that encounter, I chose to speak about my faith using metaphors and vocabulary that belong to quantum physics—like multidimensional reality—and suddenly I felt that those people started to become more interested in what I was saying. We spoke about faith and the structure of the universe, faith and black holes, and faith and time travel. I sensed that their attitude to me changed dramatically because they felt that I was talking their language. The rise in digital technology brought with it a massive change in language, communication and, most importantly, relationships. Although trying to cope with such enormous leaps in technology, Christianity still has a long way to go in expressing itself in a way that is relevant to modern life.

We must admit that technology has invaded almost every detail of our lives. Even the older generations have found themselves in a position where they have had to learn new skills in order to cope with everyday life; these are no longer a luxury but a necessity. I remember when my mother, who is over eighty years old and living with me in London away from her native Syria, asked me to teach her about Facebook because she noticed that we talked so much about news and information from home that we had read on our gadgets. Even though my mother didn't know anything about computers, she learnt how to use her iPad, and now she has a Facebook account through which she can communicate with her friends and family scattered around the world. Plus, she now has tens of books that she can read on the iPad at any time through the click of a button.

We must now accept that technology lies at the heart of our existence and affects the way that we pray, read the Scriptures, or present our faith. Faith and science, in this instance, go hand in hand to create a more balanced human being because science (in this case, technology) tries to improve human life and make it more comfortable. It can never, however, give it a purpose. On the other hand, faith brings us to the essence of our human existence, which is to build personal and intimate relationships on different levels—with ourselves, with each other, with the natural world around us and, of course, with God our Creator.

Technology can overtake our lives and affect our relationships in a negative way. It is dangerous to live our life through screens. If we look around us, we see that it is impossible to avoid screens through our televisions, computers, mobile phones and so on. We are surrounded by screens facilitating our communication between each other but without the ability to recreate the warmth and intimacy of the personal encounter. As people of faith, we need to challenge that and reassert the importance of human communication. Nothing replaces the face-to-face encounter. God took the journey to become one of us in order to meet us in the most intimate way. I don't think that any virtual human relationship could be even close to this physical encounter of God coming face-to-face with us in Christ.

We see how essential is the personal, face-to-face physical encounter in our lives. If we look at the many studies that have been made highlighting the impact of the digital world on different generations from children to the elderly, we see different opinions ranging from a minimal to severe impact on human personal relationships. For me, the reality stares us in the face that digital technology has revolutionized our existence. We all notice that even infants are able to learn very quickly how to interact with a touchscreen in front of them, to press the screen to get a picture and access the technology. I have also noticed that young parents tend to keep their children quiet by giving them a device to play with, to watch a children's programme or play an online game. This is not always negative. These days, there are a lot of educational programmes made with care targeting the learning objectives of each age group. At the same time, there are commercial programmes that are not quite as helpful.

Some computer games, I believe, could teach all of us profound lessons that stay with us for a long time. I still remember today my earliest computer game, Civilization. I had the opportunity to play this game in Germany, and it was the first game I had ever played from start to finish. This game taught me a lot, especially coming from the Middle East. It taught me that the consequences of war could be devastating for the towns at the front line of fighting. In the game, those towns were always less developed as they existed in survival mode, whereas cities far from the front line were much more developed in everything. Long periods of war, I also learnt, hinder the whole progress of civilization. Suddenly, I recognized that I had to take decisions of war and peace that would determine the present and future of the civilization that I was running in the game. That made me think a lot about reality and about how true that game is when we apply it to real life. The Middle East is definitely less developed in every way as a result of decades of wars and military conflicts, whereas Europe has flourished from the nearly eighty years of peace it has enjoyed since the Second World War. Digital technology could revolutionize every aspect of our lives and has done so, but for countries that suffer from destructive, violent crises, technology serves mostly to cause more destruction through ever more advanced military weaponry.

Being at the helm of decision-making in a game like this, I realized that I couldn't always take the decision to make peace but had to instead respond to the world around my own and sometimes I had to declare war to defend the borders of my civilization. If I look at that from the perspective of the mind of Christ, I can see the inevitability of the clashes he had with the Pharisees and the scribes and other religious leaders. Not because he chose to go through this tension but because he had to respond to the attacks against him from those people. Jesus in his life carried beautifully the tension between being a kind, merciful and generous man and being tough, challenging and confrontational. Managing this tension the way he did made him a unique and extraordinary leader who could change the face of history.

We see this tension not only with people but even with his Father. We see how he wrestled with his relationship with his Father, and although he showed total obedience, it was sometimes not without a fight. We see this in the Garden of Gethsemane when he prayed and asked his Father to release him from the option of the cross, saying: "Take this cup from me. Yet not what I will, but what you will" (Mark 14:36). We all live this struggle today, feeling sometimes overwhelmed by the challenges of modern life. As St Paul says, "We know that the whole creation has been groaning as in the pains of childbirth right up to the present time" (Romans 8:22). Sometimes, we find ourselves groaning under the pressure of keeping up with the fast pace of digital technology. Then, we must remember that Christ in Gethsemane expressed his uncertainty that his Father's love would be revealed to the world if he was to die upon the cross and asked if there was another way. After that, he accepted his fate and faced the cross because he believed that the Father was with him and would never abandon him. Like him, we must face the challenges ahead of us fortified by our faith that the Father is with us and we are not alone.

Learning the lessons of Easter

In Syria, we call Christmas the "small feast" and Easter the "big feast". This reflects the importance of each feast in the Church in the Near East. Christmas is a joyful time full of celebration with the family and wider community—although for a long time, presents were only for children until Western customs started creeping in. We have always celebrated with Christmas trees, Father Christmas and carols, which were always sung by famous singers like Fairuz and enjoyed by both Muslims and Christians alike.

Easter is different and is a more serious feast starting with Lent. In the Near East, Lent is more important than Advent and has a deeper spiritual impact. Preparations for Easter are more detailed and involved. Although we exchange painted eggs, it has never been about chocolate or Easter bunnies. In the UK, unless you are a churchgoer, you hardly realize the significance of Easter. In the Near East, when the preparations start even those who are not serious about their faith become more spiritual. When we come to Passion Week, we call it the Week of Pains in Arabic. The music of Easter is sublime both in the West and the East. Different traditions have different music. The Catholic and Protestant faiths enjoy more Western music while the Orthodox churches enrich us with more Byzantine and Eastern cultural music to express the Passion. This music is highly expressive, capturing the emotions of the pain of the cross and the joy of Easter morning. People go to enjoy both musical traditions.

Another dimension we have in the Near East is that Christianity is divided between the different religious calendars of the Eastern and Western orthodoxies, which elongates the period of celebration. Many Christians are troubled by this division, and there is an increasing call on both sides of the Church for a shared date as a symbol of Christian unity. Unfortunately, church leaders say that they want this but there has been little progress so far. Especially lately, Christians from both traditions have expressed deep frustration at this lack of progress and this has become a sore point in the body of the Church, touching a raw nerve that exposes the division of the Church at a time when Christianity is imperilled in the region as the number of Christians has dropped dramatically. Lately, Christians are increasingly fed up with church leaders they feel are failing them and look upon their leadership with dismay. They are calling for more solidarity between the different branches of Christianity in the face of persecution and emigration. During the youth ministry we had in Iraq, I was shocked to see that our gathering of around a hundred young men and women from different denominations were completely unaware of the meaning of ecumenism in Arabic, so little had it been discussed or addressed.

Despite this divided Christianity, Easter captures the imagination of Christians in the Near East. It resonates with people's reflections on the crucifixion of the region through decades of bloodshed and violence. We are all looking for the resurrection and even Muslims use this language. People are hanging on with hope that the Risen Christ can help these countries see the light at the end of this tunnel of darkness and horror that they are now experiencing. So many families are grieving loved ones. Many people feel that they are living through a long, dark Good Friday. In Arabic, this day is known as the "great Friday" or the "painful Friday", and people are yearning to see the light of the resurrection. The failing is not just by church leaders but more importantly by political leaders who have presided over a culture of corruption and silencing those who oppose them.

A lot of people are using technology today to express themselves (using either their real name or a pseudonym), to bypass the crushing hand of the political regimes in the region and speak out against all the evil that is happening in their countries. The young generation believes that social media and digital technology are instruments that we must use carefully but also widely in order to stand up against what is happening in the Near East and uncover the deep corruption of politicians who are warlords behaving like vampires sucking the blood of people there. People have reached levels of poverty and suffering that have never been witnessed before in the Near East in modern history. Christians are looking for the Risen Lord in our digital age, working hard to deploy all resources available to them to face up to those who are fully corrupt, who try to exploit them and destroy their lives. Every year, Lent and Eastertide motivate Christians and Muslims to revolt against the great thieves who are robbing the people, taking their livelihoods and throwing them into an abyss. Digital technology in the Near East is not looked on as entertainment but as an important tool for change.

I feel that Easter is different in the West. I was upset to see chocolate eggs and Easter bunnies appearing in supermarkets and shops earlier and earlier. In the year before the coronavirus pandemic, the first Easter bunny I saw was a very short time after Christmas. We have commercialized Christmas and Easter to the extent that the vast majority of people who do not go to church have no idea about the true meaning of Easter beyond Easter bunnies and chocolate eggs. Sometimes, even people who do go to church are not aware of the depth of the event of Easter. Observing the drama of the event, we miss the crucial point that Jesus lived what he preached. Perhaps the hardest lesson he preached was to love our enemies. This vital point was fulfilled when he forgave those who put him to death. His forgiveness was the ultimate embodiment of living out his words. The message of Easter can be lived on every level in our lives, whether through personal or virtual encounters via social media. This message doesn't stop at the doorstep of digital technology but is rather even more relevant today.

I remember when I was a chaplain at the London School of Economics, a member of staff who was Christian came to shadow us as chaplains and, during the Mass that my colleague was celebrating, this member of staff whispered to me, "What is this big white circle in front of the priest and why does he have a silver cup in front of him?" I then realized that this member of staff who called himself Christian didn't have a clue about his Christian faith. When I explained that the big white circle was called a wafer, symbolizing the breaking of Christ upon the cross, he looked at me with childlike wonder and asked, "What happened on the cross?" I thought, we need to talk!

Easter in the West has a Christian meaning only within the buildings of the Church. Christianity has retreated from the public space, and it has become taboo to talk publicly about faith. In secular society, people are still uncomfortable talking about their faith. If you go to buy an Easter card, for example, it is often hard to find a card depicting a cross or the resurrection. Despite this attempt to commercialize Easter, it is a more subtle and spiritual feast than Christmas. This is how it should be, dealing as it does with the death and resurrection of Christ. It is a celebration for those who truly believe that Christ is Lord who rose again from the dead. It is an inner joy for the community of believers who celebrate the extraordinary event of the resurrection.

You can secularize Christmas but not Easter. It is always easier to secularize a happy event but in what way can you make Easter a consumer-driven feast? The story of Easter is a violent and dramatic tragedy that only has true meaning if you believe that the cross redefines love and life. Through the cross, life became bigger than mere biological existence. In the Christian faith, the cross is a promise of a new and better life after death, renewing fellowship with those that you love. This is possible because Christ himself rose in a new, glorified body. When Jesus appeared to his disciples after the resurrection, he showed them his wounds. He did this in order to show them the result of loving the enemy.

Our problem today, especially in our advanced technological age, is that we love others with a calculator in one hand. We calculate what we give and also what we receive. Jesus, however, wants us to give without waiting to receive. He wants us to be neither superhuman nor subhuman. He wants us to be entirely human. The true joy of Easter, which passes all human imagination, can only be understood through the drama and sacrifice of the cross.

In our digital age, the challenge of the resurrection becomes pertinent. If we view the story of our age as one of technological advancement, how can we accept the story of Easter? How can we express the concept of the Risen Lord to those who have grown up with digital technology? For these generations, everything important can be seen and heard and be communicated through these digital tools. How can we read a two-thousand-year-old story and find meaning in it today? If we want to reach people, we need to communicate the story using the most advanced digital methods and tools and send them the message that the Lord of the resurrection is also the Lord of technology. It is not either/or. We can do that in audio-visual ways, engaging with people through film, music, forums and even through games. The aim of all this is to tell the digital generation that we can't say that we believe in Jesus without meeting him. This means feeling his presence warming our hearts.

It seems that we are very slow in embracing digital ways. We must use an entirely new language and think digitally. How can we make the story of the Passion relevant today? Jesus used familiar imagery—like the mustard seed, the shepherd and the vine—to communicate his message. What are the touchstones today that we can use to tell the Christian story without losing the true message of Christ?

During the coronavirus pandemic in 2020, many churches decided to continue their services via Facebook in order to allow the faithful to follow the prayers and link with their churches. Statistics show that the number of people who attended services or prayed online increased, reflecting how millions of lives have been affected during this challenging and extraordinary time. Even clergy who were almost totally ignorant about technology or social media found themselves in a situation where they had to learn and cooperate with members of their churches who knew how to use technology better in order to provide some spiritual sustenance to their people. Suddenly we found ourselves increasingly using the digital technology and social media at our fingertips because we needed to.

Looking at the new situation brought about by the pandemic and the subsequent lockdowns, we came to appreciate more our human fellowship and relationships that we took for granted before. Suddenly, a hug was forbidden, and a handshake could mean death. We must admit that the pandemic put us in our places and showed us how fragile our lives are and how real and ever-present is our mortality. I personally lost more than twenty close friends between the UK, Syria and Lebanon. We felt that we were driving a car at speed and then someone had slammed on the brakes, so that the rush of life changed dramatically. This made us think and re-evaluate our existence. We have lost millions of people around the world, and we have all been affected one way or another.

Easter 2020 was different from any Easter that we have lived before. We reflected on the cross in a new light and from a new perspective. The resurrection expressed our hope from a position of global tragedy. Digital technology helped us to share this solidarity of hope and we found the Risen Lord through using the gadgets and screens around us. Now the screen carried a message of love and hope and encouragement instead of the usual stream of irrelevant news and gossip. We could see that those screens turned into windows opened to beloved ones that we could no longer see in person. Many times in our lives before the pandemic, we

had postponed meeting with friends because we were busy. The invisible
virus and its power to change our lives in such a deep way made us regret
not meeting those who are dear to us.

During that difficult time, churches visited a lot of homes and people
who would not otherwise have visited a church. The pandemic taught
us a lot about our homes, both positively and negatively. We had the
opportunity to think again about our lives, where we live and our future.
Homes became more important for us because we found ourselves
spending more time there. Many people started making their houses
more like a home and felt that their homes became their sanctuary
that they needed to nurture. Many others, however, discovered that
their homes were inadequate to live in. They were places that they had
previously tolerated because they hadn't needed to spend much time in
them. The pandemic made us dream about different lives, a different
future, and different relationships.

Some clergy mentioned to me in conversation their concern that some
people would stop coming to church if the online services continued.
Personally, I don't agree with that as I feel that this period of lockdown
has made us appreciate more personal fellowship and the presence of
one another in one place. The intimacy of people gathering to worship in
one place has a completely different quality to the fellowship that people
experience via digital technology online. The Risen Lord went through
this most intimate and personal relationship with the people by being
with them, eating with them, drinking with them and socializing with
them. I don't believe that if Christ was here today, he would revert to
social media and digital fellowship. Although we use all the wonderful
resources that the digital age provides for us, that cannot in any way
replace face-to-face relationships and personal contact even at the level
of a business meeting. My emphasis on the importance of personal
presence doesn't mean in any way that we should retreat from what we
have started online. We must still cater to those who cannot come to
church for different reasons.

The drama of the pandemic appears as the cross that we were all
crucified on—bleeding, exhausted and broken-hearted. As we emerged
from this to the dawn of an Easter Sunday that had broken the darkness
of the pandemic, we were left with the hard work of restoring our

personal relationships and embracing the joy of being able to be human again. Unfortunately, as the world started to breathe again and see the resurrection at hand, another cross was planted in the heart of Europe with the vicious and evil war in Ukraine. This war is utilizing the most advanced technology of our time on an unprecedented international scale. We see this war tearing the heart of Europe and creating another bleeding wound in our world, abusing every single invention of our technological age to spread more destruction.

I see this war as another abortion of our humanity, as we fail to deal with yet another conflict. The digital revolution has turned into a curse that has destroyed millions of lives, taken us back to the darkest moment of Good Friday and pushed away the joy of Easter Sunday. We hear endless theories through audio-visual media, social media, and other methods of digital communication. Some blame the West and more blame Russia or China. We are living in an "info-demic", a period of a flood of information creating confusion over what is true or untrue. Very few people check the validity of the source of the information that they read, finding it too complicated to do so, especially if this information appears to confirm what they already think.

Many of us reject those who challenge information biases and seek to find an objective truth amidst the noise. The end result is that we have left the essence of our dignity and humanity to be taken hostage in the dungeon of the evil abuse of technology. It has manifested itself in the colossal destructive power of the modern weaponry that we have developed. It is the true face of the madness of our digital age standing in contrast to the constant cry of Christ to see ourselves through the eyes of the Culture of the Trinity, which is the culture of peace and life. The Risen Christ stands in confrontation with the evil side of our power and all of us, our lives and the very existence of humanity, are at stake.

Is the Church chasing her tail in today's world?

I always wondered why Jesus did not leave us any of his writings. After so many years of studying this fascinating personality, I have an idea why he most probably didn't write anything down. I think that he observed how religious leaders of his time built prisons out of the written word, not only that of God but also the narrative and interpretations that they built around it. Those interpretations became so rigid that they suffocated the core message. He must have experienced the impact that those written words had on people and how they restricted people's lives and pushed them into boxes with endless restrictions and narrow customs. This created a whole system of control that the Sanhedrin enforced on people and governed the detail of their lives.

Jesus used the written word, the Scriptures, very creatively. He was keen to help people to understand the sacred written word. He even created the most challenging parable, that of the Good Samaritan (Luke 10:25–37), in order to help someone who was struggling to understand the Scriptures. Jesus worked very hard to restore the role of the Scriptures and to interpret them around himself and his message. He did that with a new authority that came directly from his Father. Jesus wanted to break down these barriers between people and the loving God. The religious system alienated God and created another deity in the projection of this system, making people worship that projection rather than the loving, gracious God. Jesus had to dig deep into the structure of society in order to liberate the image of God and present him afresh to the people. He could only end this alienation by being a living example of the God he wanted people to believe in.

This is what made Jesus reveal the Culture of the Trinity that he experienced before the incarnation. Jesus observed and lived these hard restrictions and obstacles that the religious system erected in the lives and relationships of people. For this reason, I argue, he decided not to write anything down that could have been taken as another rigid set of instructions. If he wanted us to follow written instructions, he could have written these himself, but unfortunately today we sometimes treat the Bible as such. The signpost can never be the road. It remains a signpost that points us in the right direction. Today, living with the increasing domination of digital technology, we must be conscious not to let this technology alienate Jesus Christ in the same way that the written word alienated God in his time.

Unveiling the Culture of God in the life and teachings of Christ should map out how to be citizens of two kingdoms: the kingdom of God that Jesus preached about, and the kingdoms of the world in which we live today. It is important to reflect on both kingdoms and see the culture in both. First, we need to reflect on the culture that we live in here and now, including issues like globalization, the natural world and social media. This is our responsibility to reflect upon and understand. Then we must do the same and find the culture that prevails in the kingdom of God—his rule, his sovereignty and our relationship with him. Jesus Christ was the ultimate example of how to live in both kingdoms at the same time; and how to integrate belonging to the kingdom of God while living in the world today.

The more we separate the two kingdoms, the more we alienate ourselves and the person of Christ. The separation of the two defeats the purpose of the incarnation and the saving act of the loving God in Christ. We hear so much that God has nothing to do with this or that—especially when we talk about the separation between religion and state. A lot of people express surprise when I say that I am a secular priest, thinking that it is unbelievable that I agree with the separation of state and religion. It is not very hard to see the consequences of that poisonous marriage between those two institutions, not only in Christianity but in all other religions, even the most pacifist ones.

The history of Europe, with its centuries of extreme violence and destructive wars in the name of religion, that brought devastation not only to the old continent but engulfed the whole world, is the ultimate result of alienating God and Jesus Christ. How could we forget the wars between Protestants and Catholics that raged through Europe in the sixteenth, seventeenth and early eighteenth centuries, culminating in the Thirty Years' War of the first half of the seventeenth century that killed a staggering one-third of the population of Germany? In the midst of all the actions that were happening in their names, bringing God and the Lord back into the heart of society does not in any way mean bringing back the marriage between politics and religion.

I have experienced for over a decade in Syria the evil partnership between politics and religion, where terrorist groups devastated the country, killing hundreds of thousands of people and displacing millions in the name of Islam. Political Islam spread across the greater Middle East, including Egypt, North Africa, the Near East, Yemen and Libya, then spread to Africa and impacted the rest of the world. An Islamic theology that killed more Muslims than any other religious group; an ideology that is based on hate and an exclusive mentality to the extent that many of those Islamic groups went into vicious conflict with each other, with each one believing they embodied the most correct version of Islam. Unfortunately, they were able to play on the divide between the East and West, and the Western involvement in the Middle East, to recruit thousands of young Muslims from around the world, poisoning their minds with hatred and the idea that everyone who is not like them should be eliminated.

They convinced them that Islam is in a state of war with the rest of the world and that the West intended to eradicate Islam, making it their divine mission to conquer the rest of the world and kill these infidels. The point is that political Islam alienated Islam as a faith and presented the ugly face of God. I remember speaking to an imam, a dear friend of mine, saying that while we could and would offer support, it was up to him and his fellow religious leaders to stamp out this false ideology. The solution needs to come from inside Islam. We must learn from history. The Church learnt through bloodshed to remove herself from the monarchy and state and rediscover her mission to serve the people through the teachings of God in Christ.

Extreme religious ideas and ideologies use the most sophisticated digital technology to groom young people and brainwash them with their poisonous thoughts. This is happening not only with fanatical Islamic organizations but with extreme factions from all religions. As Christians, if we want to not alienate Christ and stop fanatical ideas that promote hate and enmity with other groups or religions, we need to engage with this technology and learn how to use it in order to spread faith in Christ, who is the Prince of Peace and the Ambassador of the Culture of God, the Culture of the Trinity, the Culture of Love.

Learning the lessons from history, we need to act faster and be proactive towards what is happening around us, especially after the Covid-19 pandemic. It is up to us as part of the body of Christ to prevent the digital age from alienating Jesus Christ by grabbing every opportunity to reach out to as many people as we can and present to them the Culture of God that Jesus Christ lived and revealed during his life on earth.

In the second half of the twentieth century, people in the West moved away from organized religion and the Church as an institution because they felt that the Church failed to speak to the needs of the people at that time. Spirituality was no longer connected to organized religion but was rather seen as a personal journey that people could pursue, incorporating the parts of different faiths and spiritual traditions that spoke to them. That movement sometimes took extreme forms—using drugs and chaotic sexual freedom, for example. All that pushed the Church further into the margins of society.

When I came to Germany in the early 1990s, I was shocked to see the rift between the Church and society. I found myself in a dilemma over the fact that the Church in Germany was the second biggest employer in the country after the state, but the vast majority of the institutions the Church ran didn't have any Christian ethos. I was told that this was because they didn't want religion undermining the rules. A drug rehabilitation centre, for example, was run entirely according to the latest research and without any sense of a Christ-centred spirituality. It was as if they were embarrassed by their faith.

When I came to the UK at the end of the 1990s, there was a surge in the use of early digital technology like mobile phones and dial-up internet. Even at that time, I noticed the gap between the Church and society. I felt that people were almost embarrassed to call themselves Christians. At the university where I was a chaplain, I remember a student stopping me on campus to ask me why I was bothering them with my presence there. I admired the honesty of the question, but I also felt sad at the deep rejection of religion. I looked at him and said, "I am exactly here to do that. Since I am fulfilling my mission in bothering you, can I ask why you are bothered?" He answered that all the Church does is run to catch up with society without offering any leadership or insight and, when it does, society has already moved on. I didn't feel that I could argue with him a great deal because I agreed that the Church hadn't been dealing very well with the rhythm and pace of the technological revolution.

After this conversation, I managed to build a wonderful friendship with him. He would come weekly to the chaplaincy. I understood more his frustration with the irrelevance of the Church. We started to talk about Christ, and he was amazed that the Church was not talking about the Christ I was talking about—someone who was not just a nice man but who was a radical leader who called for profound change in the society around him. Every leader who sought to make such radical changes would necessarily be hated and blocked from trying to make these changes by the leaders of the prevailing system. What we are unable to do is make Christ relevant to society because we are too busy with the bureaucratic organization of the Church. To talk about the Church in the digital age is a different subject from how Christ can change, and be relevant in, today's society. We are so busy chasing our tails that we risk overlooking the centrality of Christ the leader who has so much to speak to in our digital age. In the digital age, the world needs the figure of Christ and not another institution.

4

Jesus Christ: a counter force

In the twenty-first century, living in an ever-changing society with generations of technology invading our lives every year and feeling unable to chase the next technological development, and in an age of infinite technological possibilities, it is inevitable that controversial figureheads and opinions emerge. Every day, we see people who strive to be famous through their controversial opinions; the more controversial or shocking the better in order to attract attention. Some people rely on the originality of their views to reach the widest number of people, while others jump on the bandwagon of the latest trend. The aim of these would-be influencers is to garner the most attention and acclaim through the greatest number of followers or views.

Millions of people around the world follow and listen to the opinions of celebrities and people who emerge as "opinion formers" via social media or through being bold enough to challenge the status quo and be controversial in their thinking. Sometimes these opinions have a positive influence that inspires movements and even lobbies government. Other times controversial opinions have stirred up a storm of anger and hurt or caused a huge scandal. All this is cross-cultural and is not specific to any one country or people. Some cultures have struggled to cope with the consequences of such "opinion makers".

Is Jesus Christ a counter force to the influence of digital technology in our lives?

The interesting question that emerges is how controversial was Jesus Christ in his own time and within his own culture, without the influence of social media and without being able to reach out to his people in the same way that we can today? What made Jesus controversial and rejected by religious leaders was not that he was kind to people and taught people to be good to each other. His most controversial teaching that disturbed the religious system of the time was his understanding of love. In his time, the scribes' and Pharisees' focus was on the observance of the law so as to keep a tight grip on the lives of the people. Jesus, however, challenged this and shifted the focus away from practices and external matters to the internal, as seen in Matthew 15:

> "Are you still so dull?" Jesus asked them. "Don't you see that whatever enters the mouth goes into the stomach and then out of the body? But the things that come out of a person's mouth come from the heart, and these defile them. For out of the heart come evil thoughts—murder, adultery, sexual immorality, theft, false testimony, slander. These are what defile a person; but eating with unwashed hands does not defile them" (Matthew 15:16–20).

He said that to his disciples after they told him that the Pharisees were offended by his teaching. This shift from external behaviour to the internal was difficult to accept. What does this shift mean? Since Jesus Christ is the incarnation of the Culture of God, he reveals to us throughout his life and teachings what God finds important, not what religious leaders find important. How can we apply this in our digital culture? If evil comes from our heart as human beings, then technology in itself can never be evil. Having a highly advanced smartphone, for example, doesn't make me love or hate people. Nevertheless, if I hate then I will abuse this technology to spread hate. So, we need to be careful not to confuse our priorities and must instead look below the surface to what is empowering the technology to spread hate.

When we open a tap to find that the water flowing from it is dirty, the solution is not to change the tap but to apply a filter to purify the water. In our lives, this filter should not be applied to our behaviour or the technology we use. The true filter is in the heart, as all our thoughts—both evil and good—flow from the heart. Our thoughts, words and deeds all come from our hearts. We hear a lot of complaint about the culture that we live in today. We forget that culture is the collective interaction and life of all of us. If we want to influence our culture, we need an education that reshapes the heart. If we look at Michelangelo's statue of David, for example, we admire this masterpiece for its perfection and beauty from every angle. This is how our hearts should be. Through the Culture of God, we need to reshape our hearts to take the shape that God wants. From whichever angle we look, our hearts should be shaped by the culture and love of God.

Problems arise when our hearts are shaped by external filters rather than by the internal filter of our hearts. The hardest challenge we face in this shaping is the hidden parts that nobody sees but us. When I think, for example, of taking revenge on someone who has hurt me, nobody sees this thought but me. When we work on reshaping our hearts, we become influencers in our culture rather than letting the culture that surrounds us reshape us. The Pharisees were concerned that Jesus and his disciples were eating with defiled hands because they could not look beyond the external cosmetic observance of religion. Jesus was able to carry his audience to a deeper level of understanding of self-worth and faith.

Through our baptism and our subsequent decision to follow Jesus Christ, we receive a new heart. Once we freely open this gift and decide to use it, we allow the Holy Spirit to activate this new heart and help us to integrate it in our lives. This doesn't happen automatically, and baptism is not a magic formula. God respects our decision in accepting his gift and embracing this new heart. When we do this, we become citizens of the Culture of God. There are serious consequences to this in the way we live. When we decide to follow Christ and live according to this new heart, we must choose Christ over ourselves. St Paul puts it beautifully in his Epistle to the Galatians:

> I have been crucified with Christ and I no longer live, but Christ
> lives in me. The life I now live in the body, I live by faith in the Son
> of God, who loved me and gave himself for me (Galatians 2:20).

This existential statement shows us the choice I have to allow the Holy
Spirit to work in me and make this heart active in my life. What is
happening is that I am being replaced by Jesus. Jesus Christ takes us
outside our individualism and the egocentric view of life that prevails
today. When I consciously choose Christ to live in me, I am choosing
to embrace the Culture of God, giving Christ control over my life and
everything I do. I then become part of eternity within the Culture of God
and am no longer subject to the fear of death. St Paul explains this further
in his Epistle to the Romans when he says: "But if Christ is in you, then
even though your body is subject to death because of sin, the Spirit gives
life because of righteousness" (Romans 8:10). All this is possible only
because Jesus Christ was crucified and rose again. It is possible because
of the One who had the power to defeat death, which is the ultimate
threat to human existence. This is why in Christ we are conquerors of fear.

We all know the power of fear and how people act because of it. In fact,
a lot of politics is woven around fear. We have seen how many politicians
in the UK, for example, used to spread fear in order to promote their
political agenda. The best example of this that I can think of is, of
course, Brexit, when the UK decided to hold a referendum to leave or
stay within the European Union. I remember how both sides of the
argument compensated for a lack of clear information with a campaign
of fear—either to stay or leave. It was the ultimate example of dishonesty
that I have experienced outside the Middle East. I felt at that time that
politics and politicians had lost dignity and credibility in their desperate
attempt to exploit the emotions of the people and spread lies with very
little factual backup.

This is exactly what St Paul means when he writes to the Galatians
about Jesus, "who gave himself for our sins to rescue us from the present
evil age, according to the will of our God and Father" (Galatians 1:4).
What he means by "the present evil age" is evil hearts. From those evil
hearts comes the abuse of digital technology to manipulate the hearts
and minds of people. The Brexit campaign was a race to see who could

spread more terrifying lies faster. This issue caused deep divisions within communities in the UK. Following this came the presidency of one of the most controversial people in the United States. In President Trump's time in office, I saw divisions, lies and tension in American society that I had never before witnessed since my first trip to that country in 1986. Regardless of political affiliation, I saw for the first time an unprecedented level of hatred from the media, on the street and even between friends and colleagues. American society slipped into this state of polarization within such a short space of time.

More and more, we have entered a dangerous time when we accept or respect only those who are like us. In our digital culture, with the possibility of instant communication, we are able increasingly to build a cocoon around ourselves in which we only listen to the opinions that agree with ours and reject everything that doesn't fit with us. This is exactly the opposite of what the Culture of God wants us to embrace. When I allow Jesus Christ to free me from my selfishness and my egocentric world, I don't need to live in this cocoon anymore and I am able to engage lovingly and rationally with those who are different from me. This doesn't mean that I agree with them, but I am no longer living in a room of mirrors reflecting my own image.

Increasingly, technology is making us selfish and egocentric. The devices we use—whether computers, TVs or mobiles—even when they are switched off become mirrors reflecting our own image. When we use our devices to communicate with one another, most of us look at our own image rather than the image of the person we are communicating with. At the other extreme, people hide behind a blank screen in order to reduce their level of engagement, especially when part of a forum or a classroom.

The Covid-19 pandemic has made us use our computers and mobiles more extensively as communication devices in order to keep in touch with the outside world or do our work. They have become our only window on the outside world to connect us to other people or bring us news. This means that the number of hours we spend in front of our screens has rocketed, and we are forced to barricade ourselves behind our devices. As I write, I can see six screens spread around me—the TV, computer, two mobiles and two iPads.

We have reached a stage where digital technology has become our lifeline. During the pandemic, millions of people relied on their digital devices just to order food, while digital technology played a massive role in saving lives in and outside hospital. We are constantly making decisions concerning the use of technology, beginning with the digital alarm clock that greets us when we open our eyes in the morning, through to the coffee makers and the endless devices that surround us as we go through our day.

Those of us able to go shopping every day are acquainted with the concept of self-checkout using digital machines connected to apps on our mobiles that allow us to collect points or redeem vouchers. Even when we shop online, we are connected to websites that allow us to track our order and confirm that we received it digitally. As if this is not enough, the next generation of retail shopping uses radio frequency identification to allow you to go into a shop, identify yourself digitally, put what you want in your bag and go. Each item has an electromagnetic identity tag that charges the item to your online account, allowing you to leave the shop without having to check out manually or even speak to another living human being.

I totally understand the benefits of convenience and comfort that come with such technology, but the question is, does that make us better and more mindful human beings? The technology itself is amoral because it is like having money in your pocket—it is our decision how to spend the money that determines whether it is used for evil or good. Jesus Christ always warned against the love of money, not money itself, and this also applies to technology. The danger lies when we allow the advancement of technology to make us more narcissistic by reflecting our own image to the extent that we fall in love with ourselves and forget our place in the wider context of creation.

The Covid-19 pandemic will hopefully help remind us that all our military might was useless against an invisible virus. The world lost millions of lives to this infinitely small organism that cannot be seen or detected by the most sophisticated radars in the world. This virus smashed all the mirrors that surround us to reflect our true, vulnerable selves. It managed to kick us off the thrones of our arrogance, especially the belief that we are masters of our own destiny. Regardless of whether it was transmitted via an animal or was man-made in a lab, the truth remains that we are much less than we thought we were—in power, intelligence and even as moral beings.

Although we have learnt to cooperate more with each other, if we look in the mirror that the virus holds up to us, we see humanity as a dwarf and not the giant that we imagine ourselves to be. Although we have had moments of positive decision-making around the world, I still believe that we have ultimately failed to reveal the image of God in which we are created. The question we are asked today in our post-pandemic lives, facing further advancements in digital technology, is how we see ourselves in relationship to others and God? What can Jesus Christ teach us in building these relationships? How can we make him a counter-culture in our lives that challenges us when we are too comfortable, affirms us when we are weak and energizes us with the power of change when our lives become too stagnant?

Overcoming fear: Jesus Christ and the ethics of living in a digital society

If we understand "ethics" as the moral principles that guide our decision-making process, then we need to re-examine these principles in our society and see how we evaluate an issue and reach a moral judgement on it. The word ethics comes from the Greek word *ethos*, which can be taken as meaning habit, custom or disposition. Most of the time when we talk about ethics, it means that we are dealing with a dilemma. The sources of these moral principles are usually taken from cultural, religious or philosophical practices.

In some universities, ethics are also called moral philosophy. This discipline deals with almost every aspect of our lives. It becomes more visible when we have a problem like human cloning, abortion or damage to the environment. All these burning problems are ethical issues that should be based around moral principles. Ethics can also deal with everyday decisions, especially when it comes to building communities and social relationships. For example, is it morally acceptable to discriminate against somebody based on race, gender or sexual orientation? Having said that, ethics is inextricably linked with religion and faith. Faith also touches everything in our lives and informs our decision-making.

Living in a highly advanced digital culture presents us with new ethical dilemmas. How do we use the internet or social media? We are constantly faced with the values on which we base our moral judgements. People differ in their ethical response to different problems, usually based on their religious or cultural backgrounds. I remember when I moved from the Middle East to live in Europe in the early 1990s and for the next twenty years, I noticed that the churches in Europe and North America were deeply engaged in heated debates around sexuality. This was a completely new discussion for me. In the Middle East, it's rare to find any discussion about sexuality in the Church or the wider community. I remember when I had a discussion about sex with the youth group that I was leading in Lattakia, it was seen as quite revolutionary in the church. I was blessed that the discussion went very well to the extent that other churches heard about it and began to address the subject as well. For me, it was eye-opening to be in the middle of discussions about homosexuality, for example, in Europe—a subject that is still a matter of taboo in the Middle East.

I had the opportunity to listen to different ethical and theological arguments, but my point is that it was interesting and challenging to face this ethical dilemma that forced me to think before rushing into any moral judgement. I felt that it was far too easy to hide behind my cultural background and take sides based on this. I realized that I needed much more engagement in order to form a moral opinion. I noticed that many people used the Bible in a dangerous way to support their pre-existing opinions. In fact, they manipulated texts in the Bible to make God agree with them. I have seen this type of manipulation from all different viewpoints. I have rarely heard someone admit that, on reflection, they were wrong.

Most of the time, I heard people who had already made up their minds and then searched for verses in the Bible and other texts to support their judgement. I remember commenting in a Synod meeting that I noticed each side in the debate was arguing that God agreed with them, making it even more confusing for believers. What bothered me most was not that people had reached different conclusions, but instead that the degree of absolutism left no margin for doubt or finding a middle ground. This absolutism has generated a bitterness within the Church that is very destructive.

Humanity has wrestled with morality for thousands of years and has formed codes of conduct, the oldest of which appeared as early as the Babylonian era with the code of law that the god Shamash gave to the Babylonian king Hammurabi, who lived between 1792 and 1750 BC. The other great code of morality that swept the world of course is the Ten Commandments, a set of religious laws that was, it is believed, handed down to Moses by God, as described in Exodus 20:2–17 and Deuteronomy 5:6–21:

"I am the Lord your God, who brought you out of Egypt, out of the land of slavery.

"You shall have no other gods before me.

"You shall not make for yourself an image in the form of anything in heaven above or on the earth beneath or in the waters below. You shall not bow down to them or worship them; for I, the Lord your God, am a jealous God, punishing the children for the sin of the parents to the third and fourth generation of those who hate me, but showing love to a thousand generations of those who love me and keep my commandments.

"You shall not misuse the name of the Lord your God, for the Lord will not hold anyone guiltless who misuses his name.

"Remember the Sabbath day by keeping it holy. Six days you shall labour and do all your work, but the seventh day is a sabbath to the Lord your God. On it you shall not do any work, neither you, nor your son or daughter, nor your male or female servant, nor your animals, nor any foreigner residing in your towns. For in six days the Lord made the heavens and the earth, the sea, and all that is in them, but he rested on the seventh day. Therefore the Lord blessed the Sabbath day and made it holy.

"Honour your father and your mother, so that you may live long in the land the Lord your God is giving you.

"You shall not murder.

"You shall not commit adultery.

"You shall not steal.

"You shall not give false testimony against your neighbour.

"You shall not covet your neighbour's house. You shall not
covet your neighbour's wife, or his male or female servant, his ox
or donkey, or anything that belongs to your neighbour" (Exodus
20:2–17).

These Ten Commandments took a more prominent place in the
Christian faith after the thirteenth century. They reveal the morality of
the whole region of the Middle East at the time. Jesus Christ during his
life re-examined some of the commandments and reinterpreted them,
with the result that he created a new moral code, not as a law this time
but as a set of high moral principles. This re-evaluation is seen in what
is referred to as the Sermon on the Mount, as described in Matthew 5–7,
and the sermon on the plain in Luke 6:20–49. In these chapters, Jesus
turns the law into divine principles that we all strive to apply in our lives.
It is in fact an ethical compass that guides us when we engage with any
topic or social dilemma. As we live and breathe in our digital culture
of today, I find these divine principles that Jesus gave to be extremely
helpful in informing and enriching our ethical investigations and moral
decision-making.

How do we approach critically but lovingly the moral dilemmas that
our digital age presents to us? How can we implement the teachings of
the Lord when it comes to our relationships with each other in this highly
sophisticated technological age? Now more than ever, we need to rethink
the impact of digital technology on our lives and our relationships. In
order to be able to relate to the digital culture around us, we need to learn
how the Lord himself related to his own earthly culture. The relationship
between Jesus and our human culture is like the relationship between
salt and food. Out of this relationship, he asked us to be like him, saying:
"You are the salt of the earth. But if the salt loses its saltiness, how can
it be made salty again? It is no longer good for anything, except to be
thrown out and trampled underfoot" (Matthew 5:13).

We know that salt cannot have an impact on food unless it not only
touches the food, but is buried within it, so that it is dissolved and
enhances the flavour. The most important characteristic of salt is that it

does not point at itself. When we eat well-seasoned food, we don't say that this food is delicious because it is salty. It is delicious because the salt is balanced and allows the other components of the dish to reach their maximum flavour. It's not easy for us to enable others to give their best without taking the credit or without being visible and recognized. We live in a culture that idolizes individualism. Every one of us wants to shine brightly and every digital platform around us offers us this potential. The image of salt reflects values that lie at the heart of the Culture of God because it challenges our narcissistic human self-centredness. Salt metaphorically dies as something apart in order to allow the things around it to reach their full potential. Although salt dissolves, it is a powerful substance that alters the very structure of what it comes in contact with. It is an active agent that stirs things up. Without salt, food can taste bland and unappetizing.

This leads us to a similar metaphor, one that is referred to by St John in his narrative of the Gospel. We see Jesus talking about himself as a "kernel of wheat", saying "Very truly I tell you, unless a kernel of wheat falls to the ground and dies, it remains only a single seed. But if it dies, it produces many seeds" (John 12:24). Here, Jesus assumes that there are cracks in the ground that are necessary for the kernels of wheat to fall into. When the kernel falls inside, it interacts with the environment around it, where it absorbs moisture and nutrients. Eventually that seed dies in order to allow new life to spring up out of it. This new life is powerful enough to find its way to the surface and then grow. Jesus fell into the cracks of his culture and interacted with the environment around him. He also realized that his teachings and his project for a new humanity would not be accepted. He taught his disciples before he was arrested the meaning and the logic of Easter and prepared them for what was coming. Although they did not understand this logic before the cross and the resurrection, they later began to put the pieces together in order to see the full picture. The different narratives of the Gospel convey to us today this teaching of the meaning of Easter, which is the essence of the Culture of God.

Jesus, after his prayer in the Garden of Gethsemane, took the decision to obey his Father. That let him deep into the cracks in the ground so that the kernel of wheat could face the darkness of the ground. He who was the incarnation of the Culture of God faced alone the deepest corner of our humanity that led to his death on the cross. In the resurrection, on the morning of Easter Sunday, we see new life sprouting from the darkest days of humanity to give us the good news that the fruits of this kernel of wheat are enough for all humanity to feed on and enjoy a new quality of life with a new revelation of who God is. Today, amidst the madness of our highly technological culture, we see similar cracks and we are called to engage with those cracks. Although we shouldn't necessarily understand our role as literally dying in these cracks, we must face the darkness within this digital age.

The question is how should we "die" for our digital culture? We do this when we live every day trying to be Christ-like. In other words, when we try to be the incarnation of the Culture of God. One aspect that springs to mind as an example of this is in facing our fears. Fear is one of the most dangerous and challenging forces that can hinder our work in our lives. What do I mean by fear? One of our greatest fears today is the fear of being different, or fear of strangers or anyone who is not like me or does not agree with me. Facing that fear is essential in order to be Christ-like. Jesus overcame that fear through his faith and his relationship with God.

The Church of England, for example, admitted recently that it is a racist institution. That in itself was not a surprise for me, as I'm sure that it wasn't for many other people. I have lived and experienced that racism. One of the senior officials in the Church asked to see me one time as I had been brought to his attention. After several conversations, he told me to my enormous shock and surprise that I didn't fit in the Church and that it would be extremely difficult for people like me to find a place in the Church of England. When I asked him directly whether he was saying that the Church was a racist organization, he simply answered yes. This is a typical example of the fear that I mentioned earlier that we need to face head on. So many times in my ministry, I have seen fear in the eyes of people who hold senior positions in the Church. People like me who are outspoken and have broken through the barrier of fear are uncomfortable for an organization that, it seems to me, likes to be bland, offering few challenges and with an instinct not to cause waves. A Church like this can never be the salt that we are called to be and can never be the kernel of wheat that Jesus was. When we are afraid to face the darkness within the cracks in the earth, we become ourselves a crack that resists any seed that tries to grow and give new life. Although the Church of England has great men and women serving their communities, as an institution it has a huge fear of difference that hinders everybody from releasing their potential and playing the role of being the incarnation of the Culture of God in our current digital culture.

In the present age, although we live in a global digital revolution that impacts all cultures, fear of losing our local identity is still pervasive everywhere. The solution is not to erect barriers and build walls between ourselves and the world around us. On the contrary, it is to do as Jesus did when he decided to go through Samaria and personally meet the Samaritans, who were considered the Jews' worst enemies (as narrated in John 4). We see that fear led Peter to deny Christ (Luke 22:54–62). Peter was afraid to be associated with Jesus. He wanted to save his own skin. We also see that the rest of the disciples (except John) fled after Jesus was arrested because they were afraid. After the resurrection, we see them gathering in the upper room, scared to go out. The question that puzzles me here is what is the Church afraid of? Why is the Church of England resisting giving a bigger role and acknowledgement to people who are different? What are we protecting? And what are we afraid of losing?

Jesus tells us, after he speaks about being the kernel of wheat, that "Anyone who loves their life will lose it, while anyone who hates their life in this world will keep it for eternal life" (John 12:25). What does this mean in the Church today? It currently seems that it has no meaning. We love ourselves and love those who are like us. Those who are different apparently have no place in the life of the Church. If this is the situation inside the Church, how can we become the kernel of wheat facing the darkness of the culture that we are living in? In other words, if the salt has lost its saltiness what is it good for? Living in this sophisticated and highly technological culture demands that we renew our hearts and minds if we still want to be the force of the seed and the power of the salt.

It is our task to release the image of Jesus in our audio-visual culture today. This colossal task requires us to understand the complex reality of our human life. Our complex reality is governed by endless rules and regulations. Wherever we turn, we are faced by more rules and more instructions to follow. The only freedom we have that respects our human dignity and spirit is our faith in Christ. Our digital age requires society to move faster and faster into regulating our online/offline life and relationships. More and more voices are being raised to introduce more control over our interactions with our virtual and online existence. It has become even more challenging to find ways in which we can be Christ-like beyond the humanitarian actions that we usually revert to, like giving money to charity, attending church once a week, donating clothes to the poor or other actions that make us feel good about ourselves. Christianity is much more than that and these actions should be the natural outcome of living a life of faith in Christ.

In the Gospel according to John, Jesus says, "A new command I give you: Love one another. As I have loved you, so you must love one another" (John 13:34). This commandment is not about ethics or morality. It describes an existential state of being. St John speaks a lot in his writings about abiding in God or Christ, which means being united with Christ. In John chapter 15, Jesus says, "I am the true vine, and my Father is the gardener. He cuts off every branch in me that bears no fruit, while every branch that does bear fruit he prunes so that it will be even more fruitful" (John 15:1–2). These verses appear harsh because they involve cutting or pruning. Both the fruitful and unfruitful branches will be cut, but in different ways. The branches that do not bear fruit will be cut from the base and will be removed entirely from the vine. Those that do bear fruit will also be cut, but this time the aim is not to remove them but to inject them with new power to be fruitful. For God, being fruitful is not enough. He wants us to exceed our limitations and our abilities, and this is only possible if we, as St Paul says, do not live as we live but as Christ lives in us. Pruning also prevents the branch from wasting its energy by growing out of control or in different directions.

It is very important to continue with St John's text. If we look at verse 7, Jesus says, "If you remain in me and my words remain in you, ask whatever you wish, and it will be done for you. This is to my Father's glory, that you bear much fruit, showing yourselves to be my disciples" (John 15:7–8). What does this mean? It means that in order to be his disciples, we need to absorb and understand and abide in his word. We should not forget that after the resurrection and the ascension, he gave us the greatest gift, which is the Holy Spirit. That gift tells us that we cannot do anything relying solely on our own power. In this time, we have become a branch fixed to the vine of digital technology around us, feeling that there is no escape. We must remember that the true sap of life does not come from the vine of the culture of digital technology but from the vine that is Jesus Christ. Being a branch of the true vine does not alienate us from our culture but empowers us to influence that culture and bear witness to the true vine.

The Son of God became human in order to provide us with the real vine that carries our own nature. Because of that and coming from someone who suffered like us, we have the sap that strengthens us not only on a spiritual level but on a practical, day-to-day level. When we rely on that sap and allow the power of the Holy Spirit to work in us, we not only become fruitful but fruitful beyond our expectations. When we are aware of our attachment to the true vine, everything that comes out of us becomes the fruit of that attachment. The process of making decisions in life becomes empowered by this attachment. This is what I mean by saying that Jesus' commandment to love each other is not about being a good Christian but is about being witnesses to the work of God in Christ. Jesus is the kernel of wheat who died facing the darkness of humanity so that death for us is only a stepping stone to a new quality of life.

Many people find it very hard to forgive when they are deeply hurt, for example. It is indeed very difficult to forgive because the pain within us prevents us from taking this step towards forgiveness. Once I recognize my position in Christ and acknowledge that I am a branch of the true vine, what is humanly impossible becomes possible. Only through the strength that I get from the vine and through the strength of the Holy Spirit in me can I break through the barriers of pain and set myself free from the prison of anger and hate. I can in turn set the other free from my darkness and this is what I call forgiveness. Forgiveness is not a normal human act but is a divinely supported human act. It is the power that allows me to go beyond what is possible humanly speaking and move from being fruitful to being more fruitful. The word "more" here signifies the breakdown of my limitations.

I have noticed that many people immediately resort to using technology to hurt others in return. More than ever, I feel that we need to look into the power of forgiveness at a time when you can hurt someone through the press of a button. There are many ways in which we can hurt each other using the technology at our disposal, from sending an angry email to reacting to an online comment or image. We have seen people hurting each other by distributing pictures, or messages, or hacking into another's digital accounts. Technology has also facilitated the online distribution of acts of extreme violence and terror. With all this technology at our fingertips we need more than ever the fruit of the Spirit as St Paul describes it in Galatians 5:22:

> But the fruit of the Spirit is love, joy, peace, forbearance, kindness, goodness, faithfulness.

The availability of technology must come with huge responsibility and the ability to slow down our anger and embrace the gift of the Spirit, which is forbearance. I remember when I received a hurtful email, my dear friend Bishop Michael Marshall, who was a co-founder and president of the Awareness Foundation, stopped me from responding immediately to it and told me to wait, sleep on it and return to the email tomorrow. It felt difficult to wait twenty-four hours, especially when the hurt was so visceral. The following day, however, I felt completely different on approaching the same email. Since then, I have trained myself to wait before responding to any emotionally charged email right away and instead take time to reflect on a response.

We see a lot of anger, character assassinations and virtual violence across the digital platforms that we live in. We react impulsively to hurtful messages and any hostility facing us, and our instinct is to hit back. That is often a knee-jerk reaction. What I mean about living in Christ is recognizing that I can hit back but that I choose not to. This is not about turning the other cheek but about managing your anger and having the ability to deal with the pressure of instant communication and instant gratification by not giving in to the temptation to return the hurt. The temptations of our digital culture are different from the ones we had before. The danger here is if we act impulsively. The way that the digital culture pushes us to act or react can be handled differently if we exist in the Culture of God and within the true vine.

Facing the dark corners of our digital world as Jesus did cannot be determined by an ethical system that frees us from the fear of facing the evil around us. When we embrace the Culture of God that is in the person and the teachings of Jesus Christ, we become empowered by the Holy Spirit (not by a moral system) to engage with the digital world around us. Our relationship with the living Christ and being rooted in him empower us to live this continuous dialogue between the cross and the resurrection as we live our lives today. We are constantly experiencing the cross that manifests itself in this hectic and stressful life—as well as the inner peace that creates a space in our hearts for overcoming the pressure that may break us.

We have all experienced, especially during the pandemic, the pain of being ill, of losing loved ones, or the breakdown of relationships, losing our jobs and feeling isolated despite the digital technology that surrounds us. This accumulation of stress can generate fear in our lives, but we need to understand that being in Christ must make a difference in how we deal with this by remembering that we are not alone, that we are in partnership with Christ. Sometimes life today makes us forget this partnership and makes us feel that we have to find solutions ourselves. But it is not me, but us. It is God and me, and it is that that makes the difference that allows us to break through the fear and darkness. When we reach out in acts of kindness and mercy to help others, it is not because we want to be good or that it's morally or ethically required. We do it because it flows out of our being in Christ and our being in the Culture of God. The Culture of God is the culture of mercy, of kindness, of peace—not a set of ethical rules that we follow—and this allows us to face our own fears and our own cross in life through the power of the resurrection that is the essence of the Culture of God.

The difference between being "civilized" and being technologically advanced

We should be aware, before using the word "civilization", that this concept cannot be understood straightforwardly. Indeed, its meaning in this context is not easy to pin down. Civilization can mean cultural values and the journey of human evolution but, for some people, it can also carry the heavy burden of colonial association and a certain feeling of superiority. I want to use the word in all its controversial context because the human journey itself is also controversial and full of paradoxes and contradictions. Coming from the Middle East, as much as I observed how households there evolved technologically, making life more comfortable, I also noted how the region plunged into the dehumanization of societies through endless conflicts and wars powered by generations of advanced weaponry.

I remember vividly when my mother, having had six children and two sets of twins, trying to cope with washing and cleaning and looking after a big family with minimum help from technology, first bought an electric washing machine in the late 1960s. This made a huge difference to my mother, who was also a seamstress. This machine revolutionized the way in which she organized her time. When the electric oven arrived, this represented another leap forward in our lives. I remember the excitement in the community when mum bought a pressure cooker. These little things brought a lot of comfort and ease to families everywhere. At the same time, the leaps of technology that the region experienced were also marked by the succession of various wars in 1948, 1967, 1973 and 1980. We saw revolutionary advancements in armaments, making it easier to kill more people and cause colossal damage. Now we have smart weapons and remote technology with drones that are being tried out in conflicts in the Middle East, most recently in Syria, Iraq and Yemen.

Having lived through all that, I have seen how the creativity of the human mind can enrich our life experiences and make us more comfortable, but this creativity can also be weaponized to create even more damage and destruction. Experiencing both sides of the human mind has made me think, what makes us human? If we believe that God created us in his image, where do we see the image of God? Of course, we all think that it is impossible to see the hand of God in the dark side of human creativity. The possession of highly advanced armaments brings with it power and the temptation to dominate people and nations. If I look at the war that has been raging for more than twelve years in Syria and think of all the tools of destruction that have been used by different international powers to manipulate groups inside Syria, the result of all this is to make me wonder what direction our humanity is going in.

I still believe that the weapons trade and business have a radical influence on the world economy. I believe that we must be able to resolve our conflicts or differences by peaceful means, without reverting to violence using all the advanced technological weapons of destruction that we have invented. For the most part, the advancement of digital technology does not show the true image of our humanity. We abuse this technology in order to control diminishing natural resources. For example, finding huge reservoirs of oil and gas in the Mediterranean Sea in the last few decades has engulfed the whole region in a vicious competition to control these resources. The peoples of the Near East are suffering the most horrendous consequences of the fight between international powers for these resources. Religion is dragged into this feverish struggle for resources, creating further tension and conflict.

These conflicts become a mirror that reflects our broken humanity and how far we fall short of the love of God. The contradictions that we see in how we use digital technology leads us to our role as cultured and faithful human beings who believe in the power of love that can transform our hearts and minds. This power that is available to all should be used to challenge the abuse of technology and the evil race to dominate that some governments are trying to force on other countries and nations. As citizens of the Culture of God, the Culture of love and the Culture of the Trinity, it is our responsibility to seek ways in which humanity can manifest the love and the light that comes from the Culture of God. You may think that I am talking theoretically, but I have seen with my own eyes the power of God to transform especially young lives and make them ambassadors for peace and reconciliation in their broken communities.

It might appear as if we are trying to stop a tank by throwing a flower at it. I argue that the more flowers that we put in the hands of young people and empower them to turn these flowers into pen and paper, the more we can stand against the invasion of tanks and machine guns. I have experienced for myself how young people, using simple digital technology, are able to create life-changing initiatives within their communities to serve the suffering. I still believe with every fibre of my being that when the Culture of God breaks in and touches people's lives, we see moments of transfiguration. These young people are a mirror that reflects the transforming power of love and goodness. When the Culture of God becomes the sap that feeds a whole generation, we see how people can exceed their limits and break the barriers of what they thought possible. What is possible in our eyes can be more than possible for those armed with the Culture of God, with the faith that their humanity cannot be manipulated by technology or religion.

Humanity is filled with the work of something beyond us but within us, something outside us but also in the depths of our being. This special something is the work of the Holy Spirit that brings the culture of love, the culture of God to be united with our fragile human culture. Being civilized is not about imperial power or a sense of superiority of one nation or people over another. In this case, being civilized means being aware of the meaning of our humanity in relation to each other and at the same time to the love of God as revealed in the life, the cross and the resurrection of Jesus Christ.

Sometimes we think that because we are highly advanced technologically that makes us better. Most of the time, technology gives us power, but that does not mean that we are better or more human than those who have no technology. I have experienced this confusion between possessing sophisticated technology and thinking that we are above others. This confusion is very dangerous. Our humanity is not measured by the advancement of technology but rather by the impact of this technology, not only in improving our lives but in using it to help those who have less. I have also seen when technology is used as a camouflage to cover insecurity with a fake sense of power and superiority. On the other hand, I have also seen the work of technology in spreading prosperity and generosity. The advancement of technology is not what makes us human, but how it is used to spread peace and defeat illness and poverty.

Unfortunately, if I look at the region where I come from, I see that humanity has failed to reflect the positive side of technology. If we look at the world today, we see the feverish race to exploit resources and impose war and pain in places where these resources are found. This is totally the opposite of what advanced technology should and could do. Technology is not put to the service of humanity but rather has been used to create wars, spy on each other, and hack systems to exploit people and resources. People of faith have the responsibility to stand together against this new technological war and push governments to change their attitude regarding how to use the earth's resources.

Now more than ever, we see how small the planet is, how fragile it is and how insignificant and vulnerable we are in relation to the universe. Coming from a region like the Near East taught me to value faith and its role in making technology more humane. At the same time, it makes me critical and suspicious regarding the role of religion that can be manipulated to create more tension and more polarization, especially using advanced technology today. The journey has just started for us as human beings to live together and use our abilities and technological inventions for the service of all humanity, to lead a better life as God wants us to.

5

The Culture of God in Social Media

Jesus and his disciples went on to the villages around Caesarea Philippi. On the way he asked them, "Who do people say I am?" (Mark 8:27)

In this verse, we see that Jesus cared about what people thought of him and wanted to know the impact he had had on them. He was also interested in the image that he presented in people's minds and what kind of person he was for them. I feel that this was uncharacteristic of Jesus to care what people thought of him personally. It tells us that the identity that we share with other people does matter. Most of the time, we can't be sure if people see us the way we see ourselves. Jesus knew that people didn't recognize his identity and recognize who he truly was. So, he turned to the closest people around him: "'But what about you?' he asked. 'Who do you say I am?'" (Mark 8:29).

It's understandable that the general public wouldn't know who he was, but his challenge was to those nearest to him to discover whether they were the same as everyone else. After he posed that question and Peter's answer that he was the Messiah, Jesus opened his mind to them and shared the mind of God with them. At this point, the culture of God and their culture were not in harmony. When Jesus told them that he must suffer and die and rise again, they couldn't accept it. They didn't believe it because they didn't want to believe it. This incident reflects for me Jesus' social media moment, caring about what people thought about him and how he communicated with them.

Mark, the writer of this Gospel, shows us that Jesus cares what people think despite the fact that they are unaware of his true mission. Jesus was always aware of the image he projected and his communication with other people. His interaction with society was on different levels. Sometimes, his "social media strategy" was to communicate his thoughts through short stories or what we call the parables of Jesus, which are perfect tools for modern forms of communication like YouTube or Facebook. At other times, he spoke directly, for example in his Sermon on the Mount in the Gospel according to Matthew. This sermon would also be incredibly impressive as a thread on Twitter.

At that time, social communication was through the spoken word. Jesus embraced the art of the spoken word and I believe consciously chose not to write things down himself. Throughout his life, I imagine that there were many incidents that I would have loved to film; like, for example, when he met with Nicodemus at night. Such an image could speak volumes. Or when the woman sinner kissed his feet. That moment was beyond description and has captured the imagination of many great artists. In today's social media world that image would be sensational on Instagram.

St John went in a completely different direction in communicating the message of the Gospel and in portraying Jesus Christ. For him, the self-communication of God with humanity was the ultimate form of social media. God stopped sending messages to tell us what he wanted and instead decided to be the message himself in the form of Jesus Christ. John tells us beautifully that the clearest form of social media was when "The Word became flesh and made his dwelling among us" (John 1:14). John reveals this cosmic event when God the Almighty, who is beyond time and space, the Creator of everything, socialized with us and became one of us. This is what John means by "made his dwelling among us".

When we talk about social media, we are talking about community communication. With the incarnation, God communicated himself to the community of humanity. This communication that God chose was not via highly technological devices but via personal encounter. When we study this important field of modern-day human communication, we shouldn't forget that as Christians we must look at it while bearing in mind the perspective of the incarnation.

In Luke 8, we read of the incredible story of the woman who suffers from haemorrhaging. She decides to follow behind Jesus with the desire to touch the hem of his garment so that she might be healed. This story reminds me of our relationship with digital technology, with the digital devices that we use daily representing the edge of the garment of our digital culture. The woman wanted healing without being exposed to the crowd or directly interacting with Jesus. Likewise, most of us want to interact with digital devices and the various social media platforms that they offer without being exposed. We seek some kind of healing through using or being part of the digital culture. Social media itself, including all its platforms, past, present and future, is amoral. These platforms are tools waiting to be used and it is for us to decide how to use them.

Being social beings is part of the divine purpose of humanity. We are created to be social and to form communities. One of the inevitable consequences of being social is to communicate with one another. Early communication was verbal, through storytelling. This profound art form is millennia old. Even the early cave paintings told stories of humanity's experience. I remember going for the first time to the National Museum of Syria in Damascus and seeing the piece of clay inscribed with cuneiform, the first known alphabet in history. Ugarit (or Ras Al Shamra) was the first historic site that I ever visited, at six years old. It lies less than six kilometres from where I grew up in Lattakia. We were told at the museum that a librarian in Ugarit inscribed the entire cuneiform alphabet on a tiny piece of clay as a tool to teach his students reading and writing. I was deeply moved standing in front of this piece and couldn't help becoming emotional. My first thought was that it was not much bigger than my mobile that I can use to communicate with the whole world.

Even after thousands of years, we are still using language and images to communicate with each other, exactly like this librarian in Ugarit and the early cave-dwelling humans. Can we say that the cave walls millions of years ago were the first visual form of social media that early humans used to communicate their life, feelings and social activities? Throughout history, people have memorized stories and passed them down orally from one generation to another. That was their way of preserving their faith and traditions. Even Jesus Christ, it seems, refused to write down his teachings. Media later became a critical field that channelled stories and news all over the world. Written and audio-visual media has played a vital role in forming our social conscience and has influenced societies all over the world.

People used to trust the media more in the past. Stories used to be passed on from the few who were trained in this field, and were present at an event, to the many millions of readers and listeners. Today, this communication is no longer passed down by the few but by the many, with an even wider coverage. We also have the opportunity today to look at the same incident from multiple perspectives rather than rely on one particular source. News has stopped being the exclusive job of journalists. People can report instantly via their smartphones anywhere and everywhere they are. This does not of course replace professional reporting, especially by those who have built their credibility through hard work and dedication to their field. It is important to also note that breaking stories is not just the job of journalists. For example, the video clip that captured the largest non-nuclear explosion in history, that happened on 4 August 2020 in Beirut, was taken on the mobile phone of a bystander and was broadcast millions of times around the world.

The fact that we can send and receive news and commentary via small devices that we can put in our pockets has changed our lives forever. We are able to trace each other and be traced in return wherever we are around the world. It is possible to track everything and anything that we do online, for different purposes. We are all part of an enormous flow of data whether we like it or not. How far have we compromised our privacy without fully being aware of it? Of course, it is amazing to be able to communicate with our friends and families anytime we want day and night. It is also tempting to surrender to the comfort and convenience that social media and life online offers, but I believe that nothing can be offered for free.

There are many priceless advantages to having a life online. Moreover, we cannot undo or easily opt out of this digital culture. What we can do is to reconcile our digital culture with the Culture of God. Our God is not only the Lord of our lives; he is also the Lord of time, of past, present and future. The Culture of God can lie at the heart of living in the modern age, not only through talking about ethics but more profoundly through inviting the Culture of the Trinity, or the Culture of love, to help us shape this digital culture so that we do not become slaves to it but instead use it to reflect the image and message of God through the life and teachings of the person of Jesus Christ. It comes to my mind that being loved by God is truly unconditional and free. God expects nothing from us because we have the freedom to reject him. In the feverish world of social media, we always feel that we need to do something either to respond to something good or strike out at something bad. In the Culture of God, communication and social media aren't based on a revenge or reward model. When we receive love in that culture, we only need to learn how to be thankful.

We live today in isolated bubbles that we create by being in groups that share our views. We can easily avoid those who are different or who disagree with us. This is not how social media works in the Culture of God. God is calling us to live with and love our differences. The Trinity gives us the model for diversity that lies at the heart of the divine creation. God calls us to remember not to surrender our freedom and our lives to the service of social media, but rather it is up to us to decide how to use the tools and technology in our service. Social media platforms are gateways to different worlds that invite us to enter, but we need to keep in mind that these gateways are created and controlled by large, powerful companies that have their own commercial agenda. We need to remind ourselves that these companies are not beyond criticism. Collectively, we need to influence their direction by putting pressure on them and raising awareness of what is happening. We need to create an awareness that without us these companies cannot exist and that we are willing to raise the alarm when things go wrong.

The first task is to realize that these social media companies are neither invincible nor indispensable. We have learned over the last twenty years that social media platforms appear and disappear as new ideas emerge. Some platforms flourish and survive, while some don't. So, we shouldn't become too attached to any one platform. With all these warnings, though, we should also be grateful that God has given us the gifts to create these gateways into other worlds in order to improve the quality of our lives. There are many advantages that we should acknowledge. One of these is the interconnectivity that social media provides. We can't ignore the colossal impact of this feeling of being connected. For me personally, this connection has been profoundly important, not only in my personal life but also in my work at the Foundation. Through social media, we have connected with thousands of young people either living in or fleeing from war zones in the Middle East. At the height of the Covid pandemic in 2020, we were able to launch a programme called Awareness Live that engaged with tens of thousands of young people around the world and opened a dialogue with them about how to be agents and ambassadors for peace wherever they are. This would not have been possible without social media.

Social media is, in many ways, a beacon of education, especially by making it possible to directly access key figures in science, art and education to know their minds about the issues that concern them. They are a fount of knowledge and wisdom for millions of people. Social media platforms allow people to share their knowledge, skills and experiences at every level. We don't hesitate to go to YouTube, Tik Tok or other channels to learn a range of skills from how to bake a loaf of bread to how to build a robot. Social media can also be a profound source of support and encouragement. There is a great sense of comfort to be had from mixing with and sharing ideas with people who share similar experiences to you—either physical, sexual or cultural. Conversely, it can also be refreshing to interact with people you would be unlikely to meet in real life who offer a window into another world and ideas that can enrich and inform.

People with disabilities who without social media might never have the opportunity to communicate widely are given a platform to touch the lives of many and share their deepest thoughts to help both themselves and those who would otherwise feel isolated. Social media also provides the opportunity to form different support groups for those who need help psychologically, physically or spiritually. Something that is close to my ministry personally is the field of mental health, as we try to help young people living in areas of conflict. Social media can be a great source of support for those who suffer from various mental challenges. It is possible for people to access help and information whenever they need. A friend of mine was contacted by someone who was feeling suicidal. Through the ability to access direct contact through social media, my friend was able to save this person's life without him having to expose his identity.

Social media has also played a major role in natural disaster relief. A priest friend of mine first encountered Facebook when his parish was struck by a major earthquake. Facebook allowed him to connect with people to organize the relief work and offer invaluable information and advice. All this is thanks to one of social media's finest qualities: its ability to respond quickly to events and provide up-to-the-minute information and connections via the growth in eyewitness journalism by passers-by recording events on their mobile phones. The most potent example of this is the death of George Floyd in Minneapolis. The iconic footage of Floyd being held down with a knee on his neck led not only to worldwide outrage and the growth of the BlackLivesMatter movement, but also to the arrest and conviction of a white police officer for his murder. The fact that several governments around the world seek to restrict social media platforms indicates that they too understand well the range and impact of these platforms.

The use of the word "social" to describe this technology highlights its role in helping people to connect with others, something that has been vital in the years of the Covid pandemic with worldwide lockdowns. Unable to meet in person, friends and family can still meet virtually, offering some outlet for the loneliness and isolation endemic in lockdowns. Social media now has a prominent role in the cultural lives of people. I have seen powerful messages conveyed in short videos or text or single photos. When we communicate in this way, this helps us to create a defence of the vulnerable and the marginalized in society. We have the opportunity to be the voice of balance in a world of extremes. Being engaged with social media on a daily basis, I see that one of the most encouraging aspects of it is that it allows people to express their dreams and aspirations and their hopes for the future. This reminds me of the revelation of St Paul:

> Brothers and sisters, I do not consider myself yet to have taken hold of it. But one thing I do: Forgetting what is behind and straining toward what is ahead, I press on toward the goal to win the prize for which God has called me heavenward in Christ Jesus (Philippians 3:13–14).

Jesus reaches out to us from the future. Although we look at the story of the past, we meet him through going forward and through reaching out to what is to come. I am sure that social media will continue to develop, with different ideas emerging to rock our world. We will always be engaging with new ideas and new platforms on social media. As a result, we need to be firmly rooted in the Culture of God so we can prayerfully deal with whatever this emerging media throws at us.

However we use these platforms, we need to understand that they carry some serious risks in turning into quick fix solutions; for example, through using them as tools for revenge or harassment. They also carry the risk of helping us to build walls between people or allowing people to hide behind fake masks that hide their true identity. On the other hand, social media provides us with incredible opportunities to share our thoughts instantaneously with the whole world. Different social media platforms play the role of an amplifier and can take a small idea and give it a life and a reach that touches millions of other minds. The idea is amplified in two ways: by reaching those who are active on the platform and can spread it further, and also by reaching those who are less active but who are passive recipients. In both cases, the seed of the idea is implanted and grows.

Some ideas not only take off but also generate discussion and engagement. This is when social media platforms become transformative. Jesus Christ was a radical character and quite controversial in his time. He interacted with people on many levels and touched their lives either physically as a healer, socially as a storyteller of parables that challenged the social norms, or spiritually in his arguments and discussions with the spiritual leaders of the time. In a way, Jesus was the social media star of his time who threatened the political and religious establishment through his courage and boldness in communicating what he thought of them. In our digital culture, we see that both broadcast and digital media like controversial figures who generate discussion and engagement. Even today, both the political and religious establishment are threatened by radical figures gaining attention. Even after two thousand years, we have not learnt as a Church to appreciate outspoken and radical views or people.

I am clearly not suggesting that every radical person is like Christ. What I'm saying is that social media platforms have allowed different influencers to surface in every walk of life. After two thousand years, we still publish hundreds of books every year trying to determine who said what and why in the Bible, and are still arguing over which epistles St Paul really wrote or who was the writer of particular passages of the Gospel. Before social media, we would buy magazines featuring an article about a celebrity we liked. Today, we do not need to read so much about celebrities or politicians; instead, these people now have direct access to their followers through their own social media accounts.

We all remember how President Donald Trump used his Twitter account to reach people directly without needing to go through media interviews or statements in the Senate. He could release comments in the middle of the night from his bedroom or even, allegedly, from his bathroom. Celebrity culture has grown organically from traditional media to a variety of social media platforms to continue influencing hundreds of millions of people. There are still a huge number of people who follow the example of the celebrities they like down to the last details of what they wear, what they eat or what they drink. Our digital culture will continue to develop new and more advanced social media platforms and our lives will continue to be pressurized by having to cope with this feverish journey.

If we take our faith in Christ seriously, we must pause and reflect on how much we are the product of digital media and what image of humanity social media reflects back at us? Whatever our age, we are orbiting the gravity pull of digital technology that influences our lives dramatically in different ways. Social media is one of the most important fields of modern-day communication that defines the intersection between digital technology and human life. I believe that the more we advance in developing digital technology, the more advanced platforms will appear and disappear, and this picture is constantly changing. Because of that, we need to slow down and reflect on where we are.

Communication in general is a minefield. We need to navigate it so that we do not get hurt or hurt others. Social media can be a vicious and destructive power when used irresponsibly to hurt someone or something. At the same time, it can be an enormously creative and uplifting source of thoughts and images. This reminds me of St Paul's words to the Corinthians:

> "I have the right to do anything," you say—but not everything is beneficial. "I have the right to do anything"—but not everything is constructive (1 Corinthians 10:23).

Living with the digital technology around us gives us a sense of responsibility. When you communicate via social media, you are not talking privately with a dear friend but with potentially a much wider circle of people who may not share your own cultural background and beliefs. This is especially true when the message that we want to communicate results from our anger or frustration or the particular mood we are in. Being in the Culture of God as well as living in a technologically advanced world gives us the space to allow God to guide us in our communication. The Culture of God redefines our responsibility. God is a community and decided to enter our realm of existence through Christ in order to surround us with the essence of that loving culture. Love in its deepest form is communication and a relationship with the other.

When we talk about social media, we are talking about community communication, which is the heart of the divine culture. It is also a powerful source of information about what is happening around us. When we are active on any social media platform, the question is whether we are aware that we are also living and active in this partnership with God, the partnership of love through Christ. The two should be inseparable. How much margin do we give God to reveal to us his will? I love the passage in St Paul's letter to the Romans in which he says:

> Do not conform to the pattern of this world, but be transformed by the renewing of your mind. Then you will be able to test and approve what God's will is—his good, pleasing and perfect will (Romans 12:2).

These words of St Paul are powerful in the world of social media. When he says, "Do not conform to the pattern of this world", it means do not let the world take over and push you away from God. St Paul also raises the important question of renewal. When we live in such a changing world as the one today, we need this renewal to happen continuously. The question is how do I know the will of God? Is it the will of God for me to use Twitter or Facebook or Instagram? I often think about the reason why people revert to using social media anonymously. They treat this field of communication as a form of role play and use it on occasion to destroy other people's lives with no one knowing who they really are. When St Paul asks us not to be conformed to this world, he is asking us to question the ways that we use all the communication tools at our fingertips.

What do I write or say when I know that my identity is hidden? Who guides our words and actions when we are able to say or do things without exposing ourselves? This leads us to one of the basic questions of social media, which is why do we change our personality when we use these platforms? Some people say that they hide their true identity because they want to protect themselves. But from what? Don't we know that when we put our thoughts or images on social media that will understandably invite reactions? And that we will not like some of these reactions? I understand that sometimes we try to hide our identity when we give political or religious opinions, especially in some parts of the world, including in the Middle East. Some political or religious views could be life-threatening. Other times, people might be worried about bullying or about personal attacks that force them to hide behind a fake identity. My impression is that these platforms are a jungle rather than an ordered environment based on a set of rules. In a jungle, we live in constant fear of being attacked or exposed. This environment also allows us to nurture our aggressive side without fear of repercussion. This leads us to lower our inhibitions around hurting others, especially by reacting instantly and sometimes thoughtlessly to a particular situation.

The Culture of God doesn't regulate social media but instead challenges our motivations in being part of this world of communication. Jesus Christ showed us how important it is to be the children of light and to walk in the light:

> "Believe in the light while you have the light, so that you may become children of light." When he had finished speaking, Jesus left and hid himself from them (John 12:36).

Social media can extract the best and the worst from us. How ready are we to walk in the light in today's world? Many people believe that in our aggressive digital world there is little place for kindness and compassion. Others believe that it is a golden opportunity for us to show the world that we are indeed the children of the light. St Paul affirms that when he says in his letter to the Ephesians: "For you were once darkness, but now you are light in the Lord. Live as children of light (for the fruit of the light consists in all goodness, righteousness and truth) and find out what pleases the Lord. Have nothing to do with the fruitless deeds of darkness, but rather expose them" (Ephesians 5:8–11). In order to be the children of the light and walk in the light, we need to feel that God, who is light, is ruling our hearts and thoughts even when we are interacting with the world anonymously or if for some reason we need to hide our identity.

I believe that what comes out of us reflects the image of our hearts. When Jesus rejected cleansing rituals like washing hands before eating, he did not mean to discourage hygiene but instead rejected the idea of cleaning the surface without paying attention to our hearts and minds. In Mark 7, the Pharisees and scribes complained to Jesus when they saw some of his disciples eating bread without washing their hands. Jews at that time had a lot of religious rituals around cleaning everything from kitchen equipment to their bodies. Jesus was questioned why his followers didn't follow the traditions of their elders. They thought that this omission would embarrass him, but Jesus turned to them and said: "Isaiah was right when he prophesied about you hypocrites; as it is written: 'These people honour me with their lips, but their hearts are far from me'" (Mark 7:6).

Jesus was upset when people looked at unimportant details and ignored the meaningful side of their relationship with God. He called to the people around him and said: "Nothing outside a person can defile them by going into them. Rather, it is what comes out of a person that defiles them" (Mark 7:15). This verse applies perfectly to our relationship with social media. When we sit in the comfort of our homes interacting with the world virtually and decide to react or act, we need to remember that verse. We must control the quality of what comes out of us because what we say and do, whether people know who we are or don't, represents our hearts. It is enough that we know the truth of this, even if others don't. When we know that our words can hurt other people, how does this make us feel even if our true identity is not exposed? In this case, we are not the children of light with clean hearts and minds.

Social media is like any other method of communication, a gateway to a world that we need to explore carefully and interact with aware that we have a serious responsibility to behave knowing that our true self could be revealed and that that revelation may be a shock to us. I remember a dear friend telling me that he didn't know that he could be so vicious in his reactions until he started using social media, and that he was shocked and disturbed by this. "Why didn't I know that about myself before?" he questioned. What disturbed him most was the pleasure he felt in observing the effect of his vicious comments. He felt that his Christian faith had not illuminated all the spaces within him. In this case, the danger is when we discover the dark places within our personality that can be revealed when we interact with social media. These dark places are revealed because our reactions can sometimes be impulsive and reactive to certain situations in our lives. Because everything tends to be instant in social media, sometimes people have no control over their actions.

For me, what was interesting was when my friend told me that he was terrified that he considered his ability to destroy people through social media as entertainment, forgetting about the dignity of the person. When the divine culture encountered human culture in Christ, God revealed how his love respects human dignity. The Culture of God stands up against the destruction of life. The cross and the resurrection have taught us a new lesson about the sanctity of life. When we look at the different social media platforms, we can see that many people seek to be provocative in their interactions as a way to stand out and be noticed. The real challenge, however, is to respect human dignity and rights even when we want to be provocative. St Paul puts it thus:

> Let your conversation be always full of grace, seasoned with salt,
> so that you may know how to answer everyone (Colossians 4:6).

St Paul is suggesting that we invite the grace of God to be present in all our communication. But what is the grace of God? Grace means gift. This gift is nothing less in Christianity than God himself, as God, in Christ, communicated himself to the world. So, when we invite the grace of God to be present in our communication, we are inviting the divine culture to dwell in it. When that happens, the Culture of God rejuvenates and sanctifies our communication. In the Christian faith, the grace of God is the fruit of the Spirit. St Paul tells us what these fruits are:

> But the fruit of the Spirit is love, joy, peace, forbearance, kindness, goodness, faithfulness, gentleness and self-control(Galatians 5:22–23).

This does not mean that our communication on social media should be overly nice or bland. I do believe that we can create powerful content without being vicious or destructive. When we read articles in respected newspapers or magazines, we can find writers who apply certain filters to their writing that allow their argument to be powerful and even scandalous but presented in a respectful manner. Many people on social media claim to be experts on any number of subjects without thinking or caring about the impact of their thoughts on vulnerable people. We must also be careful to recognize that many posts on social media are propaganda from sources such as government, businesses or individuals. We all remember the scandals around how big companies use data to try to manipulate people through targeted content. Anyone can be a victim of such propaganda. Most of us don't have the patience to fact-check the sources, so enthusiastically spread this propaganda unthinkingly because it conforms to our views. We would like it to be true, so spread it without checking first.

This reminds me of the epistle of St James, in which he writes:

> My dear brothers and sisters, take note of this: Everyone should be quick to listen, slow to speak and slow to become angry (James 1:19).

The Culture of God also, by opening our hearts and minds to the presence of God, empowers us to be critical thinkers. We stop being naive in the way we communicate, and we learn how to deal with things through the wisdom that we receive through God. This is what makes us different from the world, as St Paul says to the Ephesians:

Be very careful, then, how you live—not as unwise but as wise,
making the most of every opportunity, because the days are evil
(Ephesians 5:15–16).

Communication on all social media platforms has become extremely
complex, to the extent that it has become almost impossible to distinguish
what is poisonous from what is nourishing. We have all experienced this
during the Covid pandemic. We have seen the enormous exchange of
opinions about the origins of the virus, its spread, potential cures and
then of course the endless conspiracy theories around the vaccines. I
could not believe how many people believed that the vaccine contained
a chip that controlled you or that it changed your DNA. Many people
have fallen victim to this poisonous belief. Such beliefs have spread far
and wide throughout the world of social media. People who believe in
these conspiracy theories have used digital technology to spread the truth
of their beliefs as they see it. Many other people have felt torn between
these competing theories and ideologies. As believers in Christ, we are
called to examine these various theories before we rush into taking sides.

Living in such a sophisticated technological age demands that we
who believe in God and his saving act in Jesus Christ are agents of peace
and reconciliation. It is no longer enough to conduct our relationships
according to the principles of the Culture of God in our lives; these
principles must also be extended to our virtual lives. For God, reality
is more important than ideas. The thought of the incarnation was not
enough for God, but the thought became a decision and a reality in
Christ. Through making this idea a reality, God offered himself to us.

Jesus Christ, in his own earthly culture and through his life and
teachings, has taught us that it is possible to live in both cultures
simultaneously. The resurrection of Christ is the eternal invitation of God
to all of us that the saving work that has been achieved by the crucified
and Risen Lord is still at work in the hearts and lives of believers. Today
we are able, not through our own power but through the power of the
Risen Lord, to live in both cultures. This leads us away from being selfish
and self-centred, which are two of the biggest temptations of our digital
culture. It is our responsibility, as we communicate with the world

through our relationships or via social media platforms, to be beacons of light that reflect the power of the divine culture. As Christ asked us to do:

> In the same way, let your light shine before others, that they may see your good deeds and glorify your Father in heaven (Matthew 5:16).

I join my cry in the virtual world as well as the real world with St Paul when he says: "Let us therefore make every effort to do what leads to peace and to mutual edification" (Romans 14:19).

6

Identity crisis: who are we in the digital world?

As we approach this exciting topic—the relationship between the Risen Lord and the cosmos based on new scientific explorations—we need to define some concepts and narrow down the focus of our discussion from what is a wide-ranging issue. For the last five years, one of my dreams has been to present this topic at the London Planetarium with an audio-visual discussion about the Risen Lord and the universe. I believe that Jesus Christ, the crucified and Risen Lord, is the Lord of the universe. We need to define the word "universe". Scientifically, there are different definitions. One of them regards the universe as one whole, regardless of the fact that it is expanding or shrinking and regardless of the phenomena within it like black holes and supernovas. Another theory suggests that we have baby universes, different universes that are not connected. Maybe, it is argued, we will one day be able to connect with another universe.

All these scientific theories don't diminish the fact of a Creator. The God that we believe in is not part of the universe, or universes, but rather outside all these dimensions that form existence. Cosmological science has made huge leaps accompanied by different theological and philosophical reflections, especially by Pierre Teilhard de Chardin and Andrés Torres Queiruga. The digital and technological revolution has influenced our understanding of the universe as much as it has influenced our theological language, and ways of expressing ourselves and understanding the salvific work of God in Christ.

It seems, however, that in our day-to-day language we sometimes use medieval metaphors. For example, we say "the sun is going down", even though we know that this is scientifically inaccurate, as the sun doesn't go "down" but we move around it. Nevertheless, we still use that language without thinking about it. We do the same theologically when we talk about, for example, the doctrine of creation. What do we mean by creation? Christian theologians have always written about the theory of creation out of nothing, which means that God created everything from nothing rather than using pre-existing materials. If we say that, it will mean that matter is co-eternal with God.

The word "eternal" itself has become debatable. Quantum physics is constantly redefining our understanding of time. One theory even posits that time doesn't exist at all, meaning that the word "eternal" is redundant. As a result, we see that this is not an easy subject. Time, space, dimension, reality, all these concepts that form our understanding of ourselves and everything around us, have become the subject of enormous redefinition. We also face the other question of whether reality changes according to our understanding of it. Our highly technological age creates new challenges for us, especially when we use the by-products of technology like computers and mobile phones. We are at the same time very slow to accept the reality and the vision behind these products.

Science uses experimental methodology and is often able to repeat experiments and recreate the same conditions in a way that is impossible for faith. Faith is not experimental but rather experiential and depends on personal and/or collective experience. We need to revisit the way in which we express our faith and reflect theologically and spiritually on what is happening around us. Living our faith in a rapidly changing world gives rise to many difficult questions and even barriers that prevent that faith from growing. As we continue to learn from our experiences of God as well as the world around us and as we continue to interact and engage with different cultures and rapidly growing technology that allows these cultures to interact more easily and faster, we should continually reflect on those experiences and engagements to keep our faith alive and relevant.

The Risen Lord and the stewardship of earth

This means a lot of effort on the part of clergy as well as laity to read and follow the latest developments in thinking and science so that our faith is enriched and forms an active part of the world around us. When we talk about saving the environment, for example, this discussion should lie at the heart of the Church's ministry. Every one of us who believes in Jesus Christ should reflect closely on the relationship between him and nature. When we study the parables, for example, the vast majority use metaphors from the natural world around him—the birds, the flowers, the harvest. He closely observed the world around him and communicated this intimate relationship. He even referred to himself as a seed buried in the ground that dies in order to give life:

> Very truly I tell you, unless a kernel of wheat falls to the ground and dies, it remains only a single seed. But if it dies, it produces many seeds (John 12:24).

Considering the earth as the creation of God is a huge responsibility. This should encourage us to reflect on the ethical dimension of our stewardship of earth and all its elements. The undertaking of this stewardship should not be through fear but through love of God's creation. As disciples of Christ, we learn from him that our God is a caring and loving God. This care and love extend not just to us but through us to the world around us. This must be our inspiration to respond to God's love.

We, through the use of technology, have vastly improved the living conditions of people around the world. I remember when I was growing up in my hometown of Lattakia, a coastal town in Syria, our tap water was salty, so we would buy fresh water for drinking. When we were finally able to drink water fresh from the tap, it was greeted with much rejoicing. If we look at the life expectancy of the population of Europe, it has jumped from the mid-thirties to the mid-eighties. We abolished famine in many countries around the world through scientific advances in agriculture, but we must work harder to achieve that everywhere. All this should not be at the expense of the world around us. Improvement in the human condition, however, is not what is destroying the environment. It is rather our greed for more and more luxury, whether it be more clothes, more gadgets or more exotic holidays. The threat to the environment does not come from improving people's basic living conditions, but rather from the many industries that are only concerned about profit, with exponential growth at the expense of cheap labour.

If we look at our biblical teachings as well as the teachings of Jesus Christ, Jesus reveals to us the mind and the heart of God through his life and teachings. He teaches us that earth is cared for by God and, because of that, we need to respond to the love that God has for his creation and stand up against the exploitation of its natural resources. St John reminds us that "through him all things were made; without him nothing was made that has been made" (John 1:3). St Paul confirms this and says, "For in him all things were created: things in heaven and on earth, visible and invisible, whether thrones or powers or rulers or authorities; all things have been created through him and for him" (Colossians 1:16).

As the world testifies to the glory of God and as we strive to find our place in this creation without destroying what God created, we need to understand the heart and mind of God towards our planet. The Culture of God in Jesus' teachings is a culture of peace and reconciliation. The crucified and Risen Lord reconciled us with God. When he appeared to his disciples after the resurrection, he said to them, "Peace I leave with you; my peace I give you. I do not give to you as the world gives. Do not let your hearts be troubled and do not be afraid" (John 14:27). This declaration of the inner heart of the Culture of God should be the basis of our work to find peace in ourselves, with each other and with the world around us. I do believe after having lived through so many wars and conflicts in my life, that we need to move from an aggressive and warlike economy based on destruction and greed to a peaceful economy based on reconciliation.

Very recently I heard of an exciting theory of what I would term a peace economy that made me think and reflect. This is the theory of doughnut economics developed by British economist Kate Raworth. This theory tries to reshape our basic understanding of the economy and its relationship to the world around us. It could form the basis on which we can move from a war economy to a peace economy. The theory describes two rings: an inner ring that provides us with the basic requirements for a good life—housing, clean water, food, sanitation and so on—and an outer ring that represents the natural resources that are available to us that we should respect and cherish, and the boundaries that we must not exceed if we are to avoid catastrophes like depletion of the ozone layer, climate change, biodiversity loss and so on.

The theory suggests that we need to move the people in the hollow centre of the doughnut, who are living below the social foundation necessary for a dignified life, to the safe zone between the two rings. At the same time, the theory insists that all economic functions should ensure that we do not break the outer ring's boundaries. We should not therefore seek economic growth at all costs. This theory has ignited a huge debate and engendered welcome fresh thinking around how we move our models of behaviour. There is of course no one theory that offers the cure to all our problems, but it at least opens the door to alternatives to our self-destructive economic patterns of behaviour. We should invest in ways to harness digital technology to support micro-economies and improve the living conditions of those millions existing in the hollow centre; as well as restrict our exponential growth and promote alternative technologies to power our homes or provide us with food.

I have lived for many years in the middle of a war economy that sucks life from people literally and economically. I experienced and continue to experience the after-effects of war. Again and again, we show our terrible failure to work together for the sake of the common good and instead revert immediately towards selfish and greedy politics. Unfortunately, we are still unable to learn from Christ and from the Culture of the Trinity how to build our communities based on the divine peace and love that God wants us to enjoy everywhere on earth.

I recently looked at a chart totalling the military expenditure by country. According to a recent European Commission report, global military expenditure has increased by 75 per cent over the last twenty years and stands currently at approximately £1.7 trillion annually. The top four countries by military spending in 2018 were the United States, China, Saudi Arabia and France. This tells me that we need to change our entire way of thinking. In 2021, after billions spent on the effects of a global pandemic, the UK chose to increase its spending on nuclear arms by 40 per cent. We can't claim that we are working on saving the environment while increasing the potential to destroy our planet through all-out war. In 2018, the UK government spent £14 billion on environmental protection but spent £50 billion on the military. This simple comparison highlights our need to change our worldview and to reframe our relationship with our neighbours and the world around us.

The war in Ukraine, that started in 2022, has again thrown the world into the fever of an arms race and pushed us into another Cold War, dividing the developed world into those who supported the actions of President Putin in Ukraine and those who opposed them. Even the Church entered the debate. Pope Francis recently spoke out against the war in Ukraine, saying, "Every war leaves our world worse than it was before. War is a failure of politics and of humanity, a shameful capitulation, a stinging defeat before the forces of evil." Since my years living in Lebanon, I have always believed, preached and taught against the very idea of a "holy war". I've always believed that every single war in the history of humanity is evil and destroys the sanctity of life and the dignity of humanity. I was vehemently opposed to the UK's bombing of Syria in 2015 and religious leaders' attempts to justify this action as defensible. Archbishop Welby, along with other religious leaders, argued at the time that "The just war criteria have to my mind been met."

In a time of increasing technological advancement, wars inevitably have a considerably more devastating impact on civilians. I was delighted to hear Pope Francis finally reject the concept of a just war. In the Culture of God, that is the culture of love and peace, there is no place for any justification for any war, past, present or future. The images of the destruction of Ukraine cannot but affirm that, in the digital age that we live in, in just a few weeks of war, weapons can turn cities into ash and devastate an entire population.

According to the charity World Vision, there are 689 million people worldwide living in extreme poverty on less than a dollar a day. Isn't that a scandal? Children and young people, says the report, represent two-thirds of the world's poor. The Culture of God challenges how we view leadership. As the disciples of Jesus Christ, we must provide new ways of thinking and leadership. What happened in the Passion of Christ helped us to understand our stewardship of the planet and our concept of leadership. St John relates how Jesus, after the Last Supper, wrapped a towel around his waist and washed the feet of the disciples:

> It was just before the Passover Festival. Jesus knew that the hour had come for him to leave this world and go to the Father. Having loved his own who were in the world, he loved them to the end. The evening meal was in progress, and the devil had already prompted Judas, the son of Simon Iscariot, to betray Jesus. Jesus knew that the Father had put all things under his power, and that he had come from God and was returning to God; so he got up from the meal, took off his outer clothing, and wrapped a towel around his waist. After that, he poured water into a basin and began to wash his disciples' feet, drying them with the towel that was wrapped around him (John 13:1–5).

This incident is an extraordinary event, not only in the life of Christ and the disciples, but in the lives of millions of people in the generations that followed. It is extraordinary for different reasons, one of which is the selflessness that Jesus showed his disciples. This episode is very much linked with the Gospel of St Mark, where Mark tells us:

> Then James and John, the sons of Zebedee, came to him. "Teacher," they said, "we want you to do for us whatever we ask."
>
> "What do you want me to do for you?" he asked.
>
> They replied, "Let one of us sit at your right and the other at your left in your glory."
>
> "You don't know what you are asking," Jesus said. "Can you drink the cup I drink or be baptized with the baptism I am baptized with?"
>
> "We can," they answered.
>
> Jesus said to them, "You will drink the cup I drink and be baptized with the baptism I am baptized with, but to sit at my right or left is not for me to grant. These places belong to those for whom they have been prepared."
>
> When the ten heard about this, they became indignant with James and John. Jesus called them together and said, "You know

that those who are regarded as rulers of the Gentiles lord it over them, and their high officials exercise authority over them. Not so with you. Instead, whoever wants to become great among you must be your servant, and whoever wants to be first must be slave of all. For even the Son of Man did not come to be served, but to serve, and to give his life as a ransom for many" (Mark 10:35–45).

Jesus all his life avoided presenting himself or talking about himself as a leader and instead gave us a totally new understanding of leadership. We can see this vividly in the way he dealt with his disciples arguing over who was greater. They were attracted by the glitter of authority and power. Jesus explained to them instead that he came to serve and not be served. This sentence directly links to his action at the Last Supper when he washed the feet of the disciples. It has been said many times that Jesus' style of leadership was to lead by living and acting out his beliefs. In every culture, the ruler rules, but for Christ, the ruler comes down not only to serve but also to put himself at the feet of those who would serve him.

The washing of the feet prepares us to understand the total self-giving of the King upon the cross. If we really want to turn life on earth around and save not only our environment but humanity itself, we need to look at how the Culture of God challenges our models of leadership and politics and how it can help us to reshape our response to the crises of the environment as well as the violence that is spreading in our world, the poverty destroying more lives each year and the tens of millions of refugees wandering across the face of our planet. Unless our politicians become more Christ-like in the way of leadership, we will always have corruption and the devastation of lives through poverty and man-made disasters. These leaders must engage with technology to find ways to deploy it in the service of those in great need.

Saving the environment is not only down to individuals doing their bit, although this is very important, but is also primarily the readiness of world leaders to see themselves as the servants and the good shepherds of their people. This is not a utopia. This is a realistic scenario that we need to work towards. It can't happen automatically but needs the disciples of Christ to push for it as a legitimate and valid option to rebuild the relationship between authority and the people. We live in a depleted ecological system as well as a human condition often devoid of values, principles and moral purpose. The solution to this stares us in the face. The Culture of the Trinity provides us with the ideal model for leadership, stewardship and our relationships with each other and with the creation around us.

We need to remember that the twelve people who followed Christ and were the recipients of his message after the resurrection were able to change the face of history. This gives us the encouragement and the hope that the model given to us is not theoretical but is proven and effective. How can we accept a system that allows 1 or 2 per cent of the world's population to control the resources, wealth and power of the planet? This must change and the only way to do it is to change our view of authority. This leads us to reflect on how Christ could reform our cosmological reality. God's creation is much bigger than the limits of our imagination. At the same time, the Culture of God invites us to break down more barriers between each other and between us and God so that we allow the Holy Spirit to move us from a life dominated by material possessions to a divine culture that empowers us to fulfil our true potential. Put simply, the Culture of God is the freedom to fulfil our potential and the purpose of our creation.

Belonging, believing, behaving

At the moment, we are living in a culture where most of us are possessed with a feverish desire to have more—more money, bigger houses, the latest gadgets. The more we have, the more we want. This desire comes from the vacuum we have inside us that we desperately seek to fill. Our materialistic reality has deepened every year, as has our desperation to fill this hole in us. Most of the time, we are not aware that we have turned this void into a black hole that sucks in everything around us. Our world, especially for the younger generation, is based around a celebrity culture that drives what we want to wear, how we want to look or behave. Most of the mechanisms we have developed to fill this vacuum are based on the desire for material gain.

I remember when I came to live in London in 1997, when I woke up to the horrific news of the death of Princess Diana. It was an extraordinary experience to witness the reactions of people, not only in this country but worldwide. I went with my sister to Kensington Palace, where there was a sea of flowers and messages expressing shock and profound grief. Most strikingly, people expressed their disbelief that something like this could happen to such an icon of youth and beauty. Princess Diana's life and dedication to worthy causes inspired the love of many across the world. On the day her death was announced, a Sunday, I had to preach in a church in Islington in north London. My first thought about the death of Princess Diana was that her youth, her fame and all the trappings of her life didn't protect her from her tragic death. This incident reminded us of our own mortality and the question of the meaning of life. Her death was a wake-up call. Our desperate striving to fill the gap inside us suddenly seemed unimportant and we were faced with our naked limitations.

We were brought back to square one when faced with a question that neither science nor human culture can resolve, which is the question of our human purpose. The aim of our life is beyond the remit of scientific endeavour. Shocking events, like the death of Princess Diana or the most recent pandemic, pose abiding questions about the purpose of our life and how we deal with the urge within us to want more and more. In the last century, theology was in constant engagement with philosophy. Many theologians weren't able to differentiate clearly between philosophy and theology. The German theologian Paul Tillich believed that philosophy and theology are distinguishable but at the same time inseparable. This relationship between the two disciplines helped both to flourish in the last century. But in the twenty-first century, this engagement between the two disciplines shrank and has been replaced by the engagement between theology and science. Theology acknowledges the necessity of engaging with modern science to express our understanding of our human existence on earth as well as our reality within creation.

Of course, we understand that science cannot explain the death of a young princess or the impact of celebrity culture, but it can help us to see our place in the universe and provide us with the latest research that could make theological reflections much more relevant and exciting, especially when we look at the questions around time and space. This investigation brings to the fore our sense of belonging to our earthly culture while being citizens in the Culture of God, and empowers us to embrace an advanced scientific culture without losing our journey to find a meaning to our life or to major world incidents like the death of Princess Diana or a pandemic. Jesus Christ showed us a deep sense of belonging to his earthly culture that appeared in his interactions with his community and in his teachings that were deeply rooted in that society. At the same time, he experienced a dynamic relationship with God the Father and taught his disciples how to balance and unite their own earthly society with the Culture of God.

Jesus Christ was the first ever full citizen of both the divine and human cultures. He grew up in his own earthly culture without ever ceasing to belong to the Culture of God. He talked about this openly with his society and community. He did not shy away from showing this dual belonging and taught his disciples in so many ways throughout his ministry that humanity was created to live and flourish in this dual existence of the culture of the earthly community as well as the Culture of God. St John reflected deeply on this dual citizenship in his vast theology of the word "abiding". In the narrative of his Gospel in chapter 15, he speaks about abiding in the divine, quoting Jesus as saying, "I am the vine; you are the branches. If you remain in me and I in you, you will bear much fruit; apart from me you can do nothing" (John 15:5). John uses the word *meno* sixty-five times in his writings to mean "remain", "abide", "dwell". The word *meno* suggests the idea of putting down roots in a community and feeling a sense of belonging.

John's most striking use of this word, which has had a profound impact in my life, is in the first epistle of John 4:16:

> And so we know and rely on the love God has for us.
> God is love. Whoever lives in love lives in God, and God in them (1 John 4:16).

This verse carries in it a deep sense of intimacy. In this way, when we abide in Christ, we are in Christ intimately and personally. Consequently, Christ is our home and out of that personal and intimate relationship we can say that we belong to Christ. Also, if we understand that Jesus is the light of the world, then belonging to Christ means being in the light. As John says, "Anyone who loves their brother and sister lives in the light, and there is nothing in them to make them stumble" (1 John 2:10). This is a beautiful explanation of belonging. The first belonging is being in Christ and the second is loving the people in my community. In one sentence, John summarizes the sense of this double belonging.

John uses light and love in an interchangeable way and wants us to understand that when we are rooted in love, we walk in the light. When we abide in love, we are in Christ and Christ is in us:

> This is the message we have heard from him and declare to you: God is light; in him there is no darkness at all. If we claim to have fellowship with him and yet walk in the darkness, we lie and do not live out the truth. But if we walk in the light, as he is in the light, we have fellowship with one another, and the blood of Jesus, his Son, purifies us from all sin (1 John 1:5–7).

All that is also true for our second belonging: to the community around us. How can you be in love with God, who you can't see, but not with your brothers and sisters around you? Belonging to the Culture of God in Christ must naturally flow into a sense of belonging to our earthly communities. This belonging happens through serving our community by putting ourselves at the feet of others. John goes even deeper in expressing the inseparable relationship between being in God and serving my fellow human. Being like Christ and serving our community is being true to our belonging in Christ:

> Whoever claims to love God yet hates a brother or sister is a liar. For whoever does not love their brother and sister, whom they have seen, cannot love God, whom they have not seen (1 John 4:20).

Looking at John's thoughts about abiding in God or Christ helps us understand our relationship to our human family and our earthly culture. In this way, we see one important dimension of the universal Jesus Christ. Love is a universal value that should impact our human values and cultures. Being in this highly advanced technological age can push values like love, service and human belonging to one side. Belonging to Christ and understanding the Culture of God as home for us brings those values back into the heart of our human communities. This dual belonging should always help us to see the importance of our humanity so that we reject any kind of slavery, like being sucked into our materialistic and consumerist lifestyle.

Belonging to a community opens our horizons to the idea that we are part of a wider belonging to other civilizations somewhere in the universe, which at the moment is in the realm of science fiction. This idea of the possibility of a wider belonging makes our roots in Christ, in love and in the Culture of God even more relevant. Our reality, which stems from our own identity as an individual to being part of the infinite cosmos, is strengthened by our relationship with the Risen Lord. The Culture of God that provides a model of how to live as humans helps us find our humility in the face of our place in the infinite universe around us. This should encourage us to find more loving and peaceful methods to reconcile our conflicts and resolve our differences. Everything around us tells us that we are not the centre of the universe but rather a speck in that vast existence. The cosmic figure of Christ reminds us of the dynamic and lively relationship that he had with the Father united in the Holy Spirit.

St Paul builds on the concept of abiding that St John explored throughout his writings when he speaks about "being in Christ", which for him is a multi-faceted idea. A striking example of Paul's thoughts of being in Christ that reflects belonging in Christ or having Christ as our identity is in 2 Corinthians:

> Therefore, if anyone is in Christ, the new creation has come: The old has gone, the new is here! (2 Corinthians 5:17).

For St Paul, God is active in our lives because we are in Christ. God communicates with us through him. For example, in the following passage in Ephesians, Paul says:

> Be kind and compassionate to one another, forgiving each other, just as in Christ God forgave you (Ephesians 4:32).

Those who have faith in Christ are in Christ and therefore our belonging in Christ deeply affects our second belonging in the community. Being a "new creation" means being forgiven, and that should be reflected in our actions as we live within our sense of belonging to our earthly community. One of the biggest challenges that we face in being citizens of both cultures—the Culture of God and our earthly culture—is to determine the distinction between the means and the end itself. Technology, for example, is the means and the problems arise when we see it as the end. The same applies to money. Our desires in life, whatever they may be, are means not ends. Disaster happens when the means and the ends are confused in our lives, especially when God himself becomes a means and stops being, in St John's words, the Way, the Truth and the Life. Many abhorrent things have been done in the name of God when faith becomes religious ideology.

How can digital technology affect and enhance our experience of belonging in our community-based digital culture? How can we use technology as the means to broaden our engagement with those around us? Digital technology has allowed us to expand our individual identities through social media, as well as our sense of belonging. It has brought us into closer proximity with each other and brought into question our sense of loyalty to our communities and each other. It poses the question: where do we belong when digital technology allows us to engage in communities that can be far from where we live? Do I have to exist physically in a community in order to belong? This also has an impact on the way we serve each other and how we contribute to communities that we feel we belong to.

The Culture of God does not limit us to a certain way of belonging or finding connections within a community. Instead, it provides us with the blueprint of how to live and belong in whichever community we choose. Now, as we live in the third decade of the twenty-first century, the borders have become blurred between our digital identity and sense of belonging through our physical existence in a community. We are witnessing a slow merging of the two existences.

There is a difference, however, between belonging to a country or a community and having roots there where we feel at home, and turning that sense of belonging into a destructive ideology in the name of patriotism. We have painful examples in our history, especially the Nazism that abused the German identity and turned it into a killing machine, brainwashing people into thinking that patriotism meant domination of the other. There are similar examples of religious belonging that became corrupted into a dark and sinister ideology that caused the destruction of hundreds of thousands of lives around the world at the hands of Isis and other like-minded organizations.

I have seen in my lifetime enough violence, hatred and bloodshed based on this concept of belonging, whether political or religious. In the countries where I have lived and worked, I have experienced first-hand the deepest abuse of shiny slogans about love of homeland and freedom that masked vultures and monsters sucking the life from young people and pushing them into senseless battles that have nothing to do with either God or homeland. I've seen and still see today how bloodthirsty governments, for the sake of economic gain, are ready to twist the most sacred principles to justify their evil ends.

In these cases, especially in the Near East, we see the most terrifying examples of the confusion between means and ends. We see political and religious parties and even governments using the Scriptures, sacred literature and even the lives of people as the means to satisfy their greed. The abuse of belonging can happen on different levels, from the individual to government and national organizations. Being in Christ must help us to stand up against that, especially when we see this abuse coming even from the institutional Church. Throughout my ministry in the Near East and living in the West, I could see so many cases of people being misled to believe that the only way to live is by ending the lives of others, and the only way to serve God is to submit the whole world to their specific political and religious agenda. The conviction with which this is spoken of is absolutely terrifying. It is deeply disturbing to see the loving and forgiving God that we looked at in the writings of St John and St Paul turn into a vicious and evil god who delights in annihilation and bloodshed.

These evil ideologies have used sophisticated technology to spread their ideas and groom young people around the world. We have seen fighters from across the world coming to the Middle East to fight for these ideologies because they were offered a different kind of belonging.

Trusting in that ideology gave them a sense of belonging that enabled them to carry out unspeakable acts in the name of that ideology. The marriage between a corrupted ideology and highly sophisticated technology has given birth to a new age of terror. In this case, believing and belonging breed appalling acts. On the other hand, we do not have a strong enough counterbalance to build up peacemakers who can unite efforts around the world to stop madness. Having worked in peace-building for decades, I feel that energy around the world is too fragmented and disjointed. There is no joined-up thinking that is harnessing the use of technology to offer a united vision, especially with regards to helping our children stand up to the pressure of violent ideologies.

We still have a long way to go as the body of Christ to challenge and stand up against such ideologies wherever we see them. If we want to be in Christ, who revealed the Culture of God as the culture of love and mercy, we need to translate that belonging, that new creation, into constructive and loving models for communities around the world. The deeper we go into that belonging to Christ, the wider our perspective of the love of God.

Who or what on earth defines me?

Being in Christ or abiding in Christ means being a citizen of the divine culture. This theological statement challenges us to go a step further and ask ourselves what on earth makes us who we are. The question of identity today is more relevant than ever. The culture, or cultures, that surround us are constantly trying to redefine us and our existence. Who I am can be understood from many different perspectives, including what I do for a living or how much money I have or even my age, looks or social status. What also defines me is my religion or my values. All these things are changeable, and I could lose or gain any of them.

What happens to my identity if one or more of these aspects change? What if I lost all my money, for example? Or lost my social status or even changed my religion? Who am I then? In our digital age, most people have a digital identity. We are surrounded by usernames, passwords, PIN numbers, credit cards and apps that form our digital identity. Recently, more personal aspects such as voice and face recognition and retina screening were included in our digital profile in the name of security. More and more details about us are stored by governments and big corporations. What is interesting about this is that this identity can be stolen, altered or lost, and we have many examples of this happening every day through the actions of so-called scammers worldwide.

The reality of who I am is one that is not so easily stolen or lost. I remember reading about a conference entitled Digital Humanities that took place in 2011 at one of the universities in London. At this conference the concept of the big tent was posited, which described an approach that welcomed all disciplines from academia, research and even commercial information providers to work across institutions and form a hub to discuss the so-called digital humanities and what it means to work and live in a digital culture. They also wanted to engage with theology and religious studies to work on an interface between theology and digital culture. I was uncomfortable with the title itself. Although I understand the need for such a concept, and despite the huge technological advances that have had such an impact on our understanding of humanity, I find it difficult to talk about the digital human.

I admit that humanity has been transformed by digital technology but talking about a digital humanity removes our humanity from the true identity that we as Christians believe it to be. If we want to accept the concept of digital humanity, can we also talk about artistic humanity or industrial humanity or religious humanity? We must rather consider humanity through the lens of being with Christ. The circumstances of humanity change as we move through different stages of development. All these changes alter our understanding of our humanity, but I don't think that they can remove our identity from being anchored in Christ, especially if we believe that through him everything was and is created.

The obvious question is what happens with those who lack that belief in Christ? How do they find their identity? Everything around us is moving and changing, so our identities are in a constant state of flux. We live in a rapidly changing culture. Our cultures around the world today are hugely influenced by the advancement of technology that causes a massive upheaval that some cultures are better equipped to deal with than others. Many people find that their sense of identity is shaped by the shifting world around them, which can be both a blessing and a curse, especially when this is coupled with the pressure of maintaining a digital identity that has become an essential part of living in the modern world. The question that all of us face is: what parts of my identity are really part of me and therefore unchangeable? What tells me who I am in a changing world?

The advancement of technology and transportation has radically changed our understanding of what is home. Is Syria home for me, even though I haven't lived there since I was seventeen? In what way am I Syrian and what does it mean to have this identity? A lot of concepts that shape our identity have been revisited culturally in a dramatic way—from gender, sexuality and family to our understanding of what our communities are. We also shouldn't forget that we are still dealing with the heritage of the past, such as slavery, racism, wars and colonialism. The geopolitical map of the world has shifted in a way that wouldn't have been thought of thirty years ago. It is not easy now for anyone to understand their identity at a fundamental level. Do we not need an anchor that makes us feel grounded and accepted? Many people find this sense of identity through religion, sometimes in an extreme way that makes them want to impose this same identity on others.

Can I understand myself beyond my circumstances and my experience? I am of course the product of my culture and the cultures that I have lived in but, through the lens of Christ, I should also see myself rooted beyond my cultural belonging and circumstantial influences. All these things are external factors, but the internal factor that exceeds all others is that I am created in the image of God and through and for the Son. As St John says, "through him all things were made; without him nothing was made that has been made" (John 1:3). The lens through which we look at our identity, apart from all the external factors, is how God sees us. Simply put, all the other factors differ from one person to another. They influence who we are but do not change our essential nature.

My economic and social status can play an essential role in opening or closing doors to opportunity, but God does not look at me and judge me according to my achievements, even though that may be the main way that others see me. I can't place my value or my worth on how external circumstances affect my life or my achievements in life. My worth comes from the fact that God loves me so much that he gave his only son for me. This worth makes us all human in the way that God sees us. This perspective, as limited and limiting as it might sound, is in fact the most imaginative and innovative approach that we can have to understand ourselves. It does not mean uniformity. On the contrary, it encompasses the vastness of God's love for us. It doesn't place boundaries on our identity but instead breaks down all the barriers that externally define us. The love of God is so vast that it includes us all without restricting us. Our worth is beyond any human conditions.

There is nothing we can do to deserve God's love or to make God love us more. Christian life is not about being good so that God loves us more. It is about how to respond to the incredible love that he showed in Christ Jesus. God doesn't love Peter more than Judas, but God recognizes that they responded to his love in different ways. What they both did doesn't make Peter more worthy of God's love than Judas, despite what God thinks about their actions. All my life, I have felt quite jealous of John the disciple of Christ. He claimed the title of the "beloved disciple" or the "disciple that Jesus loved". I thought why can't I, or anyone else, have this title? It felt arrogant of John to claim this and to set himself apart from the other disciples through this powerful title.

When I studied the Gospel of John in more depth, specifically the Passion stories, and especially through my discussion with a dear friend who is a Catholic priest in Italy, I realized that the story is actually quite different. When John spoke about Mary Magdalene and Peter after the resurrection, he beautifully captured the love they had for the crucified Christ. John tells us that Mary was desperately looking for the Lord's body but couldn't find it. She was in such a panic that she didn't recognize him when he spoke to her until he called her by her name. Peter and John ran to the tomb. John explains how Peter outran him and entered the tomb first.

When John spoke about himself, he didn't describe how much he loved the Lord but instead chose to drop his own identity, even his name, in order to redefine himself not by how much he loved Christ but by how much Christ loved him. He referred to himself mainly as the "disciple Jesus loved" not because he wanted to put himself on a pedestal. John tells us that Jesus said, "A new command I give you: love one another. As I have loved you, so you must love one another" (John 13:34). John took this commandment and shaped his own identity from it. He saw that the most important thing in his life and in his identity was the fact that Jesus loved him. In this way, he opened the door for us all to have the courage to embrace this identity—not that we love the Lord but that he loves us and gave himself for us. John is not setting himself apart and claiming a title to the exclusion of others but is instead inviting us all to also redefine ourselves as the person Jesus loves. In this way, everything else becomes secondary. I don't care if my passport changes, my bank changes or even if my gender changes. What matters is that Jesus loves me. This is the core of my identity.

It is deeply concerning when we judge the worth of people according to their behaviour and achievements. When a person commits a murder, it doesn't mean that God loves them less but instead it means that we, as the body of Christ, have failed to show God's love to this person and remind them that God loves them despite their brokenness. Most of the time we are quick to judge and slow to love. Because of that, we have the tendency to put value on achievements (or lack of).

The love of God has nothing to do with us being good. Love is the identity of God, and we cannot change that by being good or bad. We should view ourselves and our identity through the prism of this love. When we do that, we automatically find our home and our belonging. We also stop categorizing people according to their background, culture, sexual orientation, colour of their skin, gender identity or wealth.

Christ revealed his identity by responding to God's love and told his disciples that if they want to be great, they must be servants. According to the Gospel narrative of Mark, Jesus told them that he would die and rise again:

> They were on their way up to Jerusalem, with Jesus leading the way, and the disciples were astonished, while those who followed were afraid. Again he took the Twelve aside and told them what was going to happen to him. "We are going up to Jerusalem," he said, "and the Son of Man will be delivered over to the chief priests and the teachers of the law. They will condemn him to

death and will hand him over to the Gentiles, who will mock
him and spit on him, flog him and kill him. Three days later he
will rise" (Mark 10:32–34).

On a previous occasion, he told them what they needed to do to follow
him:

Then he called the crowd to him along with his disciples and
said: "Whoever wants to be my disciple must deny themselves
and take up their cross and follow me. For whoever wants to save
their life will lose it, but whoever loses their life for me and for
the gospel will save it. What good is it for someone to gain the
whole world, yet forfeit their soul? (Mark 8:34–36)

Jesus outlines the way to follow him, which is the way to respond to God's
love. He never stopped teaching us the way to be truly what God wants us
to be, which is to love as God loves us in Christ. This is the way that helps
us to discover our true identity beyond all the noise that increasingly
surrounds us, especially in today's digital world. Our identity lies in God,
not in what society tries to make us. Throughout our lives, when we try
to live according to that love, we go on a journey of rediscovering our
identity and fulfilling the purpose of our identity.

During the Covid-19 pandemic, many people suffered isolation,
loneliness and mental distress. In that stressful time, they felt the
importance of being part of something bigger than themselves. They
felt the need to belong to a welcoming and generous environment, with
people who cared for their needs and shared common experiences. Most
of us became more attached to our electronic devices in response to
this and took refuge in connecting with people outside our imposed
self-isolation. Our devices offered us the only means to connect us to
the world at that time and made us realize the nourishment we received
from our dialogue with others. All this was possible only through the
advance in digital technology.

It is difficult for me to feel my identity on my own. My identity reaches
beyond where and when I grew up and is formed by the relationships
that I build with others. Technology itself doesn't define me but the

relationships that I forge online (and offline) do. When I describe myself, I don't do it through the technological devices that I own. Nevertheless, I derive my identity from my activities and profiles online or in the digital marketplace. This can be dangerous because it begs the question of who am I outside of the digital forum and the identity that I create online. What makes me human and what is reality? The activities that we do online, from using social media to online banking, virtual communications, gaming and remote working and learning, create an e-identity that infuses our real-life identity.

For those who were born in the age of the internet, this concept of a digital identity is particularly strong. Young people spend much of their lives online and, through digital streaming, meet people they may never meet in real life but who can have a profound effect on the way they lead their lives. For them, there is no distinction between virtual friends met online and friends they meet in real life. Our human relationships are more fluid than ever. Our e-identity has played the role of an amplifier to broadcast the negative and selfish side of us as well as the kind and generous side.

Amid this heated debate on the advantages and disadvantages of our engagements online and offline, I ask myself this existential question: where am I heading in all this and where will I find harbour? St Augustine says in a prayer to God that our hearts will be always restless until they rest in him. Finding myself in the midst of this dilemma, I find that the Culture of God is the source of peace and stillness that helps me to stop and reflect, giving me the space to see clearly where I'm going, especially when the fog of the overstimulation and intensity of our modern world presses down on me. I believe that the Culture of the Trinity sends us an invitation to be citizens of that culture of love and generosity that Christ proclaimed when he said, "Come to me, all you who are weary and burdened, and I will give you rest" (Matthew 11:28).

Our faith in Christ unites within us the Culture of God and our modern culture. This connection between the two is the only way for us to make sense of our lives and to find a purpose for our existence. This purpose cannot be found in an object or an action but in a person who defined himself as the Way, the Truth and the Life. In him, we find our identity, our destination and the meaning of our entire reality and existence. This is our greatest power, our light in the time of darkness and our joy in times of trouble.

7

Return to the basics: Jesus Christ in the worlds of sci-fi and fantasy

When political, ideological, cultural or even religious restrictions prevent us from expressing ourselves or discussing burning issues or sensitive subjects, sci-fi and fantasy help us to break down the barriers built up by society. Most of the best works of sci-fi are those that tackle conflicts or issues that would disturb people if they were discussed openly. Take, for example, the culture of the United States in the 1960s when the tension between the Soviet Union and the United States was at its height following the Cuban Missile Crisis. *Star Trek: The Original Series* took the brave and shocking decision, led by its visionary creator Gene Roddenberry, to make one of the main characters on the bridge of the starship *Enterprise* a Russian, Pavel Chekov (played by Walter Koenig).

I'm sure it wasn't easy for the average American citizen, who had probably never travelled outside the United States, to see a Russian officer as a main character in a sci-fi series, a character who interacted with the other characters on an equal basis and had his own narrative. I'm sure that acceptance took time, but I'm also sure that it helped enormously to break some of the stereotypical prejudices about Russians who were then considered the enemy. Coming from the Middle East, it would be unimaginable even today to see an Israeli character who is not the enemy in an Arabic drama series.

It is extremely difficult for art to transcend society's taboos but, at the same time, I believe that only art can do that. One shining example of this is the West-Eastern Divan Orchestra started by pianist and composer Daniel Barenboim and cultural theorist Edward Said in 1999, which is comprised of musicians from Israel, the Palestinian Territories and other Arab countries. Science fiction and fantasy are important genres, not only in literature but also on TV and in films. They enjoy a certain margin of freedom that might be difficult for other genres to express. As well as Chekov, the Russian character in *Star Trek*, Roddenberry broke further taboos by casting a black female actor in another leading role, that of Lieutenant Uhura (played by Nichelle Nichols). This was a landmark decision in a troubled race relations environment, not only in the United States but around the world.

The deeper we go in tackling human issues and exploring the human psyche, it is inevitable that questions around human existence become important. Fantasy literature was arguably created to discuss the meaning of our existence and our relationship with the world around us. The oldest literary epic was the *Epic of Gilgamesh*, written around 2100 BC. This is also the oldest fantasy story we have that talks about heroes and gods and the interaction between the human realm and the divine realm. I grew up in Lattakia reading the *Epic of Gilgamesh*, and it has played a role in forming my consciousness and spiritual identity. It is widely known in the Near East and is one of our cultural treasures.

The story talks about a king of a city called Uruk, in modern-day Iraq, that was thought to be the first city in the world. The people of this city suffered from the cruelty of their king, Gilgamesh, and prayed to their gods to stop their suffering. The gods listened to their prayers and sent the king an equal called Enkidu. The two fight for days with no one emerging the winner, the result of which is that they become close friends and embark on a number of adventures together, including killing the Bull of Heaven, an act that angers the gods. Enkidu dies following the battle with the bull and Gilgamesh is suddenly faced with the question of his own mortality. He drops everything to go on a quest for eternal life.

On this quest he meets Utnapishtim, who survived the Great Flood and had been granted eternal life by the gods. Gilgamesh asks Utnapishtim to call upon the gods to grant him eternal life as well. Utnapishtim explains that Gilgamesh is not important enough for the gods to grant this wish. If, however, he eats a certain herb that can be found at the bottom of the sea he can renew his youth. Gilgamesh finds this herb, but a snake steals it and in eating it sheds its skin. Finally, Gilgamesh sails back to Uruk in despair. On the way back he meets a woman who tells him that his best chance of eternal life is to be a good king, which will immortalize him in the hearts of the people.

The epic was written in cuneiform, the oldest alphabet in history, that came from Ugarit (an ancient, ruined port city on the outskirts of my hometown of Lattakia). At the heart of the story of Gilgamesh is a discussion about the nature of human mortality and the desire for eternal life. This discussion continues today across all religions and philosophical thought. The epic fantasy of Gilgamesh particularly influenced the main religions that grew from that region, namely Judaism, Christianity and Islam. Most scholars, for example, believe that the flood story in Genesis was heavily influenced by the Great Flood in the story of Gilgamesh. I would like to pause here and tell you why I chose to talk about this ancient story. First of all, it is not widely known. As we are talking about sci-fi and fantasy, I believe that it is interesting to reflect upon such an internationally important piece of literature that also means a lot to me personally. When I was studying in London, for my final project I wrote a comparison between Gilgamesh and Christ. You may wonder what connection these two figures have? I would like to share a few points that I think are relevant to our reflections in this book.

As discussed, one of the most important overarching themes connecting Gilgamesh and Jesus Christ is that of eternal life. Gilgamesh is, according to the epic, two-thirds god and one-third man. Jesus Christ, according to Christian faith, is both fully God and fully man. Gilgamesh was the king of Uruk while Jesus Christ, who refused to be an earthly king, became for believers the King of Kings. His kingship is through divine appointment. The tragedy of Gilgamesh started when he realized that he was mortal, like other people, while the tragedy of Jesus started when other people realized that he could be divine and so plotted against him. Gilgamesh's obsession was with how to obtain eternal life, while Jesus' aim was to give eternal life to others through his sacrifice.

The death of the other, in Gilgamesh's case Enkidu, was necessary to the search for eternal life as the death of his friend confronted him with his own mortality. In Jesus' case, his own death was necessary for others to have eternal life. The life of others, in other words, confronted Jesus with the necessity of his own death. The death of Enkidu, which shook Gilgamesh to his core, was the result of a heroic battle. The death of Jesus was a result of confronting the evil of humanity. The gods decided to kill both Enkidu and Gilgamesh by sending them the Bull of Heaven. The divine decision was not to save Christ from his death on the cross but to raise him glorious on Easter Sunday. Gilgamesh found his salvation through rejecting his quest for eternal life by concentrating on becoming a good king so as to be immortalized in that way. For Christ, his humility and obedience to God the Father led him to accept the cross. His death and resurrection gave salvation to all those who believe in him:

> Therefore God exalted him to the highest place
> and gave him the name that is above every name (Philippians 2:9).

This quick comparison between two extraordinary kings provides us with an insight into an ancient fantasy story that is full of meanings and lessons that we can take and reflect upon today. Fantasy stories develop in all cultures around the world, through mythology, fairy stories or folk tales, in order to find answers to deep questions. I believe that studying such rich literary sources can give us a fresh engagement with our Christian faith. I remember Gene Rodenberry, the creator of *Star Trek*, saying that the inspiration behind the series came from many of these old literary sources. Indeed, one episode is based on the Gilgamesh story. For me, a sci-fi film or series in today's highly technological age goes beyond visual spectacle and special effects to engage with good stories and tackle deep questions. The context in which a sci-fi or fantasy story is written is only limited by the imagination, so can address more directly topics that would be restricted by a realistic setting.

A lot of sci-fi series, like *Babylon Five* or *Battlestar Galactica*, deal with sensitive political or religious issues in an open context that allows us to discuss them without being hamstrung by issues of identity. I remember an episode of *Star Trek: Deep Space Nine* in which the people of a planet believe that their prophets live in a wormhole and that Captain Sisko, the captain of the station between the planet and the wormhole, is an emissary between them and their prophets. The people's faith in this emissary fluctuates, as does the captain's understanding and belief in his role as emissary. This offers an insight into how issues of belief can wax and wane, grow weaker and stronger. Fluctuations of faith worry many

Christians but really, as this episode shows, this is a necessary part of the human condition.

What do sci-fi and fantasy add to our journey of faith?

Faith is the vital frontier on our journey towards understanding ourselves, the universe and God. It is a vital engagement in our citizenship of the Culture of God as well as our earthly cultures. It is not a concept that involves God necessarily all the time. It is embedded in every aspect of our human existence. When we say the word "faith", people only think about God and religion and forget that faith is an important pillar in our entire relationship system.

Before we go deeper into this process, we should define the concept that we are talking about. What is faith? The dilemma of understanding faith has occupied human existence for millennia. There are many different definitions that shed light on the meaning of this concept that goes beyond religion, philosophy or psychology. If we look at faith as a vital frontier, then we are already defining it as a threshold that we cross every time we build a relationship in our lives. We are unable to construct a relationship and make it grow without a minimum level of trust that is not only concerned with the other but also, and more importantly, ourselves.

When we cross the threshold of trust in ourselves and the other, we are then able to start the process of building that relationship. The opposite is also true. If I have no trust in myself or the other, there will be no movement towards a relationship. We are introducing here a new element in defining faith, which is movement. Faith is a continuous movement towards the other based on a realization of success or failure.

Faith must also be dynamic. Dynamic movement based on a minimum level of trust must also accept the inevitability of change. We understand that faith cannot be static. This can only happen when the energy that drives this process is love. This is how I understand faith: the threshold that we cross every time we embark on a relationship powered by the energy of love driving the dynamic movement towards the other, based on trust. We can apply this process in our relationships with each other, with the world around us and with God.

Jesus Christ is the ultimate example and image of faith. When I look at his life, I see it exactly in the terms I described. He lived in a state of constant dynamic movement towards his earthly culture and towards God, driven by love. He dealt with both relationships from a position of trust. How do we see this in his life? We see it in his teachings, in the miracles he performed, in his social relationships with his disciples and with the authorities, and in his spiritual life and his relationship with the Father. Jesus was a revolutionary in his way of breaking barriers and thresholds in order to meet his community and carry them with him to a new understanding of humanity and of God.

Although Jesus never uttered the word "religion" in his life, he dealt with the concept of faith the whole time in his encounters with other people. He was very alert to when people expressed their faith. For example, he was amazed by the faith of the Syrophoenician woman when she begged him to heal her sick daughter:

> Then Jesus said to her, "Woman, you have great faith! Your request is granted." And her daughter was healed at that moment (Matthew 15:28).

In the story of the sinful woman who anointed Christ's feet, he made the strong connection between faith and love:

> Jesus answered him, "Simon, I have something to tell you."
>
> "Tell me, teacher," he said.
>
> "Two people owed money to a certain moneylender. One owed him five hundred denarii, and the other fifty. Neither of them had the money to pay him back, so he forgave the debts of both. Now which of them will love him more?"
>
> Simon replied, "I suppose the one who had the bigger debt forgiven."
>
> "You have judged correctly," Jesus said (Luke 7:40–43).

The parable that Jesus told Simon highlights the importance and beauty of this woman's faith, which drove her to anoint his feet knowing that this would change her life. Jesus responded accordingly and said, "Your faith has saved you; go in peace" (Luke 7:50). In Christianity, faith means acknowledging the centrality of Jesus Christ and following him as a disciple. The faith that Jesus Christ revealed that makes us citizens in the Culture of God has another necessary side of it, and that is love. The will and the desire of God is that we have those two sides of the one coin: faith and love. These are totally inseparable in the life and teachings of Christ.

Sci-fi and fantasy present a more simplistic version of faith. This faith is mostly the gateway to the ethical dilemma that the story wants to tackle. The best example of this for me is in *Star Wars*, which offers us a stark representation of good and evil. Good is represented by the quasi-religious order of the Jedi; the resistance and the Republic and evil is represented by the Empire. The fight between them is clear. There are some Christian elements of redemption with the character narrative of Darth Vader in particular, but, in the end, the struggle between good and evil is fairly black and white.

The advancement of digital technology has boosted the possibilities open to the sci-fi and fantasy genres, allowing them to depict ever more complex ideas and narratives. As early as the late 1990s, for example, films like *What Dreams May Come* (1998), in which Robin Williams visits Heaven and Hell, were able to break visual barriers of what could be depicted on screen. I had never seen anything like this before and felt that it went a long way in bringing to life what had been quite abstract concepts. CGI has expanded even further on these ideas and has become an essential tool in the movie industry. The challenge now is not the limitations of our visual imagination but the interpretation of these concepts. The challenge is not to get caught up in the special effects themselves but to use them as a tool to explore further issues that can make a difference in people's lives.

In recent years, we have seen an enormous growth in reflections on a complex web of good and evil in the world of Japanese anime as a reaction to the more simplistic Western black-and-white depictions. The challenge is to go beyond the simplistic duality of good and evil and beyond trying to solve a specific ethical issue. The popular Japanese anime series *Naruto* tells the story of a young boy called Naruto (meaning "maelstrom" or "roaring gate" in Japanese), who is the most positive, hopeful, sunshine of a character ever. But he's also known as being an idiot and not very strong. However, he wants to be the leader of his village when he grows up, to be recognized by everyone and protect them. But an evil demon fox, a *kitsune* (a popular Japanese mythological creature), was sealed inside him to protect the village. His parents sacrificed themselves to seal the fox in him to save the village and also the boy's life, as the demon was attacking the village.

The boy grew up filled with a hateful demon inside him and the village fearful of him. But he still grew up with a sunshine personality and eventually convinces the fox to let go of his anger and hate towards humans, and they work together to become powerful enough to defeat the bad guy. They save everyone in his village and the surrounding villages. Throughout the series, the people slowly learn not to fear him too. He saves them all more than once, and constantly convinces bad guys to become good by talking to them; he's very good at connecting with people. It doesn't work on everyone of course, but it works on most people in the anime. In that way he gains a lot of friends who help him later and even save his life. If we look at the world of superheroes and anime, the stories set in this world at their heart deal with complex human issues like overcoming the darkness within ourselves. The characters are not always good but are instead treated as complex individuals, making them more relatable and also providing a way of discussing the moral ambiguities within us.

I remember when I watched *First Contact*, which is for me the best *Star Trek* film. Although it tries to engage with the ethical dilemma of artificial intelligence, it also deals with the question of what is humanity. The question I felt the film was trying to answer is: how much of a person can we replace with artificial parts before they lose their human identity and cease to be human? A lot of sci-fi and fantasy materials in the East and West have tried to explore the question of what is the human soul and how important is my physical body to my identity? These questions of course go back to ancient Greek philosophy that divided a person into two elements: body and soul. The sci-fi and fantasy genre digs deeper into this relationship between body and soul.

In Christian theology, we move beyond the ancient Greek duality and look instead at the person as a whole with body, soul and spirit. These components are not discrete elements, but instead, as St Paul tells us, are all part of the same person but from different perspectives. This unity is achieved through the resurrection of Christ, which did not discard the body. In Greek philosophy, the body is only a shell for something more transcendent, but, in Christianity, the resurrection of Christ revealed to us the mind of God and the love of God that includes our bodies. In that sense, the bodily resurrection of Christ is vitally important to understanding our humanity. When God became human, he sanctified matter and in doing so rejected philosophies like that of the ancient Greeks that sought to say that our physical presence was less important than our spiritual one.

At Jesus' crucifixion, the disciples and followers of Jesus felt that he was defeated. God, however, did not leave Jesus defeated but instead gave him glory and raised him from the dead. Jesus was not a superhero defeating everything in his path but was instead the blueprint for a new humanity. This blueprint shows us how to be reconciled with God. Faith, in this case, is not trust in an all-powerful force nor does it mean putting all our hope in a superhero as our saviour. In Christianity, not only was this saviour not a superhero but he was also a servant to humanity. This offers us a completely new understanding of God, faith and humanity.

I remember when I started watching *Star Trek: The Next Generation*, I was first introduced to the character Q, who was described as one of a superior race of beings. I felt that although the series never claimed that Q was God, he matched a popular understanding of God, that of an all-powerful force capable of doing anything and always seeking to test humanity. I was glad to see that Q was presented in a comical way, almost making fun of this shallow, popular understanding of God. In many works of sci-fi and fantasy, we see the concept of a saviour, the long-awaited messiah who comes to release people from pain or threat. It's very difficult for us to imagine a saviour who comes from a divine culture and still presents himself as a humble servant whose message to us is to follow his example.

The power of the saviour lies not in the might he has through supernatural abilities but instead lies in the power of love and living

that power in our everyday lives. At the heart of Christian faith is the
challenge to be like Christ. Through this journey of faith, we are able to
change our reality. The major difference between faith in the world of
sci-fi and fantasy and the Christian understanding of faith (although sci-fi
is heavily influenced by religious teachings) is that we are citizens of both
the Culture of God and the cultures of the world. The only way to have
such faith is through being the disciples of Jesus Christ.

Science fiction, fantasy and spirituality: escaping into a simpler world

In the last twenty years, I have noticed some major changes happening
in Western Europe thanks to the influx of migrants who challenged what
Christians took for granted: that faith is a private matter. People have
become more open, sharing a little about their own faith, being honest
about who they are. A dear friend of mine was asked about her Christian
faith, and she said: "After believing in Christianity, my faith belonged to
my identity. When I speak about my faith, I am not offending people—I
am talking about an essential side of who I am." The people of the
Enlightenment have moved beyond that influence to look at spirituality
in a different way, to the extent that globalization made spirituality a
product which you can choose as you wish.

Different schools of spirituality, and different religions, started using
the internet and especially social media to reach out to people. A positive
result is that there are now so many opportunities for dialogue. The
negative side is that there is now a new tension between the faiths, caused
by extremist religious views which have flourished due to the internet.
Some politicians have started talking about faith, trying to use faith to
promote themselves. We see that in the huge debate in the West about
the hijab, which started to raise valuable questions about the cultural or
religious nature of the hijab before the debate was hijacked by politicians
eager to win Muslim votes through their condemnation of the debate
itself. Some politicians in Germany, Austria and Italy used social media
to stir up anti-immigrant feeling to promote themselves, forming very
popular new populist parties based on an anti-immigration stance,

exploiting the tensions in their society that had been partly created by extreme, fanatical Muslim groups.

This is only a very brief look at the religious and spiritual issues that are bubbling to the fore within social media around the globe. Religious conflicts generally belong to a specific belief system like Islam, Christianity or Hinduism. Dealing with these conflicts has become more and more explosive. People's views range right across the spectrum from atheism to religious fanaticism. We see in Northern Ireland that the current conflict between unionists and nationalists is still labelled as being between Protestants and Catholics in a volatile situation that could implode at any time. The same is true for the situation between Sunni and Shia in Islam in the region of the Middle East and beyond.

Many people, especially in the West, have decided to either turn their back on religion or have decided to belong to spirituality schools that are beyond any formal religion. I was surprised at the number of people in the West who would call themselves spiritual but who do not identify with any particular religion. The sci-fi and fantasy genre deals deeply with spiritual matters ranging from the existence of God to the crises and conflicts between different imaginary religions. Engagement with the spiritual world is often shown in very creative ways. They can often prove helpful in suggesting ideas and solutions that we can learn from.

Fantasy and sci-fi do not attempt to replace religion or suggest a specific kind of spirituality. Instead, they try to construct a platform that can be used to explore and study spiritual or religious concepts and values. We see this in most sci-fi and anime series. These genres are able to present a specific spirituality and introduce it to a wider audience. For example, in the films *Coco* and *The Book of Life*, Disney explored Mexican spirituality and presented it in a creative and meaningful way. Sci-fi and fantasy engage in religion and spirituality in multiple ways, from dealing in core concepts like the existence of God or good and evil to exploring complex spiritual and religious journeys in a more nuanced way. One of the most popular themes of sci-fi and fantasy stories is the concept of salvation. Without salvation, there is an end of hope. Is there a solution to fix our broken human nature? In the recent Netflix film, *Don't Look Up*, you see an exploration of what happens when catastrophe prevails; when, in Christian terminology, there is the cross without the resurrection.

In our digital age, engagement with religions involves not only social media but also the role of digital technology in bringing religions closer in terms of dialogue and communication. Having said that, we need to be careful that in real life we tackle religious and spiritual tension with extra care, learning how to deploy the digital resources we have and the creative thinking of the sci-fi and fantasy genre in order to form strong peace-making alliances between religions. From my experience in interfaith dialogue and peace-building, along with my fascination with sci-fi and fantasy, I can see that even here writers avoid solving the idea of religious conflict by imagining a super-religion. Instead, they respect the particularities of each religion without trying to suggest over-simplistic solutions to religious conflict. Time and better communication should help heal the rifts between religious divisions.

Sci-fi and fantasy also respect and acknowledge spiritual practices beyond the bounds of organized religion. For example, the first officer on the starship *Voyager* is a follower of Native American spiritual practices, and his spiritual beliefs and practices are explored in different episodes. We also see deep spiritual themes embodied in *Battlestar Galatica*, in the writings of Tolkien or C. S. Lewis and animations by Hayao Miyazaki, to name but a few. What concerns us here is that looking at sci-fi and fantasy, and its rich handling of spirituality and religion, leads us to consider the rapidly increasing influence of digital technology on our lives. I don't see this as a threat to my spiritual life but rather as an opportunity increasingly to utilize the tools that digital technology provides in order to reach out to people and help them go deeper into their spirituality. We need to stand up simultaneously against religious or spiritual fanaticism and stop fanatical groups grooming young people to spread their hate-based ideologies.

Video games and the Culture of God: two sides of one journey?

A huge number of young people and adults alike have been engaging with a parallel universe balanced between the real world and the world of immersive entertainment. This unique space that occupies a considerable amount of time is the world of video games. This genre of entertainment has attracted many other fields like social media, animation, visual art, digital technology, fiction and non-fiction literature, psychology and even theology to come together to create a sophisticated world of engagement and entertainment that involves all the senses that human beings possess along with the mind and the heart. The field of gaming has made huge leaps in the last thirty years in all the fields listed above. Through the development of digital technology, games have become a powerful influence on many generations but especially among young people.

Games have moved from being divided into linear stages with well-defined tasks for each stage to game narratives featuring multiple storylines with tens of different endings involving serious decision-making that influences particular outcomes. All this is formed into an incredibly sophisticated artistic creation that offers a festival of audio-visual effects wrapped into complex and compelling stories. The experience of gaming is now being shared through social and online networks. There are also numerous conferences and gatherings aimed at gaming to share experiences and tips with other gamers and the gaming community. A lot of these games touch on spiritual and even theological themes that explore complex concepts of God, evil, ethics, suffering and redemption.

All this has been made possible through the development of our digital culture that has enabled the world of gaming to embrace so many other parts of people's lives, especially those areas that involve strategy and decision-making. Some video games allow the player to take the role of God. For example, in *The Sims* a player creates and takes control of a group of virtual people, giving them guidance and tweaking aspects as small as what they look like or the clothes they are wearing up to their potential jobs and life goals. The player gives them choices and lets them live their lives and deal with the challenges they run into and connections they make with other characters.

Other games allow the player to take the role of the devil. In this case, the attraction is that most people couldn't imagine taking that role in real life, so it becomes more exciting to think and act like a devil with full awareness that the story is a fantasy that takes place in a magnificent but artificial world with complex characters and storyline. Most games don't take these extreme positions; they place the player halfway between the two, but allow the player to choose in which direction they want to take the story, bearing in mind that each choice has different consequences that will affect the outcome. In the game series *Mass Effect*, the player controls the character, Commander Shepard. The player gets to customize their gender, appearance and skill set. After that they travel through space and undertake missions. Who the player talks to, the answers they give, and the characters they kill or let live affects the way other characters treat them, the battles they eventually fight or avoid, treaties with entire empires and the ending of the game, which changes depending on the player's choices.

The question I asked myself as I was playing some of these games and thinking about their influence on the lives of different generations was how do the games work in reshaping the player's mind? I think that they do play a role, like all other experiences in life (studying at university, choosing what kind of job we want or whether we believe in God or not). All these various aspects of our life require us to make a decision and each decision we make influences the storyline of our lives. This has led me to think about the alternative reality that games offer in order to teach us how to be responsible for our choices in life. It was very interesting for me to see that digital technology has allowed games' creators a bigger range of options that increases with every new generation of games.

I noticed that some games can remember choices or omissions made within the game itself or even earlier games in the same franchise. These choices can cause the death or survival of main characters based on earlier decisions. Although the player does not necessarily know the outcome of certain choices, the game gives the player the possibility to be curious, knowing that it's not possible to change your decision unless you want to reset the game. This made me wonder how many decisions we could make in real life out of curiosity, knowing that we could not undo our actions. Some actions that are also taken within the game world may seem benign but can have serious and unforeseen consequences. I remember saving a small child from a plague village, only for her to go on and infect the entire island, killing many thousands. Similarly, in the game series *The Walking Dead*, the player is given tough choices for the character they control; letting a character die or live can change the story completely and make other characters resent each other or even help each other to change the outcome of the entire game.

If we look at the scene of the Garden of Gethsemane and observe Christ being open and transparent in front of the Father, expressing his wish not to die and choosing his life over the cross, we see here two options. Each option has universal consequences. The first is: what if Jesus had refused the cross and chosen to live, which was a very real option? What would the consequences have been? Different writers and filmmakers have tried to explore such an outcome in their works, one of the best of which is *The Last Temptation of Christ* by Nikos Kazantzakis. Only his relationship with the Father allowed Christ to surrender his will: "Abba, Father," he said, "everything is possible for you. Take this cup from me. Yet not what I will, but what you will" (Mark 14:36). Jesus allowed the Culture of God to embrace his life completely. Because of that, he invited the Father to guide the coming events. In the Garden of Gethsemane, Jesus tells us that it is absolutely fine to put before God our thoughts, even if what we want does not match the will of God. Jesus does that with the faith that he is the Son of God, but so are we. As children of God, we are able to stand before him being open and transparent about what we want.

In our digital culture, video games allow players to explore the healthy struggle involved in decision-making. Many games have a spiritual aspect that is integral to the plot. I believe that this is a deliberate decision on the part of the games' creators that adds another layer to the complexity of the narrative structure, making the ethical choices even more interesting. The advancement of digital technology has made moral choices more diverse and nuanced. These moral choices that are faced within the game give the player freedom to explore the vision and the world of the game. This leads me to think about the freedom, or lack of it, that we experience in our lives to make choices. The life of Christ encourages us to value and use the freedom that we have in God to open new levels of thinking and communication with God and with our reality.

Some games allow players to play as a character with a clean slate to start building up the character to make them more effective. The way that players build the character, from the way they look to the skills that they develop and weapons that they choose to defend themselves, helps them to deal with the problems and obstacles that the game puts in their way. As the player explores the game, they learn new skills, collect new tools and form alliances with other characters to progress in understanding the story of the game, achieve their goals and get help in making decisions within the game. Digital technology has made this sophisticated process possible with increasingly powerful game engines that allow increased storage and memory, with better functionality and a better and more immersive game experience. Writers, artists and engineers are only restricted by their imagination in what they can create as a result of this increased functionality coupled with internet streaming speeds that improve every year.

A good example of a game with a clean slate is *Minecraft*. In survival mode, players start as a character with no skills, items or weapons in a vast open world. It's up to them to decide what they want to do. The player has complete freedom. They can gather materials and craft tools, start farms with crops and animals, build houses or anything they can dream of. They can choose to progress through the game at their own pace and play with other players as well. If they don't want to deal with the game's challenges at all and just want to build with unlimited resources, they can play in creative mode. That gives them access to a "god mod" (modification): massive open space, infinite resources, the ability to create any item or tool instantly, the ability to fly or teleport and other similar powers. The game promotes playing how a person wants.

In this parallel universe of gaming, which is constantly evolving both on a hardware and software level, we see that more and more people have access to games either online or offline. I can fully understand the dilemma that parents feel when they see their children spending more time in that universe. I also appreciate their deep concern over what benefits video games offer their children over the short and the long term.

Like everything else in life, gaming has both positives and negatives. We cannot ignore that the development of online gaming has helped to create communities and a way for people to connect with others who share the same interests—particularly during the recent pandemic that restricted the ability to meet in person. Some games have also helped people realize skills and abilities that they were not aware they had in strategic thinking, spatial awareness, planning and so on. This awareness can also spill over into choices made in real life.

We should remember that games are essentially stories but ones which require the player to be an active participant in the way the narrative progresses. Some of the actions taken within a game can mirror actions and decisions made in real life, especially when the game shows the player the consequences of their actions. This can be helpful for young adults to appreciate and explore certain situations, especially when it comes to building relationships with others. Video games have opened the gate to ease the barriers of gender, race and sexuality. Players are encouraged to form in-game relationships with other characters of the same gender, of a different race or cultural background, without any of the issues that might hinder this in real life.

Of course, I am aware that not all games are educational or have a positive impact and there is indeed another side to the coin. Some games, like other forms of art or entertainment, also have hidden messages that can affect people negatively or positively. An example of a negative impact would be the horror game *Agony*. The player assumes the role of a tormented soul in hell, without any memories, trying to navigate hell itself and seeing terrifying demons and the gruesome torture of people. An example of a positive impact would be the game *Assassin's Creed Origins* being used to teach history. The game offers a great visualization of ancient Egypt, and even has a built-in discovery tour mode where people who don't want to deal with the combat or missions can take an interactive guided tour through ancient Egypt with detailed narration.

When I look at a painting by Francis Bacon, for example, I feel especially disturbed by his religious depictions of the crucifixion and the screaming popes. When I see his series of pope paintings, I see the scream of humanity. We know that these paintings were inspired by Velasquez's portrait of Innocent X now hanging in the gallery of the

Palazzo Doria Pamphili in Rome. I know that many scholars have written extensively about these works, but they still release a powerful response in the viewer, even with no prior knowledge of the history behind them. For me, the paintings evoke a revolutionary message against violence and political and religious oppression. Any example of human creativity carries a message, consciously or unconsciously, and video games are no exception. Indeed, given the interactive way in which they are played, these messages can be even more powerful.

We must admit that most games have an element of violence, whether physical, mental or psychological. Most narratives are built around the concept of conquering, defeating the enemy and world-building. That requires a strategy that can be extremely violent. There is a huge debate surrounding the influence of the violence that is offered through gaming on people's violent actions in real life. Although I don't believe that digital violence has a serious direct effect on aggressive or violent actions in real life, we need to acknowledge that whatever we feed our minds will have an effect on shaping them in the same way that the food we eat helps in shaping our bodies. Some minds have a greater tendency towards being influenced by digital violence than others. I believe that we should be careful in casting a blanket judgement on the gaming world based on a surface analysis of violence in games.

This takes me to our engagement with the story of salvation that did not end with the ascension of the Lord but rather continues to unfold in our lives every day. I feel that Christianity is in some respects like video games and demands decisions to be made within the culture of the story. In Christianity the culture of the story is a life-changing interaction between our story and the story of God. The more that we immerse ourselves in this dynamic, the more we get to know God personally and feel the presence of Jesus Christ in our lives. The story of God becomes integrated with our story, and we become citizens in both cultures—our earthly culture and the divine culture that enables us to make decisions and face every challenge in our lives empowered by the Holy Spirit, who becomes the engine driving the interaction between the two cultures. As our digital age progresses, so should our faith in Christ grow.

The writer of the epistle to the Hebrews argues that:

> Anyone who lives on milk, being still an infant, is not acquainted
> with the teaching about righteousness. But solid food is for
> the mature, who by constant use have trained themselves to
> distinguish good from evil (Hebrews 5:13–14).

As we have grown in using our digital technology over the years, so we need to learn how to grow in our faith. As we learn how to enjoy and interact with the narrative of an interesting video game and build our character and community to fit the environment of the story, so should we build our relationship with God and invite the Lord to be the centre of our lives so that we build our character and community in harmony with the divine culture that the Lord brings to our lives. I believe that we could learn a lot from the world of gaming in how to manage our life with God and deepen the common ground between the story of God and our own story. The more that I maximize this commonality, the more I mature in my faith and experience the richness of the banquet that God sets before me. In our journey with God, we can explore the excitement of the multiple dimensions that we can experience on this journey.

Our God is, on one hand, the Creator of the universe (or universes) and, at the same time, he took the decision to become a human being living the human story alongside us. Our faith is in a God who feels for our suffering that he also suffered, and appreciates our tears and our loves because he also experienced them. He is not the transcendent being who cannot understand the experiences of limited humanity. The encounter between my story and the story of God in Christ can be incredibly exciting but also both affirming and challenging. Whether in a video game or in real life, we cannot escape the fact that we must meet the command to make decisions. One of these decisions is whether we say yes to God and embark on a journey with him or turn our backs on his offer and walk away.

Being interested in sci-fi and fantasy has helped me to shed light on new aspects of my spiritual life and inspired me to communicate with young people in the East and West. I can therefore say that the Culture of God as a culture of peace and love calls on us to progress with technological advancement without fear, but at the same time to use these resources to build harmony and love between different belief systems and schools of spirituality based on a position of respect for the other. We learn from sci-fi and fantasy that there are ways for harmony to exist in an advanced technological society. Futuristic frameworks should help us to understand our ever-changing reality without losing the prophetic vision of Jesus Christ. Christian faith is perfectly able to learn from other faiths and spirituality, as well as sci-fi and fantasy stories, in order to reach for a better future for human society. These other religions and realities do not threaten our faith in any way or undermine the centrality of Jesus Christ.

8

Digital vision and the future of Christianity

Recently I heard the British envoy to the World Health Organization evaluating how the world reacted to the Covid-19 pandemic. He said that the world had failed to cooperate in a constructive way, especially at the beginning of the pandemic. I sensed a deep disappointment in his evaluation. At the same time, I wasn't surprised by his statement. The pandemic has revealed how fragile and shallow international relationships are. His statement reminded me of one of our meetings at the Foreign Office in London at the height of the civil war in Syria. One of the senior officials leading the meeting told me that international relations are not and cannot be built on friendships and human connections but are built purely on the basis of self-interest. If the interests of one side of the civil war in Syria coincided with British interests, then they would be supported. Even though I knew that deep down, it still shocked me to have it laid out so baldly. I felt that humanity had been reduced to political interests decided by officials. People dying or suffering are subject to these political calculations.

This reasoning applies even during a global pandemic that has killed millions. I fully understand that countries cannot be run on human emotion and ethical principles alone. Politicians must weigh up national and international situations with the domestic economy. A thriving economy means by and large that they will be re-elected. Being brought up in the Near East as well as living for decades in the West made me realize the importance of the election cycle in Western countries, especially in the United States. Every president had a different strategy on the Near East and reacted, and acted, in completely different ways.

When President Clinton was in power, for example, he was passionate about finding a solution to complicated issues around the Arab-Israeli conflict. In contrast, President George W. Bush was determined instead to destroy Iraq. This inconsistency of policy reactions to the Near East is also visible in the UK. We see the massive difference between prime ministers like Tony Blair, who was fully engaged in building relationships in the Near East only to fully support the Bush administration's invasion of Iraq, and those who came after him who had dramatically different attitudes to the Near East.

The British envoy's statement highlighted the failure of the international community in the East and West to contain the pandemic quickly and save millions of lives. We have seen how countries acted entirely in the national self-interest from the outset and failed to share information and resources worldwide. This failure to share has led, in my opinion, to a global tragedy. Whether in conflicts in the Near East and Africa, or global crises like the pandemic, we see that there is barely any real sense of an international community. The world is so fragmented and there is little international will to work together to solve a conflict purely to save lives and end suffering. I feel that we are hostages to political and economic equations led by politicians or business interests and there is not nearly enough challenge to the motivation behind international decisions.

When the G7 countries met in Cornwall in June 2021, they decided to donate one billion vaccines to less developed countries. This decision left a huge number of people feeling that this was an act of charity, one that revealed the disparity between countries around the world. I'm not sure that these leaders understand how much resentment this causes in other countries, leading to the rise of more fanatical ideologies. Such failures give some political and religious leaders a reason to brainwash more young people to groom and recruit them to extreme ideologies. The open wounds of conflict and economic turmoil in the Near East and beyond, plus the results of the global pandemic, have greatly strengthened the grip of extremist leaders over the hearts and minds of young people in the region. This makes the fight against extremist terrorism even more difficult in the face of the highly sophisticated technological age that we live in.

The world has gone through different globally influential revolutions, some of which were socio-political and some technological. All have reshaped our world in the last three centuries. One of the most influential was the French Revolution. Another was the decolonization of countries in the second half of the last century. The Arab Spring was also a life-changing and influential movement in the region. On the economic level, the world went through a massive change with the Industrial Revolution, followed by the discovery of electricity in the nineteenth century that gave the world hope for a better life and changed the face of industry and the everyday life of the population. In the last century, we experienced the dawn of computing and the feverish race to explore space that took the world by storm and changed our understanding of ourselves and the world around us.

In the twenty-first century, we are experiencing another revolution in the form of our understanding of robotics, 3D printing and even quantum computing, which has reimagined the use of computers. In today's world the internet is not only a source of information and connectivity but it has also invaded the fabric of our daily lives. It has become something that we carry with us everywhere, from the watch we wear and the glasses we see through to the car we drive. In the midst of this sea of change, we look beyond the bubble of this technology and see that there are still people in the world with no electricity or fresh water, who have no schools and live in extreme poverty. Every generation of politicians promises to lift these people out of poverty, but the pace is so slow while the gap between the very rich and the very poor is growing every day. Worst of all is when the poor become a slogan for political rhetoric. So much has been promised in the name of the poor but so little delivered.

Whatever is done is done for reasons other than primarily to relieve those in suffering. Even when there was much discussion of how to help poor countries during the pandemic, it was within the context of point-scoring between the rich countries. Those who are making the case for charity turn a blind eye to the corruption within many of these poor countries or use it as an excuse to do nothing. In many cases, when people do rise up to depose their corrupt leadership, they become the victims of a proxy war that causes more suffering. I am thinking of course of the situation in Yemen, in Libya and in my country of Syria. All the countries involved in proxy wars around the world do it in the name of helping the people. The result has been devastating, with millions of dead and a staggering total of more than 70 million refugees worldwide. This leaves us with the question of who really speaks for the poor and who really works to lift their suffering?

The Culture of God that Jesus showed us and lived challenges the very essence of political and economic exploitation, beginning at a local community level up to international politics. Mark tells us in his Gospel that:

> On reaching Jerusalem, Jesus entered the temple courts and began driving out those who were buying and selling there. He overturned the tables of the money changers and the benches of those selling doves, and would not allow anyone to carry merchandise through the temple courts. And as he taught them, he said, "Is it not written: 'My house will be called a house of prayer for all nations.' But you have made it a den of robbers."
>
> The chief priests and the teachers of the law heard this and began looking for a way to kill him, for they feared him, because the whole crowd was amazed at his teaching (Mark 11:15–18).

In this extraordinary event, Jesus challenged the whole corrupt political and economic infrastructure that the chief priests and religious leaders had built around the temple. His rage was not primarily against those who were buying and selling in the temple courts because he knew that people needed to offer animal sacrifices according to the law. His rage was instead against the way that the religious leaders handled the money and the corruption that prevented the flow of money that came to the temple from being used to help the poor and relieve their suffering. His concern was not with the money as such but with what the institution of the temple did with the money, or failed to do with it, to help the community. Many social movements and ideologies have been inspired by the Culture of God that Jesus showed and taught as he lived the life of the kingdom of God. This should not be turned into a political ideology in our world but should be used to inspire change in the way that economic systems operate and lead us to ask difficult questions about how governments, charities or institutions are using money to lift the burden of poverty from hundreds of millions of people around the world.

We have to admit that in many ways we have failed as a Church to reflect and live this divine culture, especially in relation to the increasing influence of the highly technological culture that controls the movement of money and the distribution of wealth around the world. Unfortunately, the sad truth is that the digital culture of today is much more powerful than the Gospel. I do not mean that this culture is in its nature stronger than the Gospel but rather that we are overwhelmed by the influence of technology in our lives, so much so that we have lost our direction. I feel as if Christianity is moving in the opposite direction from that which Jesus Christ showed us. It is essential that we stand in front of the mirror of the Culture of God and see our failures. Otherwise, we will never be able to turn back to the path that Jesus laid out for us. In an increasingly technological society, the Church as an institution has failed to live the true faith. Instead of being strengthened and empowered by the Culture of God, which is the culture of truth and love, we find ourselves living in fear of change and facing the new era that is waiting for us if we embrace the challenge of the Culture of God.

It seems to me that we are choosing to accept the suffering of the present rather than looking towards the future because moving forward means implementing and embracing change. Failing to move towards the future shown by the Culture of God means that we do not love freedom. Instead, the Church chooses to be enslaved by present failure. We have become used to the status quo and very little change is happening in churches everywhere. I acknowledge and praise God for initiatives within the Church that show us that there are people ready to change, but these are not enough. During the pandemic, I had the opportunity to attend many online services, Bible studies and lectures. I am saddened that the vast majority of what I heard was the regurgitation of old ideas that people are fed up with because they have heard them over and over again. For example, I felt the lack of powerful, creative ways of looking at the Scriptures. I believe that to move on, we must go back to the Scriptures and study them armed with the vision of the Culture of God that provides us with new perspectives that help us to make the stories of the Scriptures more relevant in the highly technological culture that we live in.

Back to our roots: the start of the revolution

Today, our understanding of ourselves as human beings has changed dramatically due to the digital revolution that we are living through. The "I" at the heart of this revolution is different from the "I" that we understood less than 30 years ago. This change in understanding has not stopped evolving since the Renaissance, through all the revolutions that we experienced from the Enlightenment to the Industrial Revolution and today's technological revolution. The question is whether faith has progressed alongside all this radical change. Where are we today in terms of understanding who we are? I believe with all my heart that discovering the roots of faith is the best way to start a revolution. Martin Luther, for example, tried to return to the roots of faith and wanted to liberate the Scriptures and make them available to the people. Even the Renaissance was in essence a sense of going back to discover the roots of human culture through studying classical Greek and Roman culture as well as the culture of the Bible. Another example is the second Vatican Council that sought to go back to basics and rediscover the power that comes from studying the roots of faith. Our roots as Christians must lie in the Scriptures. Every time we go back to those roots, we discover a new way to connect with God and allow the Holy Spirit to refresh the Church and pump new blood and energy into her veins.

Another revolution that changed the face of Christianity, that is also linked with returning to our roots, was the translation of the Bible into different languages. This was indeed a revolution that changed the Church forever as these translations brought with them different perspectives and ways of understanding the Scriptures. Amid the digital revolution that we live in, we need a similar revolution that takes the Culture of God and turns it into a journey back to the roots of faith, and that opens the door for the Holy Spirit to lead the Church into a new era and a new future.

Jesus Christ in his life taught and proclaimed the kingdom of God, which marks the era of the sovereignty of the triune God. At the same time, it is Emmanuel that means "God with us". This theme of the kingdom of God is central to the teachings of Jesus Christ that describe a new era that he opened up for humanity. At the heart of this proclamation of the kingdom of God is change: change of heart, of mindset, of how we approach God, of our understanding of ourselves and in the dynamic relationship that Jesus created between humanity and God. The Culture of God can be understood as the way in which we live in the kingdom of God and an exploration of the mind and the heart and the passion of the Trinity. It is also a movement that takes us back to the roots of how Jesus revealed the heart and mind of God in his own earthly culture, as well as how he revealed his own identity to his disciples and further to us all down the generations.

The Culture of God that Jesus revealed has three different roles. The first is to show us the true nature of God and his interaction with us. Secondly, it empowers us to build the relationship that he desires. Lastly, the Culture of God challenges our thoughts, actions and words so that we look at Christ as our compass that leads us to the heart of the divine Trinity. In our highly evolved digital culture, we need to understand that this human journey is not going to stop and that we won't be able to undo the progress we have made. Indeed, it will progress further. Because of that, it is imperative that we as Christians keep engaging with both our culture and the roots of our faith. One of the most important aspects of this is to re-engage constantly with the Scriptures.

We see Christ turning some of the most important ways to interact with God upside down. He directs the disciples, and indeed us today, towards a different perspective that shows what God wants rather than what we think he wants. Many times in religion we get it wrong. If we look at the history of the Church, we see how many times we had to readjust and correct our interpretations, for example in the relationship between Church and State and the Church and science. One of the best examples from the life of Christ that illustrates this and has parallels with our situation today is the incident that Jesus and the disciples faced during a storm in the Sea of Galilee. The Gospel according to Mark relates this incident in the following way:

> That day when evening came, he said to his disciples, "Let us go
> over to the other side." Leaving the crowd behind, they took him
> along, just as he was, in the boat. There were also other boats
> with him. A furious squall came up, and the waves broke over

the boat, so that it was nearly swamped. Jesus was in the stern, sleeping on a cushion. The disciples woke him and said to him, "Teacher, don't you care if we drown?"

He got up, rebuked the wind and said to the waves, "Quiet! Be still!" Then the wind died down and it was completely calm.

He said to his disciples, "Why are you so afraid? Do you still have no faith?"

They were terrified and asked each other, "Who is this? Even the wind and the waves obey him!" (Mark 4:35–41)

This is an incredible scene that Mark describes in a very powerful way. We see how Jesus asks the disciples to sail into deep water, after which a huge storm appears with waves battering the boat that fills quickly with water. Many of the disciples must have faced sea storms before. So let us consider this scene from their eyes. They felt that the storm was threatening the boat and with it their lives. They also saw that it was filling with water, increasing the threat of the boat sinking. Although they were accustomed to sea storms, they began to be afraid for their lives because of the strength of the storm. At this point, we see the disciples feeling lost and unable to cope with the situation. Clearly, from the text we see that they reached a point of fear for their lives. They were obviously astounded by the sight of Jesus in a deep sleep on a cushion. You can feel how upset they were with him that he was able to sleep through this life-threatening situation.

It is also clear from the text that they did not try to understand why he was sleeping or how he was able to sleep through this crisis. The reason for this is that they were too afraid to think clearly and make sense of the situation. Fear not only confuses us but also fogs our minds and prevents us from seeing clearly and judging a situation correctly. They felt that their last option was to wake him up to make him aware of the situation. Because they were afraid, they woke him up in anger, saying, "Don't you care if we drown?" In a way, they were saying, "How dare you sleep through this?" They were accusing him of not caring and demanding that he do something to fix the situation. It reminds me of the accusation that Martha throws at Jesus when she says: "If you had been here, my brother would not have died" (John 11:21). For the disciples, it was as if the sleeping Jesus was not there. This is like when a mother moves away from a small child; the child cries, as for them it is as if their parent has disappeared entirely.

Essentially, the disciples are behaving like children, and we see this in Jesus' response and his reprimand, "Do you still have no faith?" Jesus is asking them when they are going to understand their relationship with him. He ended the storm with a word and then turned to the disciples to deal with the storm of their confusion and fear. Why is this story so important for us today? The disciples treated Jesus as a superhero or, in the language of our culture today, as an action man. They came to him to demand that he act. Most little children treat their parents in the same way because, for the child, they are also the superheroes who can fix everything and make things happen. In our present culture, we want our God to compete with these action heroes that we have created in our minds.

This can have a terrible impact on our faith. When the disciples woke Jesus up, they were unaware of his presence while he was asleep. His presence was only tangible to them when he was awake. We always want to treat God as an almighty superhero and forget something that the Nicene Creed reminds us of in the first sentence: "We believe in one God, the Father almighty." We see that the word "Father" comes before the word "almighty". The power of God comes not from the fact that he is almighty but rather from the fact that he is a loving father. Whatever our experience with our own fathers may be, this should not influence our understanding of the fatherhood that Jesus chose to describe God as. We should not project our own experience on this understanding of God.

After the storm had been quelled, the disciples were even more frightened by the display of his power, despite the fact that they wanted him to fix the situation. Sometimes, we feel as if God is not there and is silent in the face of our problems and desperation. There are two ways of dealing with this. The way of the disciples is to require action, and this is what our culture pushes us to expect. The second is to ask God to reassure us of his presence, which is the position of the crucified Christ when he cries, "*Eloi, Eloi, lema sabachthani?*" (which means "My God, my God, why have you forsaken me?") (Mark 15:34). With this cry, Jesus was not asking God for action to save him from the cross. He had resolved this with God in the Garden of Gethsemane: "Abba, Father," he said, "everything is possible for you. Take this cup from me. Yet not what I will, but what you will" (Mark 14:36). His approach to God is not to see him as an action man but rather as a supportive father who engages with him in a loving dialogue.

Our culture pushes us to project on God the dominant features of our culture, those of action, of power and of competition. The Culture of God shown in the incident of the storm is vivid because Jesus reveals to the disciples how God desires them to relate to him. Looking at this incident and exploring the Culture of God within this framework helps us to correct our understanding of who God is. Jesus reveals that he is not primarily a superhero who deals in dramatic action, otherwise he wouldn't have been so upset with the disciples and their lack of faith. Rather he wanted to teach the disciples that being in communion with him means feeling his presence all the time, even when they think he is not there. He wanted them to be mature in their understanding of his identity and the identity of God the Father, who loves humanity as a father, acts like a father and is powerful in his love as a father.

He challenges the disciples' notion of faith. They had faith because they decided to wake him up in the belief that he could solve the situation, but this is not the kind of faith that Jesus demands. I asked myself when I was studying this text how the disciples would have reacted had they truly understood Jesus? How could they have behaved in a way that would have met his approval as true disciples? One option would have been for one of them to do what Jesus did and stop the storm with a word through the power of their faith in him. John relates how Jesus said, "Very truly I tell you, whoever believes in me will do the works I have been doing, and they will do even greater things than these, because I am going to the Father" (John 14:12). Another option could be to have faith that they would survive because Jesus was on the boat; or to pray for guidance to endure the storm. There are options other than rushing to wake him up. Jesus asks why they were afraid that they had been abandoned when their faith should show them that they had not been abandoned even while he slept.

It is logical for us to ask the question of what to say to a Ukrainian, a Yemeni or a Syrian family who have lost everything as a result of a missile attack that levelled their homes and cities. Where is a merciful and compassionate God in this situation? I heard this same question posed by a senior politician in this country. The prevailing culture pushes us to compare our God to the Marvel superheroes that we see on our screens and in the cinema. Our God is and will always be a loser in this comparison as God is not a superhero who saves the day through a magnificent display of power. The power of God is within us. We should all stand up to challenge war and those who spread it. We shouldn't be discouraged that our God is not a Superman, or Batman or Captain America. Our God is the God of love who works with us and through us. It is catastrophic when a church tries to justify and defend any kind of war as that goes against the very heart of the Culture of God. Our faith in the God of love and life should empower us to raise our voice and challenge the ways of dealing with the storms in our lives. We must act as people of faith to find different ways to solve our differences and conflicts. Tens of billions of dollars have been spent in a senseless war that has destroyed a country in the heart of Europe as the world was emerging from another catastrophe caused by the Covid pandemic. We are all guilty of reverting to violence to resolve our differences, with hidden economic agendas that form the tapestry behind the political conflicts that we see. Our God is not Spiderman, and we are not watching a movie. Our God is in the middle of the storm ready to partner with us to bring a better life to humanity.

Looking for love in all the wrong places

Recently, I was approached separately by three people from different cultures and backgrounds who all shared one common dilemma. They all fell in love with people they had met online and had never met in person. Their relationships developed online using text, voice and camera. All three felt that they were deeply in love and ready to sacrifice anything for these online relationships. Sadly, all three of these relationships failed, leaving these people feeling devastated and broken-hearted. These three people spanned the decades from their early twenties to their early forties. They all believed that the person they were in love with had deceived them. Two of the three believe in God but did not get any succour from their faith.

We had many long discussions about love and reality and how much we can rely on digital technology to claim that we know another person. I felt the sincerity of their feelings but also felt that all three suffered from a sense of disorientation and were unable to distinguish between the presence of people in their everyday lives and the online presence of people they loved. They allowed their imagination and emotions to take over and fill the missing pieces of these online relationships. They had all taken at face value the truth of the information they had about these people online and built on it according to their own desires and needs. They didn't seem to realize that these people only existed online according to the image that they chose to present. Instead, they felt betrayed that these people who they thought they knew had other facets and characteristics off camera and in real life.

These three were quick to commit to a relationship and fall in love with someone they barely knew and who was in reality a fantasy figure. They entered these relationships with huge expectations. They didn't use digital technology to get to know that person better and to find out more about them. Instead of using technology as a starting point in relationships, it became an end point. They didn't want their image of the other to change or evolve through a process of getting to know each other because they were in love with the image that they had created in their head. The excitement of online dating, with its immediate gratification from direct texting and the apparent intimacy of face-to-face calls, was very compelling.

The pieces that they built to fill the gaps in their knowledge of the other were specific to what they needed. One partner, for example, mentioned to my friend that she was going to a museum with a friend, which pleased my friend greatly as he was interested in art. It later turned out that she wasn't interested in art, but he had assumed that she was because that fulfilled a need in him for that kind of connection. In digital relationships, there are a lot more gaps for your imagination to fill than in real life. We all have the problem of loving someone by projecting what we like or need onto the other, but this is just magnified online. We try to find ourselves in the other in order to love them. This reminds me of the myth of Narcissus, who believed that his reflection in the pond was someone else and fell in love with that person. He couldn't see outside of himself and couldn't see that it was only his reflection in the pond. These three people saw much of their own reflection in the people that they fell in love with online.

When we go outside of ourselves, we make ourselves vulnerable. It is difficult for us to move beyond our comfort zone in order to know the other. By recognizing someone as a person in their own right, we give them the freedom to choose whether to be in love with us or not. True love demands freedom and love needs this freedom in order not to be possessive. If I'm not giving you the freedom to choose, I am saying that I own you. Sometimes the illusion is so beautiful and seductive, we don't allow any space for anything that can challenge this image. We are ready to do anything to keep this illusion alive. In this case, we become like Narcissus who yearned to kiss his reflection in the pond but instead withered away from the impossibility of this love. This love is possessive and selfish. It does not allow any margin of possibility to discover that the other is not for me or to allow the other to see that I am not for them.

A dear friend in Italy once drew my attention to the fact that when we switch off our devices, the screen turns black and becomes a mirror that reflects our own image. That reflection had a powerful effect on me. The digital world, as busy and information-packed as it is, can also be extremely lonely. When I switch off my device, all that is left is my own image on the screen. My ministry among young people in Syria and Iraq while living in the West has given me insight into the role of digital communication in these different cultures. In the Near East, personal relationships lie at the heart of society. We invest a lot of time and effort and ourselves in building personal relationships with others in our community. Some people then fall into the trap of thinking that digital technology can offer the same quality of relationships online as they have in real life. Nevertheless, if we use digital technology to get to know people and expand our horizons without imposing further expectations, it can open doors onto the world.

It's not easy to love or be loved online. In Christianity, the incarnation is an essential part of faith that God became one of us. There is nothing that can replace someone's physical presence. God recognized the need to take this journey and become one of us. His love demanded that he experience our world even if it meant limiting himself to space and time and exposing himself to pain and human loss and suffering. This did not prevent him from taking this journey because he loved us. When I pray to God the Father through the Son, I know that God knows how I feel because he has experienced that himself. When St John says, "Whoever lives in love lives in God, and God in them" (1 John 4:16), he is talking about the love that made God vulnerable to hurt and suffering to the extent that he faced death in the ugliest way possible.

If we take this and apply it to our digital world, it exposes the disadvantages that exist in building human relationships online. Online relationships lack the most important aspect, which is the physical presence of the person. Whatever experiences we share digitally, the physical dimension is lacking and that should not be underestimated. Online encounters, however, provide opportunities that we didn't have before to get to know each other. My advice as a minister to young people is that we need to differentiate between getting to know someone online and liking that person and being in love with them. It is a huge blessing to be able to widen our circle of acquaintance, especially if we are aware of the pros and cons of such encounters. We shouldn't confuse infatuation with being in love with a person, which needs much more than the interface that the digital world can offer.

The possibility of going out of myself in order to be with the other and allow them the space to be themselves with me shrinks considerably without the ability to meet face-to-face. The physical dimension of human relationships is quite powerful and physical attraction can easily dominate our feelings for somebody. This can cause us much confusion so that we cannot differentiate between being in love or in lust with another. We live in a time when quick fixes are very common, and this can have an enormous impact on our ability to build stable and long-lasting relationships. The Culture of God challenges this quick-fix culture and our selfishness in conducting relationships. The model that the Trinity provides us with is that the Father gives himself to the Son entirely in love, and the Son returns that love and gives himself entirely to the Father. The Son takes nothing for himself in a dynamic relationship that is enabled by the power of the Holy Spirit.

The relationship between the Father and the Son doesn't require them to blend into one another. This unique relationship allows the Son to remain the Son and the Father to remain the Father. Neither loses their identity. This is how we understand the freedom that should exist in love that respects the identity of the other and rejoices in being with the other and giving the other ourselves, not in order to own them but rather unconditionally in an act of love. Being in the kingdom of God that Jesus Christ taught about is to adopt this culture of the Trinity that empowers us to respect our own identity as well as protecting and respecting the identity of the other. This is the foundation of our understanding of love as Christians based on the mind and passion of God revealed in the life and teachings of Jesus Christ.

This kind of love is also like faith, which exists for the other and not only for ourselves. We see such love and faith in different ways when we look at Jesus' encounters with people like Jairus, one of the leaders of the synagogue. He came to Jesus to plead for the life of his sick daughter and begged him to come to his home to heal her. This incident shows Jesus' respect for Jairus' love for his daughter and faith in him that allowed Jairus to open himself up and plead for those he loved. It shows how we go out of ourselves to bring those we love to the presence of God. It makes us consider how, when we plead for others, we allow ourselves to exist for the other and not always revolve around ourselves and our own needs. On the way to the house, Jesus was delayed and the child died. Jesus encouraged Jairus to hang on to his faith even in the face of the death of his daughter. He continued to journey to the house and brought her back to life.

The question for us today is: are we able in the present digital age to keep our faith and go beyond our ego in order to love people as they are rather than imposing on them what we want them to be? Our digital culture introduced into our emotional life and our relationships with other people a strong virtual dimension that didn't exist only a decade or so ago. This dimension is present through the communication technology of social media and video technology. We must acknowledge that this has shortened the distances between people and made communication with friends and loved ones much easier and more convenient. This close proximity through virtual means, however, has also made us more vulnerable. When we get hurt it is more difficult to deal with because of the physical distance between us. We can only rely on virtual means to communicate and resolve our hurt, and this can amplify the negative side of digital communication and highlights the importance of face-to-face encounters in solving our problems.

The Culture of God is a culture that embraces the incarnation. God desired the personal encounter with humanity. This means that we should not underestimate the effects of the lack of physical connection. We have felt this absence most keenly during the Covid pandemic of 2020. The press media continually showed us the consequences of this absence of physical contact from friends and loved ones. We saw the harm caused by people's inability to communicate physically with their loved ones. Many people had to rely more and more on virtual communication apps like Zoom, Facebook and Instagram. Although these forms of technology kept us going, they couldn't replace the physical encounter. That time made me appreciate more my birth culture in the Near East, where physical intimacy is of utmost importance and is the cornerstone of human relationships.

I believe that love demands physical existence. Although it can benefit from the digital technology at our fingertips, it cannot take priority. Love is connected intrinsically with generosity and hospitality. In the saving acts of Jesus Christ, God revealed beyond any shadow of doubt that his culture is manifested through his generous self-giving, even up to the cross, and his hospitality in offering life in its fullness to humanity through the resurrection of Jesus. We see in that act the ultimate expression of the culture of the Trinity. We are called as Christians in every age and in every generation, regardless of our scientific or technological advances, to know and experience personally the glory of this act of self-giving. St Paul says in his letter to the Philippians:

> I want to know Christ—yes, to know the power of his resurrection and participation in his sufferings, becoming like him in his death, and so, somehow, attaining to the resurrection from the dead.

> Not that I have already obtained all this, or have already
> arrived at my goal, but I press on to take hold of that for which
> Christ Jesus took hold of me (Philippians 3:10–12).

The verb "to know" that St Paul uses here reminds me of the words of the Virgin Mary when she responded to the angel after he announced her pregnancy, saying (in some translations), "How shall this be, seeing I know not a man?" (Luke 1:34). To know in this context means "to build a relationship". To know Christ in St Paul's writings means to have a relationship with Christ. In this living, breathing relationship, we experience the power of his resurrection. Our afflictions and suffering are in fellowship with the suffering of Christ on the cross. For the sake of knowing him in this way, Paul is ready to consider all the advantages in his life as garbage. His aim is to win Christ even if the result is to lose everything else. This leads us to look at the gains we have in today's digital age. We need, as always, to find the balance between the opportunities released by technology that allows us to reach out to people beyond our immediate physical circle and the limitations and challenges that this technology presents. Such technology is like money; in itself, it's neither bad nor good. The question that we always face is how to use it without hurting others or hurting ourselves.

The roadmap to the Culture of God

> For it is we who are the circumcision, we who serve God by his
> Spirit, who boast in Christ Jesus, and who put no confidence
> in the flesh—though I myself have reasons for such confidence.
>
> If someone else thinks they have reasons to put confidence
> in the flesh, I have more: circumcised on the eighth day, of the
> people of Israel, of the tribe of Benjamin, a Hebrew of Hebrews; in
> regard to the law, a Pharisee; as for zeal, persecuting the church;
> as for righteousness based on the law, faultless (Philippians
> 3:3–6).

This text of St Paul's letter to the Philippians reminds me of our life in the East and in the West. In both sets of cultures, people are hugely preoccupied with what they can gain, including materialistic gains like money and possessions as well as non-materialistic gains like success, fame, family and social connections, power and of course influence. Most people these days seek some, if not all, of these gains to the extent that our highly technological cultures feed the frenzy of their pursuit. We see from the text that Paul had a lot to boast about: things that he inherited and things that he achieved. He had to list them in order to tell the Philippian church what he could have enjoyed if he had focused on either his inheritance or his achievements.

I remember a dear friend who had no immediate family, or extended family, who found a computer program that helped him to trace back to his ancestors. He became obsessed with that because he wanted so much to be linked to an important person in history. One day he came to me to tell me gleefully that the program had traced his line of descent to one of the English kings. He was truly excited and proud to be able to boast of this. It's amazing what a software program can do by linking a man with no living family to an old king. We all need something to be proud of that brings us affirmation, either through inheritance or achievement or association.

One of St Paul's biggest achievements was in persecuting the Church. After listing all these achievements, he continues to write one of the most beautiful verses in all his writings:

> But whatever were gains to me I now consider loss for the sake of Christ. What is more, I consider everything a loss because of the surpassing worth of knowing Christ Jesus my Lord, for whose sake I have lost all things. I consider them garbage, that I may gain Christ and be found in him, not having a righteousness of my own that comes from the law, but that which is through faith in Christ—the righteousness that comes from God on the basis of faith (Philippians 3:7–9).

We see Paul shocking everybody by casting all his earthly jewels at the feet of Christ and raising his relationship with Christ as his ultimate achievement. Not only that, but considering everything else not a close second or third but as no more than garbage. Someone today could, like Paul, describe themselves thus: "Had my first communion at 12, am a white Anglo-Saxon, from a Christian family, a churchwarden, with a PhD in computer science, a higher-band taxpayer, own a detached house and a luxury sports car, am a social media influencer with hundreds of thousands of followers, have travelled the world and can afford to send my children to private school, and my friends are influential people from the City, law and the media." The question is would that person continue to say with Paul that "all this is worthless in the face of my faith in Christ for whose sake I have lost things and consider them garbage that I may gain Christ"? How realistic is that today?

Paul could only say that because he was filled with the love of God and the Lord Jesus Christ. St Paul had to enter a fight about his identity before Christ and after Christ. Only in Christ, when he was rooted in Christ, was he able to consider all his gains as garbage. He reached a point where he had a John the Baptist-type experience where he decreased, and Christ increased within him. Only then could he regard everything that he achieved and inherited as worthless compared to the new identity that being in Christ gave him. Today, our culture is centred around me and my desire for love, acceptance and inclusion. Our culture is all about my success and everything depends on what I do, right or wrong. The philosopher, Michael Sandel, argues that we are obsessed with our merit and that my identity depends on what I do, what I earn, what I have and what I achieve but never considers everyone else who helps me to be who I am.

The question today is how I relate to my identity in our digital culture that gives me different digital identities and allows me to create a different identity for different platforms. It puts me in the centre and everything that happens depends on me and what I do. It's up to me to justify or excuse anything that I do. We have lost a sense of belonging to other people. Who am I without other people? Our digital culture feeds our ego and helps us to forget our debt of gratitude to those around us without whom we could not say "I have achieved this or created that". Sadly, this also applies to our relationship with God, in which I also put myself in the centre, judging God according to what I do. For example, I may say:

"God hates me because I am not doing what he wants," or "he loves me because I am doing his work."

In the 1960s, there was a philosophical discussion around "to be or to have; for example, in the writings of Erich Fromm. In the third decade of the twenty-first century, we have moved beyond this discussion of being or having to face our digital reality that reintroduces us to the concept of community. Today we are all part of different communities, all of which are real, including our digital community. What happens to me in my life no longer depends just on me, or who I am, but on who I am in relationship within my communities. What St Paul gives us in his letter to the Philippians could be extremely helpful today in putting our understanding of our identity in perspective. St Paul sees everything in his past and present as nothing compared to his eagerness and zeal to know Christ. Today we talk about the total digital transformation of society that includes not only the transformation of the economy but also, and more importantly, the transformation of the individual. The transformation of the market has little value without the digital transformation of the customer. Our identity is being transformed more and more into a digital identity.

We have all experienced the invasion of computer codes, PIN numbers, digital fingerprints and face recognition technology into the details of our lives. We have also experienced—especially during the Covid-19 pandemic—heated debates around digital vaccine passports and the different apps that keep the health authorities in touch with millions of people on a daily basis. We are going through a total digital transformation on every level in our lives. In the middle of this existential and life-changing transformation that is altering the essence of who we are, how do we understand our identity in relation to the Culture of God? I am sure that in the future we will experience bigger transformations even than this. We will have even more advanced technology with which to identify ourselves to each other and to our communities. St Paul provides us with an incredible metaphor for his understanding of his identity. He borrows vocabulary from the ancient Olympic Games when he speaks about the concept of conquering the goal. In his time, athletes were not competing for a medal but to conquer the goal of the game they were participating in and by extension mastering it, which is in itself a military concept.

This reminds us of how, in classical Arabic, when we want to describe someone obtaining first or second place, we say he invaded or conquered the first or second position. We use this same word to speak about an army invading or conquering a target. St Paul admits that he has not reached or conquered his goal, but he is still seeking to conquer or overcome it. He then quickly admits that, for the same goal, Jesus himself conquered Paul. As we seek to obtain knowledge of Jesus Christ and deepen our relationship with him, we need to understand that we cannot do that unless we allow Christ to conquer us. What does this mean in the light of this journey of digital transformation? It should mean for those who believe in Christ exactly what it meant to Paul: to open our hearts and lives, to be conquered by Christ, so that we are able to know him and have a living, breathing, dynamic relationship with him. This helps me know the power of his bodily resurrection. When I know the power of his resurrection, I am in fellowship with him and share his suffering. That brings me the transformative power that empowers me to live and interpret the digital transformation in my life.

When Christ conquers us, we put our digital transformation under his feet, as St Paul says in 1 Corinthians 15:27: "For he 'has put everything under his feet.' Now when it says that 'everything' has been put under him, it is clear that this does not include God himself, who put everything under Christ." The challenge today of going through this digital journey of transformation and, at the same time, living and experiencing the power of the resurrection of Christ and allowing him to conquer us, is enormous. Christ's conquest is the conquest of the Culture of God. It is allowing God to take the upper hand in everything about us. This conquest presents a serious challenge to how to live the Culture of God in our ever-changing digital culture.

St Paul reveals to us the heart of the Culture of God, which does not recognize or value all these worldly gains. Knowing Christ and making him the ultimate gain in life through a living relationship with him is something that religion cannot help us to achieve. When we consider Christianity a religion, clergy become religious leaders and put themselves on a collision course with Christ and the Culture of God, which cannot be experienced and lived through being more and more religious. Religion is a social phenomenon that limits and tames the power of faith through its rituals, rigid doctrines, legalistic morality and problematic religious institutions. When someone asked Jesus about the most important commandment, the answer was simple:

> Love the Lord your God with all your heart and with all your soul and with all your mind and with all your strength. The second is this: 'Love your neighbour as yourself.' There is no commandment greater than these (Mark 12:30–31).

Later, Jesus gave us something beyond these commandments that he called the "new commandment":

> My children, I will be with you only a little longer. You will look for me, and just as I told the Jews, so I tell you now: where I am going, you cannot come.
>
> A new command I give you: love one another. As I have loved you, so you must love one another. By this everyone will know that you are my disciples, if you love one another (John 13:33–35).

The question is: why did he call this a new commandment? He went beyond what he described before as the "great commandments" to ask us to love one another, but this time "as he loved us". This commandment is a game changer in the history of humanity as it is linked to the revolutionary teaching that he gave before, which is "love your enemy". We see Jesus loving Judas and washing his feet along with those of the other disciples although he knew that he would betray him. He also loved Peter and washed his feet as well, although he knew that he would deny him.

Today, we need to ask ourselves: who is Judas in my life and who is Peter and how can I love them? Sometimes we confuse loving the person with having to accept what they did. When Jesus loved Judas and Peter, he did not condone what they were going to do. It is essential, when we love Judas in our lives, to be aware of the evil things that they do. At the same time, we should not be held hostage by our hate for such people and their actions. The only way to free ourselves from the bitterness of hate and its consequences is to hold on to the value of forgiveness. We must insist on holding on to that value, not because it is easy but because it is difficult to achieve, and also because we know through our experiences that the liberation forgiveness provides is magnificent. To insist on forgiving is to practise the new commandment of Jesus. This new commandment takes us to another level of existence, which is to exchange that kind of love with each other. A love that led Christ to the cross. That kind of love made God raise Jesus from the dead victorious because he lived what he taught.

Living in a highly technological age should not mean that we sell our souls to that technology, but rather transform ourselves through the same kind of love that Jesus taught us through this commandment and through his own life. We are able to face our digital transformation with a deeper level of awareness that being the disciples of Christ means to love and to live what Jesus Christ himself taught and lived in his life. It is also to be aware that it is not through our power that we achieve this but through the power of the Risen Jesus, not the digital Jesus.

Lightning Source UK Ltd.
Milton Keynes UK
UKHW010826080223
416669UK00011B/1455